D0491484

CANDLE
ILLUSTRATED
BIBLE
ENCYCLOPEDIA

EDITED BY TIM DOWLEY

CONTRIBUTORS:
DR STEPHEN MOTYER
DR DAVID PAYNE   DR MARY EVANS
ROBERT BACKHOUSE

CANDLE
BOOKS

Copyright © 2005 Lion Hudson plc/
Tim Dowley & Peter Wyart trading
as Three's Company

Published in 2005 by Candle Books
(a publishing imprint of Lion
Hudson plc).
ISBN 1 85985 544 X
Distributed by Marston Book
Services Ltd, PO Box 269,
Abingdon, Oxon
OX14 4YN

All rights reserved. No part of this
publication may be reproduced,
stored in a retrieval system, or
transmitted in any form or by any
means – for example, electronic,
photocopy, recording – without
the prior written permission of the
publisher.

Worldwide co-edition produced by
Lion Hudson plc, Mayfield House,
256 Banbury Road, Oxford
OX2 7DH,
Tel: +44 (0) 1865 302750
Fax: +44 (0) 1865 302757
e-mail: coed@lionhudson.com
www.lionhudson.com

Printed in Singapore

Picture acknowledgments

Photographs
Tim Dowley: pp.12, 13, 14, 21, 25,
30 bottom, 42, 51, 52, 55, 73, 79,
87, 90, 98, 100, 104, 106 bottom,
109, 113 top, 115, 118, 119, 122,
124, 130, 140, 141 top, 158, 166-67,
179, 186, 1900, 191, 199, 216, 219,
227, 228
Peter Wyart: pp. 9, 17, 19, 24, 30
top, 31, 72, 80, 83, 94, 97, 103, 106
top, 113 bottom, 114 top, 119
inset, 120, 126, 141 bottom, 163,
168-69, 184, 196, 203, 221, 226

Maps
Hardlines

Timeline:
Tony Cantale

Illustrations
Frank Baber: p. 160 top
Brian Bartles: pp. 142-43, 217
Shirley Bellwood: p. 95
Peter Dennis: pp. 1, 2, 3, 9, 10
bottom, 13, 15, 16 top, 17, 18, 19,
22, 23 top
Jeremy Gower: pp. 29, 152 top
James Macdonald: pp. 54, 65, 76,
92, 100, 227, 234
Bob Moulder: pp. 172-73
Trevor Parkin: pp. 43, 56, 136-37
Alan Parry: pp. 72, 79, 91, 93, 128,
129, 131, 132, 133, 134, 135, 144-
45, 146, 147, 149, 152 bottom, 153,
156-57, 158-59, 160 bottom, 161,
164-75, 180-81
Kate Pascoe: p. 185
Francis Phillipps: p. 78
David Price: p. 23 bottom
Richard Scott: pp. 8, 10 top, 16
bottom, 45, 55, 68, 69, 89, 104,
115, 116, 139, 140, 164, 165, 179,
193, 194, 196, 197, 198, 200, 201,
202, 203, 204, 206, 207, 208, 209,
210-11, 211, 212, 213, 214, 215,
216, 217, 218, 219, 232, 233
Annabel Spenceley: pp. 81, 231
Paul Wyart: p. 184

DUNDEE CITY
COUNCIL

LOCATION
C'STON

ACCESSION NUMBER
COO 415 595X

SUPPLIER   PRICE
Bert   £9.99

CLASS No.   DATE
220.3   9/1/06

Contents

How the Bible Came to Us

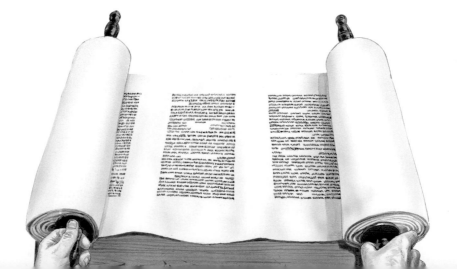

What is the Bible?

The Bible is made up of a 'library'of 66 books, 39 in the Old Testament, 27 in the New. The writings of the **OLD TESTAMENT** first appeared as separate scrolls in Hebrew; we do not know how or when they were first gathered into a single volume. The 39 books of the Old Testament vary in authorship and style and can be divided into four major groupings:

Law
Sometimes called the Pentateuch, or 'five scrolls'.

History
Tracing the story of God's people from their entry into the Promised Land to the Exile.

Poetry and Wisdom
Full of proverbs, riddles, parables, warnings and wise sayings.

Prophecy
God's prophets explained what had happened in the past; spoke out against evil in the present; and told of what God would do in the future.

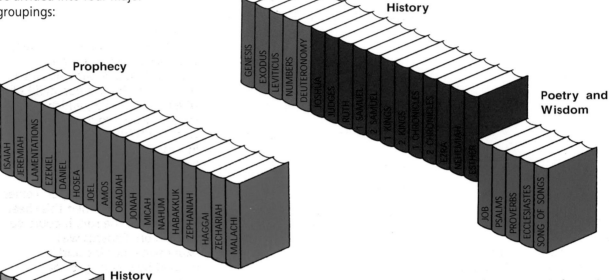

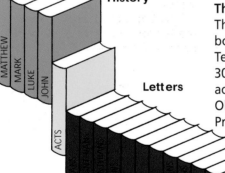

The Apocrypha
The Apocrypha is a collection of books and additions to the Old Testament books written between 300 B.C. and A.D. 100. They were not accepted by the Jews as part of the Old Testament Scripture, and most Protestant denominations do not accept them as part of genuine Scripture.

The books are interesting and valuable historical documents that range from historical narratives to pious fiction.

The 27 books of the **NEW TESTAMENT** were written in Greek and can also be divided into different types of writing:

History
The book of Acts and the four Gospels. The Gospels, however, are not simply historical records; they were written to persuade readers to believe in Jesus, and form portraits of Jesus as the Messiah.

Letters
These include Paul's letters to churches in various cities, his letters to individual Christians, and letters written by other apostles.

Revelation
This book opens with letters to seven churches in Asia Minor, but continues with disturbing visions about the Last Days.

How the Bible was written down

Clay tablets
In ancient Babylonia clay for writing was shaped into thin, flat, rectangular bricks. Words were pressed into the soft clay with a wedge-shaped stylus, and the clay then baked in the sun. Archaeologists have found whole 'libraries' of these clay tablets.

Papyrus
Before the pyramids were built, the ancient Egyptians had learned to make papyrus paper from the pith (or inner stalk) of Nile papyrus reeds, which grew in marshy areas around Egypt. Still wet, the thick stems were laid out in rows on top of each other and beaten until they melded together into a flat paper surface. (Our word 'paper' comes from 'papyrus'.) When this sheet had dried in the sun, it could be written on. Papyrus was expensive – but it could be re-used by washing, or by scraping.

Egyptian pens were brushes made from reeds, and ink was derived from plants and insects.

Stone
The first permanent writing surface was stone. In the Bible, the first reference to writing is to the Ten Commandments, which were written on stone. The first pen was a chisel.

Ordinary people often used broken bits of pottery, called 'sherds', to write memos, bills and even shopping lists.

Ink was made from soot mixed with oil or gum.

Leather
The skins of sheep, goats, calves and antelopes were dried, scraped and cleaned to make a smooth material called parchment. (The Hebrew word for book means 'scrape'.) Then the skins were stretched and beaten flat ready for writing on.

Pens were made from reeds, with one end cut to a sloping edge and then split.

Waxed boards
Writing boards were made from pieces of wood or ivory covered with wax. They were used by the Assyrians, Greeks and Romans. Two boards were sometimes hinged together. Any pointed stick made a pen.

The languages of the Bible

Writing

The first writing consisted of simple pictures, with one picture for each word. Writing like this, with over 800 pictures, has been found in Babylonia (modern Iraq) and is over 5,000 years old.

Hieroglyphs

The Egyptians made up their own little pictures to represent words, or parts of words. They painted them on papyrus sheets – and on walls.

Cuneiform writing

The Babylonians did not have access to papyrus, and it was not easy to draw on clay. For this reason their pictures became increasingly simplified, until words became standard shapes pressed into the clay with wedge-shaped sticks. The word 'cuneiform' means wedge-shaped.

A Jewish rabbi teaches boys to read the Scripture. They are using writing boards; he is reading from a scroll.

The alphabet

In Canaan about 1500 B.C. someone had the clever idea of making up a symbol – a letter – for each sound in the language. They found that they needed about 25 letters.

There was now no longer any need to learn hundreds of different shapes for hundreds of different words. Any word could be written down just by listening to its sounds and choosing the matching letters. This simple idea quickly spread to other languages.

a
b
g
d
h
w
z
h
t
y
k

l
m
n
s

p
s
q
r
s
t

Hebrew

The Old Testament tells the story of the Israelite people. Their language was Hebrew, and most of the Old Testament is written in Hebrew. The Hebrew alphabet has 22 consonants, but no vowels (vowel sounds had to be added by the reader). Hebrew is read from right to left, so the first page of the Hebrew Bible is our last page.

A Hebrew scroll.

Aramaic

Aramaic was spoken by the Persians, who were the major power in the Middle East for 200 years from about 550 B.C. Aramaic became the language used by traders in that region. Parts of the Old Testament books of Daniel, Ezra and Jeremiah were written in Aramaic.

By New Testament times, Aramaic was the everyday language of the Jews, and Jesus would have spoken it. However, Hebrew remained the language for prayer and worship. Educated people still understood Hebrew, but when the Hebrew Bible was read aloud in synagogue services, a translator often gave the meaning in Aramaic.

Some manuscripts of parts of the Old Testament in Aramaic, called 'Targums', have survived. They help us to discover the words of the original Hebrew.

The Greek alphabet

A — A	K — K
B — B	Λ — L
Γ — G	M — M
Δ — D	N — N
E — E	Ξ — O
Y — U	O — O
Z — Z	Π — P
H — H	P — R
Θ — TH	Σ — S
I — I	T — T

Greek

In 331 B.C. the Greek general Alexander the Great conquered Persia. He now ruled the known ancient world, and 'common' Greek became the language that most people understood.

When the followers of Jesus wrote the New Testament, they wanted the whole known world to hear the good news, so they wrote in Greek, translating the Aramaic spoken by Jesus into the Greek language. In just a few places they retained original Aramaic words. For example *abba* is an Aramaic word meaning dad.

When Jesus spoke to Jairus' daughter, he said, *'Talitha, koum'* – these were his actual Aramaic words. The Gospel writers gave us a Greek translation, which in English is, 'Get up, my child' (Mark 5:41).

There are 24 letters in the Greek alphabet, which was the first alphabet to include letters for vowels. Sentences – and books – were written from left to right.

In Revelation, God says: 'I am the Alpha and the Omega' – the first and last letters of the Greek alphabet – 'who is, and who was, and who is to come' (Revelation 1:8)

The earliest evidence

Possibly the earliest part of the New Testament so far discovered is a papyrus fragment, only 6 x 9 centimetres (2 x 3 inches), containing a few lines from John's Gospel. It is written in Greek, dates from about A.D. 130, and is known as the 'John Rylands fragment'.

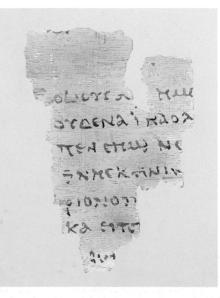

Who wrote the Bible?

The Bible we have today is usually one very thick book of more than 1,000 pages. But different parts of the Bible were written by different people over a very long period of time – probably as much as 1,500 to 2,000 years. It was only later that the many different parts were collected together into a single book.

Oral tradition

The first stories in the Bible go back to pre-history, long before writing was invented. They were passed on in the same way as children's playground songs are passed on today – by being constantly repeated. Passing stories on in this way is often called oral (or spoken) tradition. Round the camp-fires in the evenings, at worship, at work or at war, people sang the songs and told the stories that they had learned as children. Because these stories were about God, they were treated with great respect. Every word was important, and had to be repeated correctly.

Jewish scribe.

In writing

Scholars are not sure when the books of the Old Testament were first written down; the period of their writing covered several centuries. Much of the Old Testament was probably collected together and revised during the period of the Exile by scribes such as Ezra. By the third century B.C. the Jews recognised a number of their books as 'holy', and directly inspired by God. They were formally agreed at the Synod of Jamnia in A.D. 90, and are the books we know as the Old Testament – though we have them in a different order.

What about the New Testament?

Jesus of Nazareth was born hundreds of years after the writings mentioned earlier, just 2,000 years ago. But stories about Jesus were at first passed on by word of mouth too. Matthew, Mark, Luke and John wrote the four Gospels based on eye-witness accounts of Jesus' life. So the stories about Jesus' birth at Bethlehem, his life and miracles, which we know from the Gospels of Matthew, Mark, Luke and John, were all written down before about A.D. 100.

The apostle Paul and others wrote letters to explain to believers about the faith and instruct them in Christian behaviour. The first of these letters appeared before the Gospels, from around A.D. 50.

As the apostles and first generation of Christians began to die, the younger believers began the attempt to assemble a collection of authentic writings that would preserve a more permanent record of Jesus and his teachings. By about A.D. 100, most of the writings we now know as the New Testament were recognised as inspired by the Church; and by about A.D. 200 the New Testament as we know it today, with its 27 books, was recognised.

The contents of various Old Testaments

The Jewish Bible, the Septuagint (an early Greek translation of the Old Testament), the Roman Catholic Old Testament and the Protestant Old Testament all vary a little in the number of their constituent books and in their order. The chart helps compare the four different versions. (See also page 76.)

RABBINIC CANON 24 BOOKS	SEPTUAGINT 51 BOOKS	ROMAN CATHOLIC O.T. 46 BOOKS	PROTESTANT O.T. 39 BOOKS
The Law	**Law**	**Law**	**Law**
Genesis	Genesis	Genesis	Genesis
Exodus	Exodus	Exodus	Exodus
Leviticus	Leviticus	Leviticus	Leviticus
Numbers	Numbers	Numbers	Numbers
Deuteronomy	Deuteronomy	Deuteronomy	Deuteronomy
The Prophets	**History**	**History**	**History**
The Former Prophets			
Joshua	Joshua	Joshua	Joshua
Judges	Judges	Judges	Judges
1–2 Samuel	Ruth	Ruth	Ruth
1–2 Kings	1 Kingdoms (1 Samuel)	1 Samuel (1 Kingdoms)	1 Samuel
The Latter Prophets	2 Kingdoms (2 Samuel)	2 Samuel (2 Kingdoms)	2 Samuel
Isaiah	3 Kingdoms (1 Kings)	1 Kings (3 Kingdoms)	1 Kings
Jeremiah	4 Kingdoms (2 Kings)	2 Kings (4 Kingdoms)	2 Kings
Ezekiel	1 Paralipomena (1 Chronicles)	1 Chronicles (Paralipomena)	1 Chronicles
The Twelve	2 Paralipomena (2 Chronicles)	2 Chronicles (2 Paralipomena)	2 Chronicles
Hosea	1 Esdras (Apocryphal Ezra)	Ezra	Ezra
Joel	2 Esdras (Ezra-Nehemiah)	Nehemiah	Nehemiah
Amos	Esther (with Apocryphal additions)	Tobit	Esther
Obadiah	Judith	Judith	
Jonah	Tobit	Esther (with additions)	
Micah	1 Maccabees	1 Maccabees	
Nahum	2 Maccabees	2 Maccabees	
Habakkuk	3 Maccabees		
Zephaniah	4 Maccabees	**Poetry**	**Poetry**
Haggai		Job	Job
Zechariah	**Poetry**	Psalms	Psalms
Malachi	Psalms	Proverbs	Proverbs
	Odes (including the prayer of Manasseh)	Ecclesiastes	Eccesiastes
The Writings	Proverbs	Song of Songs	Song of Songs
Poetry	Ecclesiastes	Wisdom of Solomon	
Psalms	Song of Songs	Ecclesiasticus (The Wisdom of Jesus the son of Sirach)	
Proverbs	Job		
Job	Wisdom (of Solomon)		
Rolls–'the Festival Scrolls'	Sirach (Ecclesiasticus or The Wisdom of Jesus the son of Sirach)	**Prophecy**	**Prophecy**
Song of Songs	Psalms of Solomon	Isaiah	Isaiah
Ruth		Jeremiah	Jeremiah
Lamentations		Lamentations	Lamentations
Ecclesiastes	**Prophecy**	Baruch (including the Letter of Jeremiah)	Ezekiel
Esther	Hosea	Ezekiel	Daniel
Others (History)	Amos	Daniel (including Susanna, The Song of the three young men, Bel and Dragon)	Hosea
Daniel	Micah	Hosea	Joel
Ezra-Nehemiah	Joel	Joel	Amos
1–2 Chronicles	Obadiah	Amos	Obadiah
	Jonah	Obadiah	Jonah
	Naham	Jonah	Micah
	Habakuk	Micah	Nahum
	Zechariah	Nahum	Habakkuk
	Haggai	Habakkuk	Zephaniah
	Zechariah	Zephaniah	Haggai
	Malachi	Haggai	Zechariah
	Isaiah	Zechariah	Malachi
	Jeremiah	Malachi	
	Baruch		
	Lamentations		
	Letter of Jeremiah		
	Ezekiel		
	Daniel (with apocryphal additions, including the Prayer of Azariah, the Song of the Three Children, Susanna and Bel and the Dragon)		

Scrolls from the Dead Sea

In 1947 a Bedouin shepherd-boy tending his flock in the barren hills west of the Dead Sea noticed a hole in nearby cliffs. He tossed a stone inside, and heard the sound of breaking crockery. Intrigued, he went to explore and found a number of earthenware jars. Exploring further, he discovered that inside the jars were rolls of leather parchment covered in ancient Hebrew writing. At first no one was interested in his find; but when some archaeologists saw the scrolls, there was real excitement.

Eventually about 400 scrolls were found in caves near a place called Qumran. They turned out to be the library of a Jewish religious sect called the Essenes, and include parts of every book in the Hebrew Old Testament except Esther. The ascetic Essene community lived nearby around the time of Christ, and built a settlement which has been excavated to reveal a watchtower, refectory, scriptorium – where the Dead Sea Scrolls were probably copied – ritual baths, pottery and a cemetery.

Carbon 14 dating has shown that the Dead Sea Scrolls were written between 200 B.C. and A.D. 70. The Isaiah Scroll is almost complete, and is 1,000 years older than our next oldest surviving copy of Isaiah; yet the two texts are almost identical. This shows how accurate the copyists were – and how seriously they took their job.

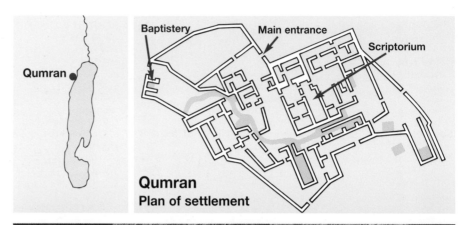

Qumran

Qumran
Plan of settlement

In these caves near Qumran a Bedouin shepherd found the Dead Sea Scrolls.

Some of the Dead Sea Scrolls are now housed in the Shrine of the Book, Jerusalem.

A number of the Dead Sea Scrolls were made of copper.

Excavated remains of the Essene community at Qumran, near the Dead Sea.

Part of the Isaiah Scroll, the oldest and longest of the Dead Sea Scrolls.

The scroll

When the Bible was written, books with pages had not been invented. Instead, people wrote on scrolls. These were made from sheets of papyrus, parchment or even thin copper, sewn or glued together to form a long strip, up to 10 metres (30 feet) long and 30 centimetres (12 inches) wide. Each end was wound round a wooden rod, and the reader unrolled the scroll with one hand and rolled it up with the other. When not in use, scrolls were wrapped in cloths and stored in tall jars to preserve them.

The apostle Paul wrote from prison in Rome asking Timothy to bring him his 'scrolls, especially the parchments' (2 Timothy 4:13).

The earliest Christian writings were on papyrus scrolls.

The Qumran scrolls were found in jars like this.

13

The book arrives

Scrolls were cumbersome to carry, and it was time-consuming to find a short Bible passage on a long scroll.

In the second century Christians collected together the books of the New Testament. They were probably the first people to do away with the scroll. Instead, they hit on the idea of collecting together several sheets of papyrus or parchment, folding them in half, sewing along the fold, and then adding more folded sheets. This forerunner of our 'book' was sometimes also given a harder cover. This early type of book was called a codex (plural codices).

The book had arrived.

Above: St Catherine's Monastery, Sinai.
Below: Overall view of St Catherine's.

Constantine Tischendorf, discoverer of the *Codex Sinaiticus.*

Codex Sinaiticus

Our earliest complete copy of the New Testament was written out not long after A.D. 300. It is called *Codex Sinaiticus* because it was found at the foot of Mount Sinai, in St Catherine's Monastery.

In 1844 a German scholar called Constantine Tischendorf was visiting this remote monastery and discovered some parchments with early Greek writing. The manuscripts turned out to be part of the Old Testament, and dated from the fourth century A.D. Excited by his discovery, Tischendorf made a return visit to the monastery and eventually found enough sheets to make an almost complete Bible. Today the *Codex Sinaiticus* is preserved in the British Museum, London.

Other important early manuscripts of the Bible in Greek include the *Codex Vaticanus*, now in the Vatican Library, Rome, and the *Codex Alexandrinus*, also in the British Museum.

Pages of the *Codex Sinaiticus*.

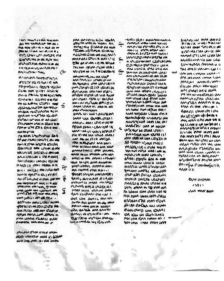

A page from the *Codex Sinaiticus*.

15

How the Bible came down to us

Copying was lengthy and laborious.

Jewish scribes

The Jewish scribes were important figures, because in early times they were often the only people who could read and write. They drew up wills and other legal documents, and kept records.

When new copies of Old Testament scrolls were needed, every word had to be written out by hand. The scribes had the sacred task of preserving, copying out and explaining the teaching of the Old Testament.

To make sure that each scribe understood the importance of his work, and to stop him making mistakes, careful rules were followed. For example:
• *Each day he had to start his work with prayer.*
• *The name of God had to be left blank, to be filled in later by a different scribe, using a 'purer' ink.*
• *At the end of a section of a book, the scribe counted the lines, the words and the letters in the original and checked them with his copy. He also found and checked the middle word of each section.*

Sometimes mistakes were made. But it has been computed that mistakes averaged only one mistake in every 1,580 letters.

Septuagint

The Old Testament was first translated from Hebrew into Greek in the second and third centuries B.C. This translation was known as the Septuagint. 'Septuagint' comes from the Latin for 70; there is a tradition that 70 (or perhaps 72) scholars made this translation. It is sometimes written as LXX (70 in Roman numerals).

Jewish people had spread all over the Mediterranean world, and often spoke Greek rather than Hebrew. This translation was made in Alexandria, Egypt, for the legendary great library there.

Monks

The word 'monk' comes from a Greek word meaning 'someone who lives alone'. The first Christian monk was Antony, who lived by himself in the deserts of Egypt from about A.D. 270 to 290. Others followed his example. More often men (and, separately, women) lived in a group in a monastery, spending their days in prayer, Bible study and useful work such as farming or nursing.

Copyists

During the Dark Ages, after the Roman Empire had collapsed, the monks protected and passed on the Bible. When a Bible was worn out, they spent years making a fresh copy. Every codex had to be copied out by hand. This was a long and laborious process.

Mistakes were sometimes made, perhaps by the monk or scribe becoming tired, or because of the poor light in which he was working. Sometimes the scribe would even change things deliberately because he wanted to put the Scriptures into his own words or make them fit his own point of view.

Often the monks worked in a scriptorium, or writing room, each monk writing in silence at his desk. Because of the danger of fire destroying the manuscripts, the room had no heat and no lighting. The work was tiring. There was a saying, 'Two fingers hold the pen but the whole body toils.'

A medieval monk copies a page of the Bible.

The first translations

By A.D. 300 the New Testament had been translated into several languages, including Latin and Syriac – a language spoken in what is today Turkey. The Syriac Bible was called the Peshitta, or 'simple' version. Syriac missionaries took the gospel – and the Bible – as far as China, India, Armenia and Georgia.

The Armenian and Georgian alphabets were probably created to allow the Bible to be translated into both these languages. The Bible was also translated into Coptic, a form of ancient Egyptian – the language of the North African Christians– and Sahedic, a dialect of Coptics.

A book for the Goths
By the fourth century, the language of the Germanic Ostrogoths had never been written down. Around A.D. 350 Bishop Ulfilas translated the Bible

Jerome translated the Vulgate in Bethlehem.

into the language of the Ostrogoths and committed it to writing.

Jerome
A scholar called Jerome, born in northern Italy in about A.D. 345,

A leather-bound copy of the Vulgate.

became very concerned about copyists' mistakes. He travelled widely, learning many languages and transcribing many parts of the Scriptures.

Around A.D. 382, Pope Damasus asked Jerome to make a completely new translation of the Gospels, the Psalms and other Old Testament books, in an attempt to get rid of mistakes that had crept in.

The Vulgate
At this time most Christians in the West spoke Latin, and found it hard to understand the Greek New Testament. Many Latin translations had been made, but they were neither well-written nor accurate. So Jerome, who went to live in seclusion in a monastery in Bethlehem in 386, set about translating into Latin the original Hebrew and Greek texts of the entire Bible. A Jewish rabbi helped him learn Hebrew and translate directly from the Old Testament. His task was to take him 23 years.

Jerome's translation gradually increased in popularity. Known as the Vulgate, meaning 'Common Version', from the eighth century until 1609 it was the only Bible used by the Roman Catholic Church.

Jerome translated the Bible with the help of a Jewish rabbi.

Precious books

and northern England, wandering from place to place explaining about their Christian faith, and setting up monasteries. These monks brought with them the skills to create beautiful and imaginative Celtic designs. Superbly decorated books were produced in remote monasteries on bleak cliffs and islands. A monk might spend his whole life working on one book, thus demonstrating his love for God.

The Book of Kells

In the Irish Book of Kells one small design, only 1.6 square centimetres (1/4 square inch) in size is made up of 158 tiny interlaced shapes. This illuminated book of the Gospels in Latin is perhaps the greatest masterpiece of Celtic and Anglo-Saxon art. It was begun in the seventh century in the monastery at Iona, western Scotland. After a Viking raid, it was taken for safe-keeping to the monastery of Kells in Ireland, where it was completed. It consists of 339 leaves, 33 x 25 centimetres (13 x 10 inches) in size, and every page is richly decorated. The Book of Kells is today preserved at Trinity College, Dublin, Ireland.

Irish monks travelled to Scotland, taking with them their faith and their Bibles.

Decorating the book

Books were made from parchment (the skin of a a calf, sheep or goat) or from vellum (a very fine parchment). After a monk had finished copying out the Latin words in a beautiful, elegant script, his work was checked.

In time, instead of merely copying the Latin words, the monks began to decorate the page as well. The resulting decorated books are known as illuminated manuscripts.

Sometimes the copyists would add a painted border with an intricate pattern to the page. Also the first letter of a paragraph or chapter would be enlarged almost to fill the page, and then be decorated with patterns, flowers or even little figures. The monks created intricate, interlocking designs of curves, spirals, scrolls, shields, and tiny detailed paintings of animals and birds. They used water-colour paints that they had to make up themselves, and sometimes gold-leaf was added for a rich

effect. Quill pens – made from sharpened feathers – and very basic brushes were the only tools available, but the results were exquisite.

Irish tradition

In the fifth and sixth centuries Irish monks travelled to Scotland

Copying a page of Scripture by hand.

The first page of Luke's Gospel, from the Lindisfarne Gospels.

An ornamented page from the Lindisfarne Gospels.

Ruins of the monastery of Lindisfarne, north-east England.

Lindisfarne Gospels

In A.D. 635 a monastery was set up on Lindisfarne, a small island off the coast of north-east England. The Lindisfarne Gospels, particularly fine examples of illuminated manuscripts, were copied out and illuminated there around A.D. 700. A priest called Aldred added an Anglo-Saxon translation between the lines of Latin text some 300 years later.

A medieval monk reads from a chained illuminated Bible.

The Golden Gospels

The Golden Gospels are a magnificent series of illuminated manuscripts of the Gospels, created in eighth-century France under the guidance of Alcuin, who came from York, England. The lettering in these manuscripts was mainly in gold, and the decoration in silver and gold, all on purple-stained vellum.

A sixth-century copy of Ulfilas' translation of the Bible for the Goths was similarly written in gold and silver on a purple-painted parchment.

Bibles in chains

Most Bibles were much less ornate than the Book of Kells or the Golden Gospels. But even plain books took years to copy and then bind with leather into a huge heavy volume. They were also very valuable, so when a finished Bible was put on display in a monastery chapel or in a cathedral, it would often be chained to the reading desk to stop anyone from stealing it.

The Bible
for the people

Peter Waldo.

In the Middle Ages most Bibles, however beautiful, were still written in Latin – a language which ordinary people could not understand. Some men were determined to change this – by translating the Bible into the vernacular.

Waldo's versions
About 1175, Peter Waldo, a wealthy merchant living in Lyons, France, became a Christian. Taking Jesus' words literally, he gave away all his possessions.

Waldo's followers, called Waldensians, translated the Bible into the Provençal language – and probably also into Italian, German, Piedmontese (north Italian) and Catalan (spoken in north-east Spain).

An alphabet for Russia
In the ninth century Cyril and Methodius, two Christian brothers from Thessalonica in Greece, embarked on a mission to the Slavs of Eastern Europe. As part of their task, they translated the Bible into the Old Slavonic language. To write out their

John Wyclif

The very first translation of any part of the Bible into Anglo-Saxon was a version of the Psalms, made about A.D. 700 by Bishop Aldhelm of Sherborne. Later the Venerable Bede, abbot at Jarrow, north-east England, translated part of John's Gospel before his death in 735.

Heresy!
John Wyclif (1329–1384) longed for the Bible to be translated into English, so that ordinary people could understand its message. It angered him that priests could decide which part of the Bible to read out and how to interpret it. Wyclif taught at Oxford University until he was thrown out for attacking these and other failings in the Church.

translation, they invented an alphabet that was the forerunner of the Cyrillic alphabet – named after Cyril – still used today in south-east Europe and Russia.

Here are the names of the Gospel writers in Russian, in Cyrillic script:

Матфея

Марка

Луки

Иоанна

John Hus

In fifteenth-century Prague, the capital of Bohemia (now the Czech Republic) John Hus (1374–1415), rector of Charles University, began to speak out against the greed, immorality and ambition of priests. He was greatly influenced by Wyclif's teachings. As a result of his outspoken views, Hus was accused of heresy, imprisoned, and eventually burned at the stake.

However, Hus' followers started to translate the Bible into Czech, and a Czech New Testament was published in 1475.

John Hus, the Czech reformer.

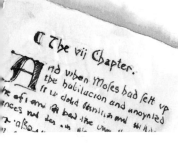

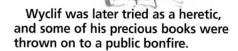

Wyclif was later tried as a heretic, and some of his precious books were thrown on to a public bonfire.

Wyclif's Bible
Some of Wyclif's followers, such as Nicholas of Hereford and John Purvey, translated the entire Bible into English, a task they finished in 1384. In 1408 this 'Wyclif Bible' was banned, but hundreds of copies were made and secretly sold.

Ordinary people could rarely read, so Wyclif's followers – poor priests or 'Lollards' – travelled from town to town reading and explaining the Bible. Some were burned at the stake as heretics, with Bibles tied around their necks. However some 170 copies of this version still survive today.

Printing the Bible on an early press.

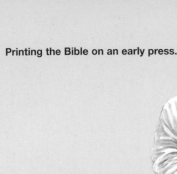

An early printed Bible.

No more copying!

In 1450 occurred an event that was radically to affect the story of the Bible: printing was invented. (Or re-invented – the Chinese had been printing books since A.D. 868.)

In Mainz, Germany, Johann Gutenberg discovered that he could print on to parchment with wooden letters dipped in dye. Using this method, he could make hundreds of printed books, instead of just one hand-written volume.

Gutenberg next experimented with metal type: the age of printed books had begun.

The first complete book printed by Gutenberg was the Latin Bible, in 1456. In 1978 one of the few surviving Gutenberg Bibles was bought for £1,265,000.

Although Johann Gutenberg and the people of Mainz tried to keep their invention secret, word soon got out, and before long presses were springing up all over Europe, from Rome and Paris to Cracow and London. The first printing press in England was set up by William Caxton in London in 1476.

Soon there were printed Bibles everywhere. The first printed Hebrew Old Testament appeared at Soncino, Italy, in 1488, produced by a group of Italian Jews.

Greek Testament

A famous Dutch scholar, Desiderius Erasmus, prepared the first printed edition of the Greek New Testament, which was printed in Basel, Switzerland, in 1516. This formed the basis for many modern European translations of the New Testament, including important English and German translations.

Erasmus of Rotterdam, c.1466-1536.

Two great translators

William Tyndale.

The great reformer

In the fifteenth and sixteenth centuries huge changes took place in Europe. More people were being educated, forming their own opinion about society and religion. Things were badly awry in the Church: many priests were dishonest or lazy, some teaching their own ideas without reference to the Bible.

One person prepared to stand up and criticise this was a German priest called Martin Luther, born in 1483. Becoming a monk, Luther strove to lead a good life, but felt he could never be as good as God wanted. While reading the book of Romans, he suddenly recognised that grace is a gift of God. It was a breakthrough!

Church doors were often used as notice-boards, and in October 1517 Martin Luther nailed to the door of Wittenberg church a list of 95 religious reforms that he believed needed implementing. Because of his stand, Luther became known as a 'reformer' and his actions led to the huge changes in the Church which we call the Reformation.

Fugitive

Luther was outlawed for his stand, and fled into hiding at Wartburg Castle. There he began to translate the Bible into German; he wanted others to experience the joy he had found through reading it.

Luther believed that a good translation had to be made direct from the original language, and that it should be in everyday speech. The complete 'Luther Bible' was published in 1532, one of the first in the language of ordinary people. Even today Luther's translation remains the best-loved of German Bibles, and it helped shape the modern German language.

A Bible for ploughboys

Although Wyclif's Bible had been in English, it was hand-written and contained many mistakes of translation and copying. Even after the invention of printing, there was still no printed Bible that English people could read in their own language.

Leaders in Church and State thought it dangerous for ordinary people to read the Bible for themselves and decide what to believe. So it was illegal to translate or print any part of the Bible. But the Englishman William Tyndale declared to a priest, 'If God spare my life . . . I will cause the boy that drives the plough to know more of the Bible than you do.'

Bible smugglers

William Tyndale (1494–1536) is the greatest English Bible translator. Exiled in Germany, he translated the New Testament from the original Greek. In 1526 printed copies were smuggled into England hidden in sacks of grain and crates of fish; King Henry VIII ordered them to be burnt. Before Tyndale could finish translating the Old Testament he was betrayed, ambushed and burnt at the stake in Belgium. As he died, he prayed, 'Lord, open the King of England's eyes.'

Martin Luther.

Changing language for a changing world

For 300 years English-speaking Protestants read the Authorised Version of the Bible. Recently many new translations have come out. Why do we have new translations? One reason is that language changes over the years.

Today Bible Society translators often re-translate the Bible into languages in which the Scriptures are already available. They are anxious to ensure that the translation is as accurate as possible. For this reason, translation is usually done by native speakers, with advice from missionaries and trained linguists. A native speaker can make the gospel more alive when he puts it into his own language, so that it doesn't sound like a translation.

The language used in a Bible translation mustn't sound old-fashioned or be difficult to understand. For this reason, new translations of world languages such as English, Spanish, French and Chinese are often made in 'everyday' language. The Bible must be as fresh and meaningful for today's readers as it was for the people who first read it in Greek 2,000 years ago.

The Bible must be as fresh today as it was for its original readers.

John 3:16 world-wide

English – Good News Bible
For God loved the world so much that he gave his only Son, so that everyone who believes in him may not die but have eternal life.

Modern German
Gott liebte die Menschen so sehr, dass er seinen einzigen Sohn hergab. Nun wird jeder, der sich auf den Sohn Gottes verlässt, nicht zugrunde gehen, sondern ewig leben.

Malay
Karena demikianlah Allah mengashi isi doienia ini sewhingga dikaroeni-akannja Anaknja jang toenggal itoe, soepaja barang siapa jang partjaja akan Dia djangan binasa, melainkan beroléh hidoep jang kekal.

Modern French
Car Dieu a tellement aimé le monde qu'il a donné son Fils unique, afin que tout homme qui croit en lui ne meure pas mais qu'il ait la vie éternelle.

Modern Spanish
Pues Dios amó tanto al mundo, que dio a su Hijo único, para que todo aquel que cree en él, no perezca, sino que tenga vida eterna.

Tahitian
I aroha mai te Atua I to te ao, e ua tae roa I te horoa mai I ta 'na Tamaiti fanau tahi, ia ore ia pohe te faaroo ia 'na ra, roiaa ra te ora mure ore.

Setswana
Gonne Modimo o ratile lehatshe yalo, oa ba oa naea Morwa òna eo o tsecweñ a le esi, gore moñwe le moñwe eo o dumèlañ mo go èna a se ka a hèla, me a nè le botshelò yo bo sa khurleñ.

Aymara
Cunalaycutejja Diosaji uqhama acapacharu muni, jupa sapa jathata Yokaparu churi, take qhitití juparu iyausisqui ucajja, jan chhakhtasiñap-ataqui, ucatsipana wiñaya jacañaniñapataqui.

RULES FOR TRANSLATORS

When translating the Bible into another language:
- *Do not add anything*
- *Do not miss anything out*
- *Do not alter the meaning*
- *Find words that communicate to new readers the purpose and feeling of the original*

The History of Bible Times

The Bible and archaeology

Archaeological milestones

Probably the earliest recorded attempt at what might be called archaeological excavation was made in 1738 at Herculaneum in southern Italy. Herculaneum, like Pompeii, which was first excavated in 1748, was covered when Mount Vesuvius erupted in A.D. 79. The 'excavations' consisted of tunnels into the hardened mud lava, allowing the excavators to remove treasures from the buried city. There was none of the systematic, scientific removal of layers of earth, carefully recorded, measured, drawn and reported, which characterises modern archaeological excavations.

The search for ancient treasure was extended to the Middle East in 1799 by the discovery, by a Napoleonic officer, of a stone with a trilingual inscription, the famous 'Rosetta Stone', which, once deciphered, unlocked the language and history of ancient Egypt, written in previously undeciphirable hieroglyphics on its buildings and tombs. Throughout the nineteenth century, entrepreneurs filled the museums of Europe with antiquities taken from the Middle East. Expeditions also went to Mesopotamia. Paul Botta ravaged Khorsabad, ten miles north of Nineveh, in 1842, and filled the Louvre in Paris with antiquities from the reign of Sargon II, an Assyrian monarch. From 1845, Sir Austen Layard filled the British Museum with treasures from Nineveh, from the reign of another Assyrian king, Ashurnasirpal II.

Reading the tablets

Between 1846 and 1855, Sir Henry Rawlinson deciphered the cuneiform script of the Old Persian language on the trilingual Behistun Rock, the 'Rosetta Stone of the East'. Soon the Elamite and Akkadian languages were also deciphered, and the history of Assyria and Babylonia was opened to the world, through the translation of stone inscriptions and clay tablets, approximately 500,000 of which have now been discovered.

Since Palestine itself, the land comprising modern Jordan, Israel and Syria, seemed to be largely devoid of valuable artefacts, the first scholars there undertook geographical surveys and the identification of ancient sites. Palestinian excavation began in Jerusalem in 1850, but the early work was not scientific.

Homer's Troy

Heinrich Schliemann, the German excavator of Homer's Troy and Mycenae, first introduced scientific methodology into archaeology. At Troy, in 1870, Schliemann discovered that the distinctive mounds which dot the countryside of the Middle East are the accumulated layers of

The 'Rosetta Stone', the famous key to Egyptian hieroglyphics.

Heinrich Schliemann (*top*) addresses a London meeting.

Sir Austen Layard supervises the removal of a giant bull from Nineveh.

ancient cities, which have been destroyed and rebuilt time and again over the centuries. Beneath each mound (or *tell*, as they are called in Hebrew and Arabic) lay an ancient city or portion of a city. By cutting through these layers, as one might slice a cake, the history of the site could be uncovered from the most recent period of occupation (at the surface) to the earliest (at the bottom). Then 20 years later, the English Egyptologist, Sir Flinders Petrie, working briefly at Tell Hesi in Palestine, observed that each layer in the tell contained its own unique type of ceramic pottery. By carefully recording the pottery in each layer, he observed changes in cultural occupation. He saw that some of the pottery had different forms, which he recognised from his work in Egypt, where he had found similar pottery in contexts which could be dated from inscriptions found at the levels in which the pottery was discovered. In this way originated 'ceramic typology', the most important technique in modern Palestinian archaeology for dating stratigraphic levels which do not contain inscriptions or coins.

Pots and dates

Petrie's discovery was revolutionary. Since ancient people often made their own pottery, when they moved on they did not bother to take it with them because it was so inexpensive. Since pottery was virtually imperishable, every layer of a tell contains an abundance of potsherds. Once this was recognised, a chronology based on ceramic typology had to be established, so that more precise dates could be given to the changes in pottery styles, which could be distinguished as precisely as changes in car models today.

The man who recognised this was the pre-eminent Middle-Eastern archaeologist, William Foxwell Albright. Working at Tell Beit Mirsim in southern Palestine from 1926–32, he excavated a well-stratified mound with enough pottery in each stratum to record scientifically the typological and chronological evolution of their major forms. His work remains the basis of all modern ceramic typology.

Some of the largest excavations in Palestine – for example, at Jerusalem, Samaria, Jericho, Tanaach, Megiddo, Gezer, Lachish and Hazor – were carried out before this method of dating had matured. Most of these sites have been re-excavated since World War II by archaeologists using not only a highly-refined pottery chronology but also modern scientific techniques.

Three legendary archaeologists

Three of the greatest archaeologists of the twentieth century are regarded as biblical archaeologists.

• W. F. Albright, of Johns Hopkins University, was perhaps the greatest archaeological mind in history. His work was often directed against radical German critics, who attacked the historical credibility of the Bible.

• Nelson Glueck, one of Albright's students, was an ordained rabbi, and described how he used the Bible as a map when making his archaeological surveys.

• Another of Albright's students, Professor G. Ernest Wright, was one of the greatest authorities on archaeological methodology. He pointed out that the biblical archaeologist 'must be . . . concerned with stratigraphy and typology, upon which the methodology of modern archaeology rests . . . yet his chief concern is not with methods or pots or weapons in themselves alone. His central and absorbing interest is the understanding and exposition of the Scriptures.'

How archaeologists work

The methods of archaeology have come a long way since the tunnels into ancient Herculaneum, and much progress has been made since the early part of the twentieth century, when well-meaning but ill-equipped diggers attacked sites with spades, wheelbarrows and hundreds of hired labourers operating on a baksheesh system, paying each worker at the current market price for every artefact found.

A scientific approach
The techniques of excavation have evolved into what is now a highly scientific, carefully controlled and very expensive operation. The cost, and the demand for ever greater accuracy, have helped transform excavation into an organisation of highly-specialised experts pooling their skills in an expedition resembling an outdoor scientific laboratory. There are five major tasks in modern archaeological expeditions: surveying, excavating, recording, interpreting and publishing. First, every new site must be approached by surveying for miles around to discover as much as possible about the geographical and historical setting in which the site evolved.

The grid method
Following the survey of the surrounding area, the site chosen is plotted from above, on a grid divided into 5 metre (15 foot) squares. Each square will be numbered, and only a representative number of squares are dug–not the whole site. This allows later excavators to check and correct errors, if necessary, as archaeological

methods continue to improve. Many sites have been 're-dug' in this way, including Gezer, Jericho, Hazor and Lachish. The squares are dug in successive strata, peeling off one layer at a time, including any pits that penetrate into lower levels. This method is known as the Kenyon-Wheeler method (after the British archaeologists Dame Kathleen Kenyon and Sir Mortimer Wheeler), and provides the greatest possible control. The work is done under the eye of area supervisors, one to each square, who keep careful records of everything that happens in that square.

Any object or small area that needs to be identified separately and recorded by itself is known as a *locus*, which may be a mere change in the colour of the soil, or something as large as a stone floor or wall. Each *locus* is given a number and all data relevant to it will be recorded under that number.

Recording the dig
Top-plans are drawn, showing the square from a bird's-eye view as it appears at the end of each working day, and listing all the *loci* visible at that time. Dig photos are taken of important stages, and are later used for publication. When the digging is finished, the baulk, or exposed wall of a square, is carefully drawn and becomes the guide to the analysis of the chronological history of the square.

By putting all the baulk drawings together, the archaeologist has the basis for analysing the entire excavated site. Just as the number of layers in a cake can be determined by cutting a slice, so the history of a site exists in its stratigraphy. This is the single most important index to the site, and for this reason the baulks are kept trimmed and their *loci* identified by sticking tags with *locus* numbers on to their walls.

Nothing is more important than keeping careful records on a dig. By its nature, archaeology is systematic destruction, and nothing will ever be seen again exactly the way it was when it was dug. Thus photography,

Workers open a new square during a recent dig at Capernaum, Israel.

Archaeological methods

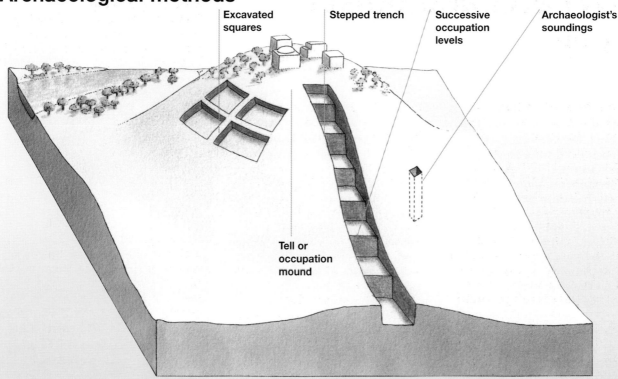

Excavated squares

Stepped trench

Successive occupation levels

Archaeologist's soundings

Tell or occupation mound

elevations, scale drawings, supervisors' observations and impressions kept in diaries are essential elements in modern excavations.

Understanding the dig
All of this is necessary for the next step – interpretation. This is, of course, the ultimate purpose of any dig, and the most difficult part of the process. Normally, supervisors, volunteer diggers and excavation directors interpret the data in the same way.

The 'new archaeology'
Recent decades have seen the use of many advanced scientific techniques in field archaeology: ground and aerial photo-grammetry, magnetometers and resistivity instruments, laser-guided and computerised transits for shooting elevations and making surveys, infra-red photography, neutron activation analysis of pottery, thin section and petrographic analysis of temper and clay, thermoluminescence, flotation

of pollen samples and settlement pattern analysis. All these are part of the 'new archaeology' and have helped transform excavation techniques.

It is now possible to date discoveries more accurately than years ago. In addition to noting the stratum in which an artefact or structure appears (the successively lower strata are progressively earlier, if the strata are scaled and undisturbed) we can now place that object in a related pottery chronology which dates the stratum for us.

Dates and coins
The discovery of coins is very important to dating, because coins carry names, and often dates, on them. Carbon 14 may be applied to organic matter, which, once a portion is burnt, gives off radio-active carbon 14 at a rate which may be measured by a type of geiger-counter. Under ideal conditions, a dating accurate to +/-200 years may be obtained from the

amount of carbon detected. Potassium argon dating may be used for much older inorganic materials. For sites later than the Hellenistic period, a chronological typology for glass similar to that for ceramic pottery is being developed.

Interpreting the data
The interpretation of archaeological data is usually done by parallelism. This indispensable procedure requires knowledge of what has already been dug at sites elsewhere with similar time-frames. A particular find is compared to these parallel sites, which hopefully will have been adequately dated, and may thus increase confidence in the interpretation given to that object at the site in question. Caution must be used, or a fruitless cycle of circular reasoning and conjecture may result. Computers are increasingly being used to catalogue finds, and make the retrieval of otherwise unknown parallels rapid and effective.

The Bible and history

There are limits to the achievements of archaeology. Much has been achieved since Heinrich Schliemann dug at Troy, but archaeology remains an inexact science. The data extracted from an excavation can often be interpreted in a number of different ways, and can be dated only within relative degrees of certainty. Absoluteness is rare. How old is man? How old is the earth? When did Abraham live? What was the date of the Exodus? Was the conquest of Canaan an invasion or just a social upheaval within the land itself? Did Moses write the Pentateuch? Neither biblical criticism nor archaeological excavation has been able to answer these and other issues conclusively.

At times archaeology and biblical scholarship seem to work against each other. Part of the problem lies in a failure adequately to understand the biblical text, and part in a misunderstanding of the archaeological evidence. Some sites may be wrongly identified, while others may be inadequately dug or erroneously evaluated. Archaeology can often help us understand something more clearly, but it rarely injects certainty into biblical uncertainties. To claim too much for it is to misunderstand its contribution.

The acts of God
The Bible is a collection of many books written over hundreds of years from the viewpoint of Judaistic monotheism. Its authors never intended to write history in the modern sense; their purpose was to demonstrate the acts of God in Jewish history. Archaeology's main contribution to the study of the Bible is as an important means of clarifying and dramatising the history in which the biblical faith originated.

The Bible was not written in a vacuum, nor did the events it records take place in a vacuum. The Jews interacted with the ancient cultures with which they came into contact; the Bible records those interactions, both good and bad. Biblical archaeology penetrates and clarifies that area of ancient history which gave birth to the Bible.

What mean these stones?
What is the value of archaeological discoveries to the reader of the Bible? Archaeology's major contribution is not apologetic. Certainly, some difficulties are clarified by the results of archaeological work. For instance, stone

Sennacherib's prism records events of his reign.

Herodion, site of Herod the Great's stronghold and palace.

Part of the extensive excavations at Masada, near the Dead Sea in Israel.

inscriptions were found in Thessaloniki, Greece, containing the term *politarch*, a term which Luke used in Acts 17:6 in referring to Roman authorities, but which critics of the Bible had rejected as erroneous because no record of such a term existed prior to the discovery. On the other hand, attempts to find Joshua's Jericho or Solomon's Jerusalem have been largely disappointing.

Exciting discoveries
Nevertheless, many exciting discoveries have been made which illustrate the Bible beautifully: the Clay Prism of Sennacherib, mentioning the Judean king Hezekiah; the Black Obelisk of Shalmanezer portraying Jehu, the Jewish king, bowing before him; the Babylonian Chronicle, providing the basis for dating the destruction of the Temple in Jerusalem in 587 B.C.; the Cyrus Cylinder, showing the Persian monarch's policy of assisting nations like the Jews to return and rebuild their cities and temples; the inscription in the pavement of the theatre courtyard in Corinth containing the name of Erastus, the city treasurer, who is

probably mentioned in Romans 16:23; the winter palace of Herod the Great in Jericho, and the site where he was buried in Herodium.

However, an eminent archaeologist, the late Roland de Vaux, warned: 'Archaeology cannot "prove" the Bible. The truth of the Bible is of a religious order. . . . This spiritual truth can neither be proven nor contradicted, nor can it be confirmed or invalidated by the material discoveries of archaeology. However, the Bible is written in large part as history . . . it is concerning this "historical" truth of the Bible that one asks confirmation from archaeology.'

The value of archaeology
The great value of archaeology to the student of the Bible lies in its ability to place our biblical faith in its historical setting, and to demonstrate the cultural setting in which biblical events took place. For those who love the Bible, there is no experience like standing on the Mount of Olives in Jerusalem and looking out over the results of archaeological excavation in the Holy City: here is part of Nehemiah's rebuilt walls; there are the steps that led

up to the Temple during the days of Jesus; here is Hezekiah's tunnel, leading to the Pool of Siloam, where Jesus made the blind man see; there are the beautiful stones on the pinnacle of the Temple which the disciples pointed out to Jesus. And what a thrill to walk through the remains of the chariot-city of Solomon and Ahab at Megiddo; to linger among the ruins of Caesarea Maritima, Herod the Great's magnificent city on the Mediterranean; and to stroll among the pools built by the Essenes at Qumran, where the Dead Sea Scrolls were found. The aqueducts of Caesarea, the bathhouses of Masada and Jericho, the synagogues of Galilee, the water-tunnels of Megiddo, Hazor, Gezer and Jerusalem, the fortifications of Lachish, the altars of Beersheba and Mount Ebal, the *fora* and temples of Samaria and Jerash, the theatres of Amman and Ephesus, all create an indelible impression of the civilisation that once inhabited these ruins. We are hence able to reconstruct in our minds these cities as they existed in the time of Abraham, Solomon, Jesus and Paul.

A historical context
The story of Jesus does not begin, 'Once upon a time in a faraway land . . .', but rather, 'After Jesus was born in Bethlehem in Judea, during the time of King Herod . . .' (Matthew 2:1). What a thrill it is to traverse the hills of Judea and walk the streets of Bethlehem, to wander through Nazareth and take a boat-ride on the Sea of Galilee and walk the streets of Jerusalem's Old City. How exciting to watch each turn of the archaeologist's spade, knowing that it was here, in these very places, here in historical and geographical reality, that the most precious heritage of human history was bequeathed to humankind. This is the value of biblical archaeology – its ability to locate the faith in the realities of ancient history.

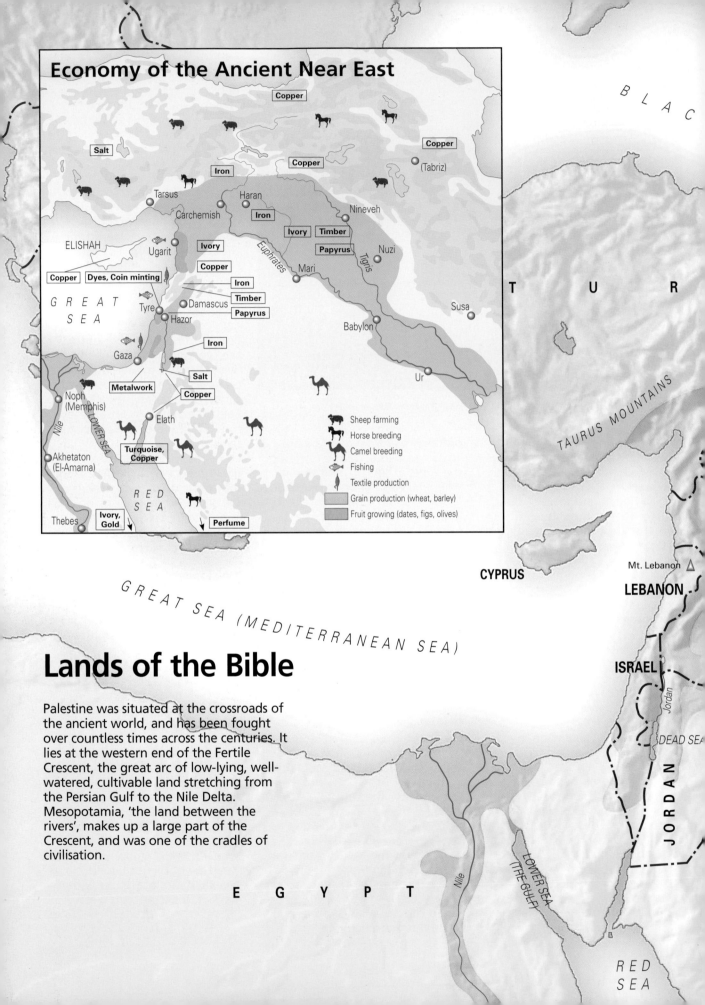

Economy of the Ancient Near East

Copper

Salt

Iron

Copper

Copper
(Tabriz)

Tarsus

Haran

Nineveh

Carchemish

Iron

Ivory | Timber

Papyrus

Nuzi

ELISHAH

Ugarit

Ivory

Copper

Mari

Susa

Copper | Dyes, Coin minting

Iron

GREAT
SEA

Tyre

Damascus

Timber

Papyrus

Hazor

Babylon

Gaza

Iron

Ur

Salt

Metalwork

Copper

Noph
(Memphis)

Elath

Akhetaton
(El-Amarna)

Turquoise,
Copper

RED
SEA

Thebes

Ivory,
Gold

Perfume

- 🐑 Sheep farming
- 🐎 Horse breeding
- 🐫 Camel breeding
- 🐟 Fishing
- Textile production
- Grain production (wheat, barley)
- Fruit growing (dates, figs, olives)

BLAC

TUR

TAURUS MOUNTAINS

CYPRUS

Mt. Lebanon △

LEBANON

ISRAEL

Jordan

DEAD SEA

JORDAN

GREAT SEA (MEDITERRANEAN SEA)

Lands of the Bible

Palestine was situated at the crossroads of
the ancient world, and has been fought
over countless times across the centuries. It
lies at the western end of the Fertile
Crescent, the great arc of low-lying, well-
watered, cultivable land stretching from
the Persian Gulf to the Nile Delta.
Mesopotamia, 'the land between the
rivers', makes up a large part of the
Crescent, and was one of the cradles of
civilisation.

E G Y P T

Nile

LOWER SEA
(THE GULF)

RED
SEA

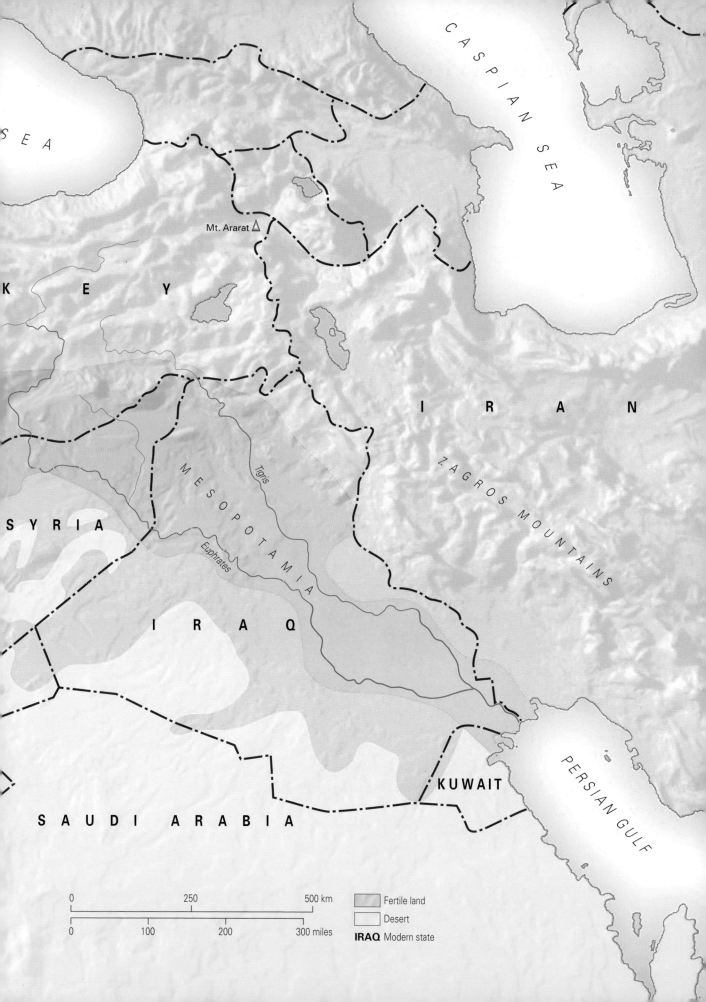

CASPIAN SEA

SEA

Mt. Ararat △

K E Y

S Y R I A

I R A N

ZAGROS MOUNTAINS

M E S O P O T A M I A

Tigris

Euphrates

I R A Q

KUWAIT

PERSIAN GULF

S A U D I   A R A B I A

0		250		500 km

0	100	200	300 miles

Fertile land

Desert

IRAQ Modern state

Bible timeline

Abraham, the first of Israel's patriarchs, receives God's call to leave his home in Ur, Mesopotamia, and go in search of a new home. This will be Israel, the land promised by God for the Israelites. Abraham is further called by God to sacrifice his son

1950-1550 Middle Bronze Age

Beginning of Egyptian Middle Kingdom – second great age of Egypt **2134**

Great pyramids built in Egypt **c.2685**

■ Wooden ships developed in Crete **c.2000**

■ Settlement of Melanesia by immigrants from Indonesia **c.2000**

■ Stonehenge started in Britain **c.2000**

■ Hittite Empire founded **c.2000**

Code of Hammurabi – first written set of laws

ISRAEL / THE JEWS

The patriarchs

Jacob **1800-1700** ●

■ Abram leaves Ur **c.1925**

● Isaac **1900-1720**

Note on dating:
Insufficient historical sources mean that sometimes dates of events and lives of figures cannot be corroborated. In these instances dating must be conjectural.

Dates of national leaders refer to their reigns and single dates of individuals refer to their births.

Key

■ Significant events

♕ Hebrew/Jewish kings

♕ All other colours – non-Hebrew rulers/kings

● Hebrew/Jewish people other than rulers

● Non-Hebrew people other than rulers

✸ Battles/points of conflict

2100 B.C.   *2000*   *1900*   *1800*

Isaac as a test of his loyalty to God. Jacob, grandson of Abraham, fathers twelve children, who become the ancestors of the tribes that settle in Canaan and form the new nation of Israel. Joseph, one of Jacob's sons, is sold into slavery and taken to Egypt. He rises to power and becomes grand vizier to the Pharaoh. Joseph's brothers come to Egypt at a time of famine in the Middle East and the family of Jacob is reunited. The community of Israelites lives near the Nile Delta. They become slaves of the Egyptian Pharaoh and build the store city of Rameses. The Israelites live in Egypt for some 400 years.

Shang ideograms from China. Clockwise from top left: city– a man kneeling in submission beneath an earthen enclosure; city wall; chariot.

Hyksos rule in Egypt *c.***1640-1570** ■

First urban civilisation in China *c.***1600** ■

merian epic of
gamesh **?**

■ Palace at Knossos
  destroyed and rebuilt **1720**

New Kingdom begins in Egypt
– Egypt's greatest era **1552** ■

Development of Brahma
worship *c.***1450** ■

Ideographic script in
use in China *c.***1500** ■

Greek language written down
for the first time *c.***1450** ■

Israel in Egypt *c.***1700-1280**

Joseph **1750-1640**

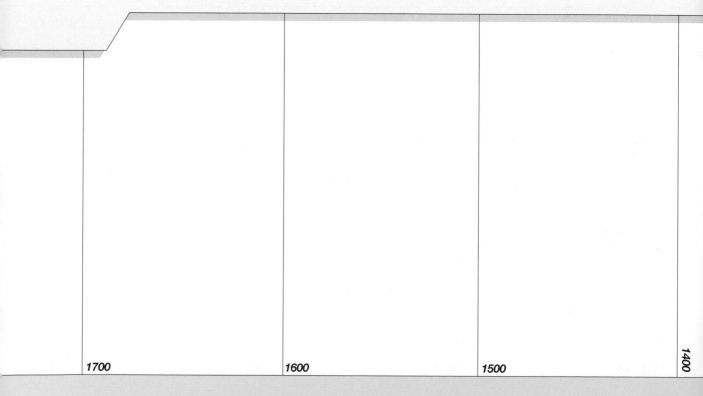

1700   1600   1500   1400

Moses champions the cause of freedom and leads the Exodus of Israelites from Egypt by crossing the Sea of Reeds. They begin a 40-year period in the wilderness, during which they receive a God-given law code, which includes the Ten Commandments, at Mount Sinai.

Joshua succeeds Moses and leads the Israelites across the River Jordan into Canaan. Military leaders, known as judges, fight campaigns against neighbouring enemies such as the Canaanites, Midianites, and Israel's greatest foe, the Philistines, whom Samson challenges. Eli and then Samuel preside over the priesthood at Shiloh, but Israel lacks military leadership and looks for a king, who is found in the person of Saul. But it is David who unites the Israelites to defeat the Philistines. He captures Jerusalem and makes it the new state capital and national shrine, lasting over 400 years. The Temple at Jerusalem is built by David's successor Solomon, who expands David's empire to its greatest extent. Unrest between the north

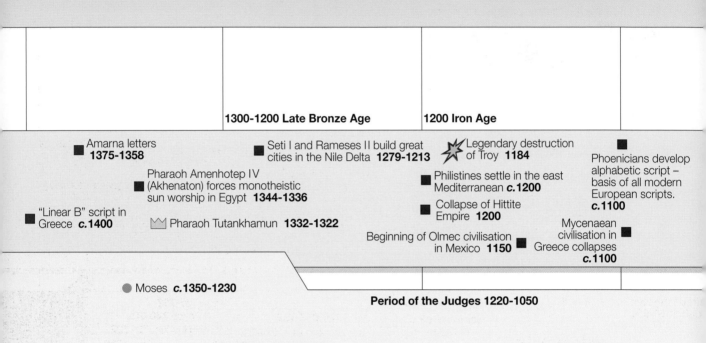

1300-1200 Late Bronze Age   **1200 Iron Age**

■ Amarna letters **1375-1358**

Seti I and Rameses II build great cities in the Nile Delta **1279-1213**

Legendary destruction of Troy **1184**

■ Phoenicians develop alphabetic script – basis of all modern European scripts. *c.***1100**

■ Pharaoh Amenhotep IV (Akhenaton) forces monotheistic sun worship in Egypt **1344-1336**

Philistines settle in the east Mediterranean *c.***1200**

■ "Linear B" script in Greece *c.***1400**

Pharaoh Tutankhamun **1332-1322**

Collapse of Hittite Empire **1200**

Mycenaean civilisation in Greece collapses *c.***1100**

Beginning of Olmec civilisation in Mexico **1150**

● Moses *c.***1350-1230**

Period of the Judges 1220-1050

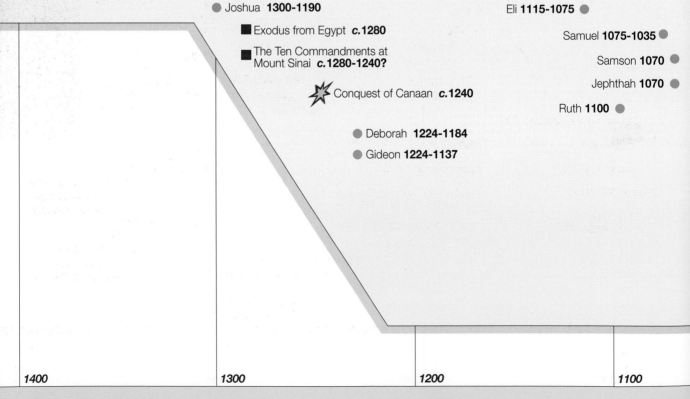

● Joshua **1300-1190**

Eli **1115-1075** ●

■ Exodus from Egypt *c.***1280**

Samuel **1075-1035** ●

■ The Ten Commandments at Mount Sinai *c.***1280-1240?**

Samson **1070** ●

Conquest of Canaan *c.***1240**

Jephthah **1070** ●

Ruth **1100** ●

● Deborah **1224-1184**

● Gideon **1224-1137**

1400   *1300*   *1200*   *1100*

and south of Israel results in civil war and the division of the land into two kingdoms: Israel (north) and Judah (south). Jerusalem remains the capital of Judah, and Samaria emerges as the northern capital.

Elijah typifies Israel's prophets in their crusade against idolatry, especially the worship of the Canaanite god Baal. Amos and Hosea condemn Israel's social injustice and religious complacency, and foretell political disaster. This is fulfilled in the invasion by the Assyrians, who capture Samaria and take many Israelites into exile. The smaller state of Judah also becomes subject to the Assyrian king, Sennacherib. Hezekiah of Judah tries to rebel but loses half his kingdom. The prophet Isaiah comforts the Judeans during this time.

With the waning of Assyrian power Josiah instigates religious reform in Judah. First the Egyptians, then the Babylonians emerge as major powers in the Middle East. Under Nebuchadnezzar Babylon besieges Jerusalem and in 587 destroys the

Phoenician characters representing an ox (left) and a bow.

K W

- Etruscans arrive in Italy *c.*1000
- Phoenicians found Carthage 814
- Golden age of Tyre (Phoenicia) *c.*900
- Indo-Aryans reach Ganges Valley and start to lay basis of urban civilisation *c.*800
- Kingdom of Kush (Nubia) founded *c.*900
- First Olympic Games 776
- Homer composes *Iliad* and *The Odyssey* *c.*750
- Legendary founding of Rome 753
- Tiglath-Pileser III expands Assyrian Empire 744
- Damascus falls to Assyria 732

United kingdom of Israel and Judah 1050-930

Kingdom of Israel 930-722

Samaria – capital of Israel *c.*879

- Jeroboam I **930-910**
- Nadab **910**
- Baasha **908**
- Elah **886**
- Zimri **885**
- Tibni **885-880**
- Omri **885-874**

- Jehoahaz **813-798**
- Jehoash **798-781**
- Jeroboam II **781-753**
- Ahab **874-853**
- Elijah *c.***870-850**
- Ahaziah **853-852**
- Joram **852-841**
- Elisha *c.***850-790**
- Jehu **841-813**

- Hosea **755-732**
- Pekah **740-732**
- Hoshea **731-722**
- Amos **760**
- Jonah **760**
- Zechariah **753-752**
- Shallum **752**
- Menahem **752-742**
- Pekahiah **742-740**

Assyria Ascendant

Fall of Samaria **722**

Sargon II **722-705**

Philistines destroy Shiloh **1050**

The kingdom divides 930

Saul **1050-1011**

Kingdom of Judah 930-587

- David **1011-970**
- Solomon **970-930**
- Building of the Jerusalem Temple **966-959**

- Rehoboam **931-913**
- Pharaoh Shishak (Sheshonq) invades Palestine **925**
- Abijah **913-911**
- Asa **911-870**
- Jehoshaphat **870-848**
- Jehoram **848-841**
- Ahaziah **841**
- Athaliah **841-835**
- Joash **835-796**

- Joel *c.***810-750**
- Amaziah **796-767**
- Uzziah (Azariah) **767-740**
- Micah **742-687**
- Isaiah **742-700**
- Jotham **740-732**
- Ahaz **732-716**
- Hezekiah **716-687**
- Assyria besieges Jerusalem *c.***704**

city and Temple. A major part of the Judean population is deported to Babylon. The prophets Ezekiel and Daniel comfort the Israelites in exile. The more tolerant Persians eclipse the Babylonians as the major Middle-Eastern power, and under Cyrus allow the Israelites to return home. The first group, under Sheshbazzar, and the second group, under Zerubbabel and Joshua, begin the rebuilding of the Temple.

Nehemiah is later appointed governor of Judea and oversees the rebuilding of Jerusalem's walls. The priest Ezra reinstitutes the Law, giving the people a new religious identity as Jews. Jews in the diaspora (dispersion) could worship in synagogues; observance of the Law (now known as the Torah), not Temple sacrifice, becomes the mainstay of Judaism. The Old Testament period ends with Ezra and Nehemiah.

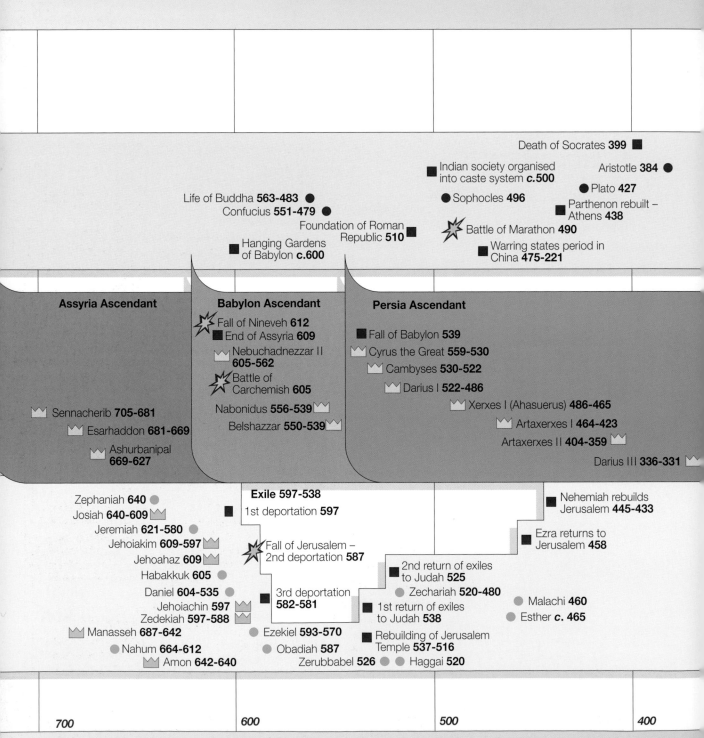

Death of Socrates 399

Indian society organised into caste system c.500

Aristotle 384

Plato 427

Life of Buddha 563-483

Sophocles 496

Confucius 551-479

Parthenon rebuilt – Athens 438

Foundation of Roman Republic 510

Battle of Marathon 490

Hanging Gardens of Babylon c.600

Warring states period in China 475-221

Assyria Ascendant

Babylon Ascendant

Fall of Nineveh 612
End of Assyria 609
Nebuchadnezzar II 605-562
Battle of Carchemish 605
Nabonidus 556-539
Belshazzar 550-539

Persia Ascendant

Fall of Babylon 539
Cyrus the Great 559-530
Cambyses 530-522
Darius I 522-486
Xerxes I (Ahasuerus) 486-465
Artaxerxes I 464-423
Artaxerxes II 404-359
Darius III 336-331

Sennacherib 705-681
Esarhaddon 681-669
Ashurbanipal 669-627

Zephaniah 640
Josiah 640-609
Jeremiah 621-580
Jehoiakim 609-597
Jehoahaz 609
Habakkuk 605
Daniel 604-535
Jehoiachin 597
Zedekiah 597-588
Manasseh 687-642
Nahum 664-612
Amon 642-640

Exile 597-538
1st deportation 597

Fall of Jerusalem – 2nd deportation 587

3rd deportation 582-581

Ezekiel 593-570
Obadiah 587
Zerubbabel 526

2nd return of exiles to Judah 525
Zechariah 520-480
1st return of exiles to Judah 538
Rebuilding of Jerusalem Temple 537-516
Haggai 520

Nehemiah rebuilds Jerusalem 445-433
Ezra returns to Jerusalem 458
Malachi 460
Esther c. 465

700   600   500   400

The Maccabees overthrow Seleucid power and the Jews achieve independence under the Hasmoneans. Apocalyptic literature, such as the book of Daniel, appears predicting God's final dramatic entry into human history. The idea is developed of the coming of a messiah, who will liberate the Jews from their oppressors. The Essenes believe the Jews need spiritual reformation to be saved.

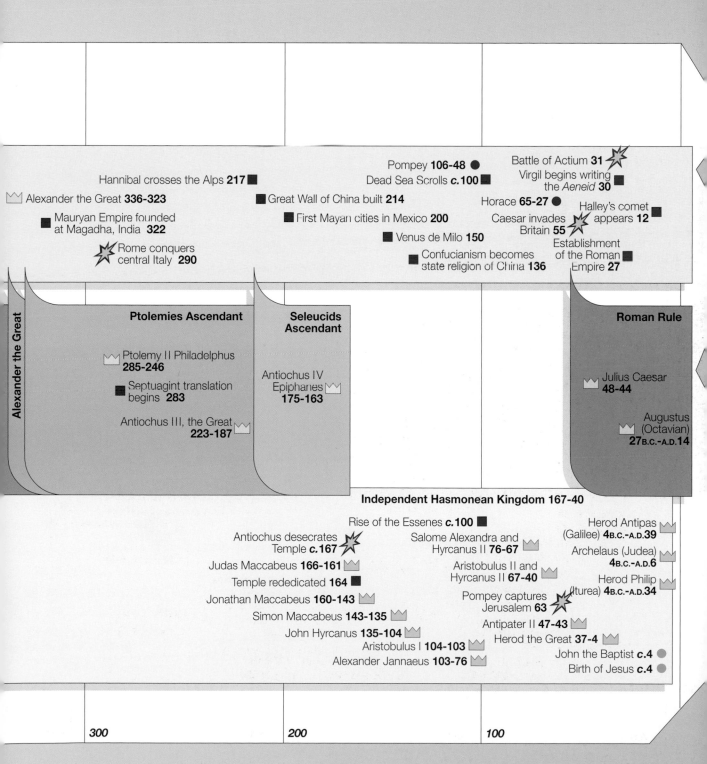

Hannibal crosses the Alps **217** ■
Alexander the Great **336-323**
Mauryan Empire founded at Magadha, India **322** ■
Rome conquers central Italy **290**

Pompey **106-48** ●
Dead Sea Scrolls **c.100** ■
Great Wall of China built **214** ■
First Mayan cities in Mexico **200** ■
Venus de Milo **150** ■
Confucianism becomes state religion of China **136** ■

Battle of Actium **31**
Virgil begins writing the *Aeneid* **30** ■
Horace **65-27** ●
Caesar invades Britain **55**
Halley's comet appears **12** ■
Establishment of the Roman Empire **27** ■

Alexander the Great

Ptolemies Ascendant
Ptolemy II Philadelphus **285-246**
Septuagint translation begins **283** ■
Antiochus III, the Great **223-187**

Seleucids Ascendant
Antiochus IV Epiphanes **175-163**

Roman Rule
Julius Caesar **48-44**
Augustus (Octavian) **27 B.C.-A.D.14**

Independent Hasmonean Kingdom 167-40

Rise of the Essenes **c.100** ■
Antiochus desecrates Temple **c.167**
Judas Maccabeus **166-161**
Temple rededicated **164** ■
Jonathan Maccabeus **160-143**
Simon Maccabeus **143-135**
John Hyrcanus **135-104**
Aristobulus I **104-103**
Alexander Jannaeus **103-76**

Salome Alexandra and Hyrcanus II **76-67**
Aristobulus II and Hyrcanus II **67-40**
Pompey captures Jerusalem **63**
Antipater II **47-43**
Herod the Great **37-4**

Herod Antipas (Galilee) **4 B.C.-A.D.39**
Archelaus (Judea) **4 B.C.-A.D.6**
Herod Philip (Iturea) **4 B.C.-A.D.34**
John the Baptist **c.4** ●
Birth of Jesus **c.4** ●

300   *200*   *100*

At the time of Jesus' birth, the Romans control Palestine. John the Baptist heralds a messiah whom many Jews, especially the Zealot party, think of as a successor to King David who will overthrow the Romans. Jesus' ministry of teaching and healing in Galilee challenges the Jewish authorities. In time he is seen as a serious political threat, which results in a Jewish conspiracy to have him put to death. Jesus is crucified at the Jewish festival of Passover. His gospel is preached by the apostles, whose mission is given divine sanction at the Feast of Pentecost. A leading Pharisee and Roman citizen named Saul (Paul) receives a blinding vision of the risen Christ on the road to Damascus. He converts to Christianity and leads the mission to the Gentiles, undertaking at least three journeys to Greece and Asia Minor. His letters form the basis of early Christian doctrine.

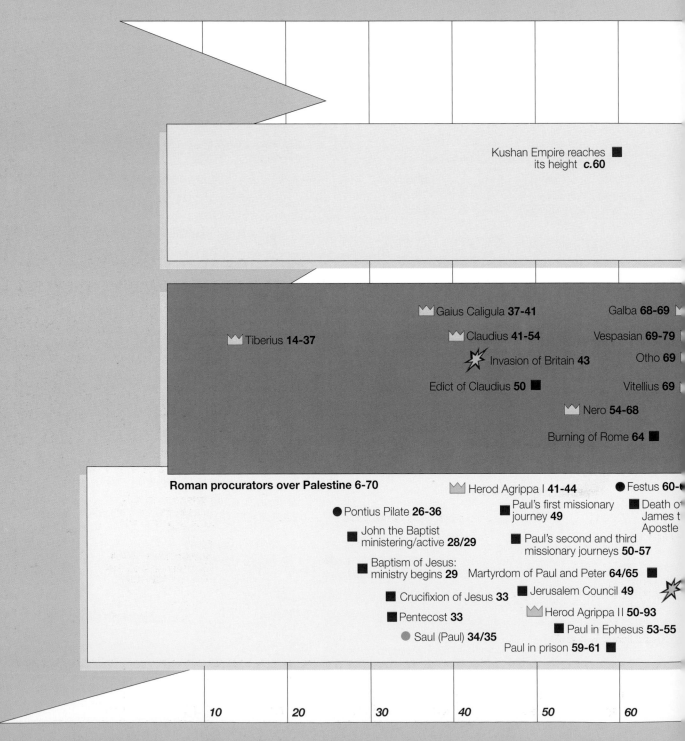

Kushan Empire reaches its height *c.*60

Gaius Caligula **37-41**   Galba **68-69**

Tiberius **14-37**   Claudius **41-54**   Vespasian **69-79**

Invasion of Britain **43**   Otho **69**

Edict of Claudius **50**   Vitellius **69**

Nero **54-68**

Burning of Rome **64**

Roman procurators over Palestine 6-70   Herod Agrippa I **41-44**   Festus **60-**

Paul's first missionary   Death o
journey **49**   James t
Pontius Pilate **26-36**   Apostle

John the Baptist
ministering/active **28/29**   Paul's second and third
missionary journeys **50-57**

Baptism of Jesus:
ministry begins **29**   Martyrdom of Paul and Peter **64/65**

Crucifixion of Jesus **33**   Jerusalem Council **49**

Pentecost **33**   Herod Agrippa II **50-93**

Paul in Ephesus **53-55**

Saul (Paul) **34/35**   Paul in prison **59-61**

10   *20*   *30*   *40*   *50*   *60*

Peter leads the mission to the Jews, and James is the head of the Jerusalem church. All three are martyred, and persecution of Christians increases to the end of the century. Jewish revolts against Rome result in the destruction of Jerusalem and the Temple, and the mass suicide of Jews at Masada. Many Jews and Christians flee from Palestine.

John, possibly the beloved disciple, is banished to the island of Patmos where he writes the book of Revelation, addressed to seven churches of Asia Minor.

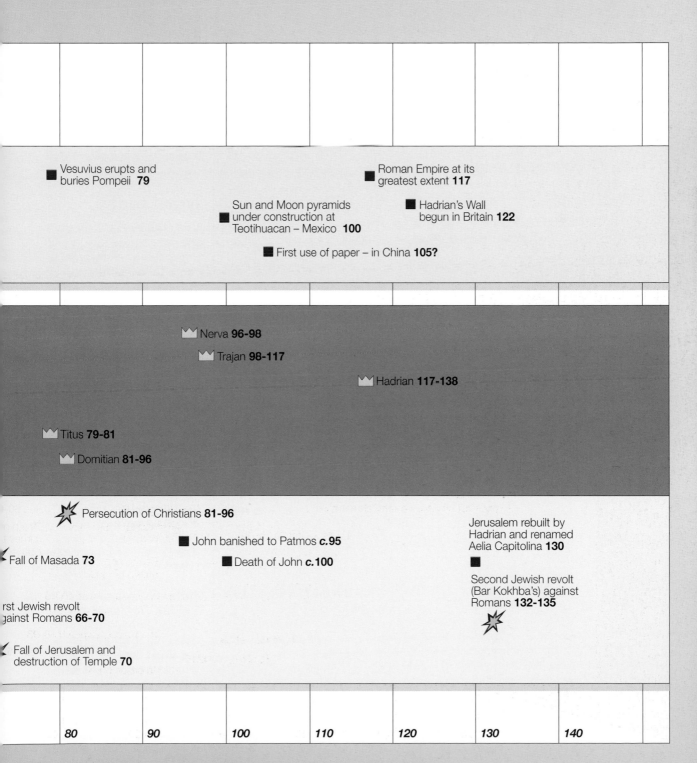

Vesuvius erupts and buries Pompeii **79**

Roman Empire at its greatest extent **117**

Sun and Moon pyramids under construction at Teotihuacan – Mexico **100**

Hadrian's Wall begun in Britain **122**

First use of paper – in China **105?**

Nerva **96-98**

Trajan **98-117**

Hadrian **117-138**

Titus **79-81**

Domitian **81-96**

Persecution of Christians **81-96**

John banished to Patmos *c.***95**

Fall of Masada **73**

Death of John *c.***100**

Jerusalem rebuilt by Hadrian and renamed Aelia Capitolina **130**

rst Jewish revolt ainst Romans **66-70**

Second Jewish revolt (Bar Kokhba's) against Romans **132-135**

Fall of Jerusalem and destruction of Temple **70**

80   *90*   *100*   *110*   *120*   *130*   *140*

The modern State of Israel

Boundaries as in 1994

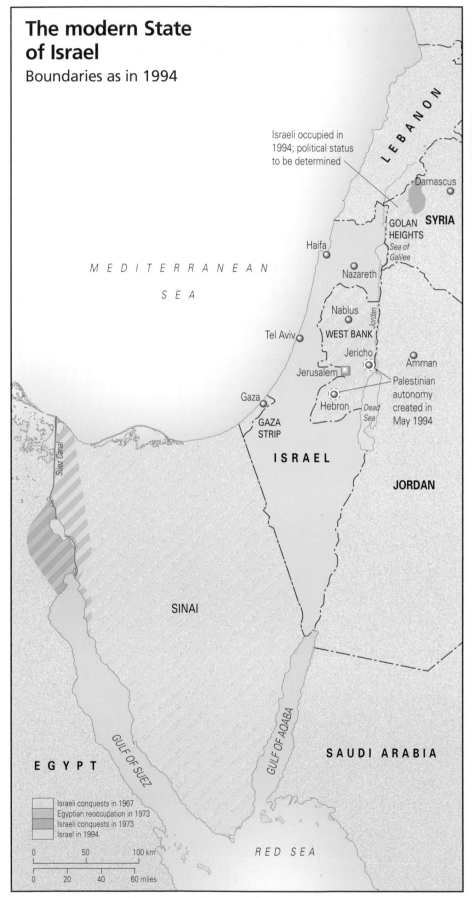

Israeli occupied in 1994; political status to be determined

LEBANON

Damascus

GOLAN HEIGHTS

SYRIA

Sea of Galilee

Haifa

Nazareth

M E D I T E R R A N E A N   S E A

Nablus

Jordan

WEST BANK

Tel Aviv

Jericho

Jerusalem

Amman

Palestinian autonomy created in May 1994

Gaza

Hebron

Dead Sea

GAZA STRIP

ISRAEL

JORDAN

SINAI

Suez Canal

GULF OF SUEZ

GULF OF AQABA

SAUDI ARABIA

E G Y P T

Israeli conquests in 1967
Egyptian reoccupation in 1973
Israeli conquests in 1973
Israel in 1994

| 0 | 50 | 100 km |
| 0 | 20 | 40 | 60 miles |

RED SEA

Tel-Aviv, capital of Israel, viewed from the ancient town of Jaffa (Joppa).

Israel today

With the rise of Zionism in the late nineteenth century, many Jewish immigrants came to Palestine from Europe. After the British conquered Palestine during World War I, the League of Nations mandated them to administer the country. The British Balfour Declaration promised a Jewish national homeland in Palestine. However, the aspirations of the Jews and the rise of Arab nationalism led to violent clashes between the Jewish and the Arab populations.

Independence

In 1947, with the British about to leave Palestine, the Arabs attacked the Jews. Israel's War of Independence (1948–49) broke out, ending in the proclamation of the State of Israel. In 1967 the Six-Day War finally brought the whole of Jerusalem into Israeli hands, together with the West Bank territories, which have been in dispute ever since.

Introducing the Old Testament

What is the Old Testament?

An artist's impression of the assault on Lachish by Assyria.

The Old Testament is a history of the nation of Israel. It tells the story of how this particular people was chosen by God, how they constantly rebelled against him and how they were rescued by him. It describes God's love for them, his patience with them and judgement upon them.

The Old Testament is also a library, a collection of 39 different books. It brings together the writings of many different people using many different styles. It includes family stories – detailed accounts of births, marriages and deaths – and national history – victories, defeats, and tales of good and bad kings. It also includes poetry, law, sermons and dramas, as well as prophets' predictions, warnings and encouragement.

The Old Testament is also the handbook for Israel's religion. It gives instructions for Israel's religious rites and celebrations, and sets out patterns of behaviour. It explains how to worship and describes what religious buildings should be like; it explains how religious taxes are to be paid and what gifts should be offered.

The Old Testament is also a collection of teachings about God. It describes what it means to belong to God – to be his people – and explains who God is and what he does. It shows how God can be worshipped and tells why he deserves worship.

The Old Testament is also communication. It is presented as God's own word to his people – dynamic, and potentially life-changing.

For many people the Old Testament is a closed book. The following pages give an outline of Old Testament history, a description of Old Testament literature, a summary of the main elements of Old Testament religion and an account of some Old Testament teachings. An attempt has been made to provide a context in which the Old Testament can be better understood and appreciated.

The Old Testament was never intended to be a closed book; it is hoped you will be encouraged to open it.

An eastern shepherd rests his flock in the shade of a tree.

Old Testament time chart

Abraham
Abraham set out from Mesopotamia on his great journey to the Promised Land.
God promised that through him all people would be blessed (Genesis 12:1–25:11). He was given a son, Isaac, in his old age (Genesis 21:1-7; 24:1–28:9).

Jacob
Isaac's son Jacob was forced by famine to go down to Egypt; his people settled there, and, years later, were forced into slavery (Genesis 25:19–35:29; 43:1–50:14).

Moses
Moses led the Hebrew people, Abraham's descendants, out of Egypt (Exodus 1:1–12:51). In the wilderness they were given the Ten Commandments. Eventually, after the death of Moses, the Israelites entered the Promised Land and occupied it (Joshua 1:1–12:24).

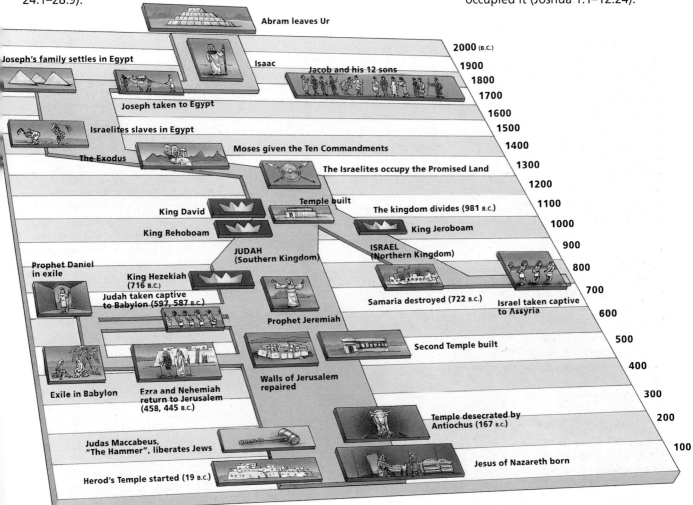

Abram leaves Ur

2000 (B.C.)
1900
1800
1700
1600
1500
1400
1300
1200
1100
1000
900
800
700
600
500
400
300
200
100

Joseph's family settles in Egypt
Isaac
Jacob and his 12 sons
Joseph taken to Egypt
Israelites slaves in Egypt
The Exodus
Moses given the Ten Commandments
The Israelites occupy the Promised Land
Temple built
King David
The kingdom divides (981 B.C.)
King Rehoboam
King Jeroboam
JUDAH (Southern Kingdom)
ISRAEL (Northern Kingdom)
Prophet Daniel in exile
King Hezekiah (716 B.C.)
Judah taken captive to Babylon (597, 587 B.C.)
Samaria destroyed (722 B.C.)
Israel taken captive to Assyria
Prophet Jeremiah
Second Temple built
Exile in Babylon
Ezra and Nehemiah return to Jerusalem (458, 445 B.C.)
Walls of Jerusalem repaired
Temple desecrated by Antiochus (167 B.C.)
Judas Maccabeus, "The Hammer", liberates Jews
Jesus of Nazareth born
Herod's Temple started (19 B.C.)

Judges and kings
As the nation of Israel developed, they were led first by judges (Judges 2:16–16:31; 1 Samuel 1:1–8:22) and then by a succession of kings (1 Samuel 9:1–31:13; 2 Samuel 1:1–24:23; 1 Kings 1:1–11:43). After the death of Solomon, the kingdom divided into Israel and Judah (1 Kings 12:1–22:53; 2 Kings 1:1–25:30).

Captivity
When the Assyrian Empire rose to power, Israel was threatened with invasion. Despite God's warnings to his people through the prophets, the northern kingdom (Israel) was taken into captivity by Assyria in 722 B.C., and the southern kingdom (Judah) by Babylon in 587 B.C. (2 Kings 17:1-23; 25:1-30).

Return
The Jews only returned from Exile in Babylon to Palestine by stages, to set about reclaiming their land and rebuilding Jerusalem and the Temple (Ezra 1:1–6:22; Nehemiah 1:1–7:73a). Many of the Jews did not make this journey back to Palestine.

Creation and covenant

Creation

Genesis 1–3, Psalms, Isaiah 40–55 and Job 38–42

It is taken for granted in the Old Testament that God exists – and that he created the world. Most of the writers' earliest thinking about God relates to the Exodus from Egypt or to the covenant. Yet God's creative activity is a vital part of Old Testament teaching.

Two creation stories
There are two creation stories in Genesis 1–2, neither of them written in scientific terms, but both expressing truth.

Genesis 1 is a structured account of creation, which is totally God-centred. God sees, creates, says, divides, calls, blesses and makes. We learn that the world is ordered and purposeful; it is made the way that God intended – 'God saw that it was good.' The climax of this creation is humanity; human beings are created to relate to God and to each other, and to take responsibility for their own actions and the world around them.

God's work in creation is presented in Genesis 1 as finished, yet also continuing. God is the Lord of nature, who rules and maintains creation. He is not merely the initiator of life, but the one who sustains life, enabling the created world and the life it contains to continue.

The Garden of Eden
The Genesis 2 account is more human-centred. It does not recount the creation of the world, but the story of what happened in a garden in one part of God's creation. But the central teaching of both accounts is the same: the world is created by God and belongs to God; human beings relate to God and are responsible to God.

God the Creator
Outside Genesis, when creation and God the Creator are mentioned, the focus of thought usually includes:
• The intricacy and complexity of the creation
• The order and structure of creation
• The beauty and power of creation
• The purpose of creation: it involves God's will
• The uniqueness of the Creator
• The power and sovereignty of the Creator.

The consequences of creation
The Old Testament teaching about creation brings meaning to a world of meaninglessness. All life belongs to God; he has the right to make demands on human beings. They are accountable to him, and owe him awe and worship as their Creator. God, as the everlasting Creator, also has an ongoing responsibility to his creatures. He knows, understands, comforts, strengthens and enables his creation. He created the world and subdued chaos, and was also willing to subdue chaos in the lives of his people.

Problems in the world
Yet the Old Testament writers are also aware of the problems in the world. Creation as it exists today is not beautiful in every aspect; alongside it is an ugliness which is not solely the result of human mismanagement. The story of the Fall, found in Genesis 3, is only the first of many reflections on how it is possible to comprehend the glory and the dreadfulness of the created world as it is.

A Flood account on tablet XI of the Assyrian version of Epic of Gilgamesh. In Genesis God committed himself never again to use a flood to destroy the earth.

Covenant

Genesis 12–25, Exodus, Deuteronomy, 2 Samuel 7 and Jeremiah 31

God created the whole world, but set up a covenant relationship solely with Israel. Covenants, or treaties – common within the Ancient Near East – were a kind of contract formalising an alliance between partners. They were not necessarily equal partnerships, but called for commitment and responsibility from both sides. The Old Testament develops this concept when it speaks of the relationship between God and his people as a covenant. Covenant is a very significant element of Old Testament teaching.

Contemporary treaties

The covenant between God and Israel is similar to contemporary treaties between imperial powers and vassal states. These so-called 'suzerainty' treaties followed a common pattern: they set out the history of the agreement, laid down rules the vassal must keep, formulated arrangements to keep the covenant document safe and to give periodic public readings, explained the benefits or protection that would be provided, and described the punishment for breaking the rules.

'I will be your God . . . '

In Israel, the covenant is established by God alone; he sets the terms. It is seen as a relationship between God and Israel. The so-called covenant formula 'You/they will be my people and I will be your/their God' is repeated in different forms many times, and lies at the heart of Israel's understanding of her life and faith.

However, the covenant was not forced upon Israel without her consent. She had the freedom to accept and confirm the relationship. The obligations of the covenant were not arbitrary; they summarised what it meant to be holy, and explained how Israel should behave if she were to enter this relationship with a holy God.

Judgement

If human responsibility is taken seriously, judgement and punishment also become involved, guaranteeing the covenant, and opening up the possibility of repentance, forgiveness and restoration.

However, the setting aside of the covenant also remains a possibility. The commitment that God makes is unbreakable; yet the covenant ends the moment its obligations are broken. It is clear that, with Israel's constant disobedience and disloyalty, it was only God's grace and mercy that allowed the covenant to continue.

Five covenants are mentioned in the Old Testament

1. *The Noahic covenant*, made between God and the whole creation. This was unconditional, with no human obligations; God committed himself never again to use a flood to destroy the earth.
2. *The Abrahamic covenant*, in which God made promises to Abraham and his family. The obligations on Abraham and his family are not spelt out in detail, but they were called upon to remain in relationship with, and obedient to, God.
3. *The Mosaic, or Sinaitic, covenant*, the major covenant with Israel – so called because Moses acted as go-between when it was set up between God and Israel at Sinai.
4. *The Davidic covenant*, in which God made special promises to David about his descendants.
5. *The new covenant*. Jeremiah and Ezekiel speak of a new relationship, in which God's law will be written on people's hearts and they will know and follow God.

> Now if you obey me fully and keep my covenant, then out of all nations you will be my treasured possession.
> Exodus 19:5

A chosen family

Genesis

When we read the Old Testament, we quickly realise that history is story. The history of the people of Israel is the story of real people, in real situations, making real decisions, taking real actions and making real mistakes.

The preface
The first few pages of the Old Testament contain the history of the beginnings of the world, painted in broad brush-strokes. We learn that all people were created by God and were intended to live in ideal circumstances, sharing their everyday lives with God. But people were created able to make choices; they chose to go it alone and hence spoilt things.

The 39 Old Testament books go on to tell how God picked a particular family – the Abraham clan – that grew into a particular nation – Israel. He chose them to be his special people, to show the world what would happen if people shared their lives with God. Sadly, on many occasions, this family and this nation spoilt their opportunities too.

But, as the story unfolds, we learn about God, his love for these people, his willingness to forgive and his great sense of justice. We get an idea of how things could have been if the people really had followed God's plans. A sense of hope kept them going.

Abraham's family
We learn initially about four generations of the chosen family. Abraham and Sarah, business people from the great city of Ur, in Mesopotamia, were called by God to leave their home and family and go to live in the land of Canaan. Much of the story revolves around the relationship of Abraham and his family with this God whom they were learning to know.

God promised them that the new land to which they were going would one day belong to their family, although at the outset they lived there as visitors; yet for many years Abraham and Sarah had no children. Eventually, when they were too old to have children, Isaac, the son God had promised, was born. Isaac's name means 'laughter', and everybody seemed to love him.

Jacob the deceiver
Isaac's son, Jacob, was different; his name means 'usurper', or perhaps 'deceiver', and he lived up to his name. He deceived his brother, his father and his uncle in his attempts to get his own way. Later he had twelve sons and a daughter, by four different women, and made a favourite of Joseph, one of the boys. Although Jacob matured and learned more about God, his family behaved dysfunctionally.

Joseph's story
Eventually Joseph's brothers grew so jealous of him that they sold him as a slave to traders travelling to Egypt, but told their father that a wild animal had killed him. However, in Egypt, Joseph grew from a spoilt boy into a gifted leader. Although he was wrongfully jailed, even in prison he was respected. A chain of events led ultimately to his being

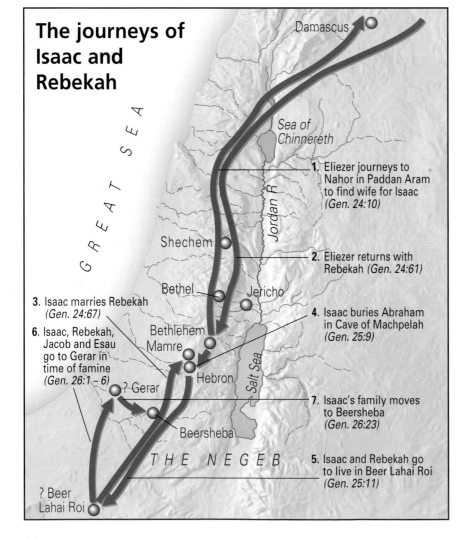

The journeys of Isaac and Rebekah

GREAT SEA

Damascus

Sea of Chinnereth

Jordan R

Shechem

Bethel

Jericho

Bethlehem

Mamre

Hebron

? Gerar

Beersheba

Salt Sea

THE NEGEB

? Beer Lahai Roi

1. Eliezer journeys to Nahor in Paddan Aram to find wife for Isaac (Gen. 24:10)

2. Eliezer returns with Rebekah (Gen. 24:61)

3. Isaac marries Rebekah (Gen. 24:67)

4. Isaac buries Abraham in Cave of Machpelah (Gen. 25:9)

5. Isaac and Rebekah go to live in Beer Lahai Roi (Gen. 25:11)

6. Isaac, Rebekah, Jacob and Esau go to Gerar in time of famine (Gen. 26:1 – 6)

7. Isaac's family moves to Beersheba (Gen. 26:23)

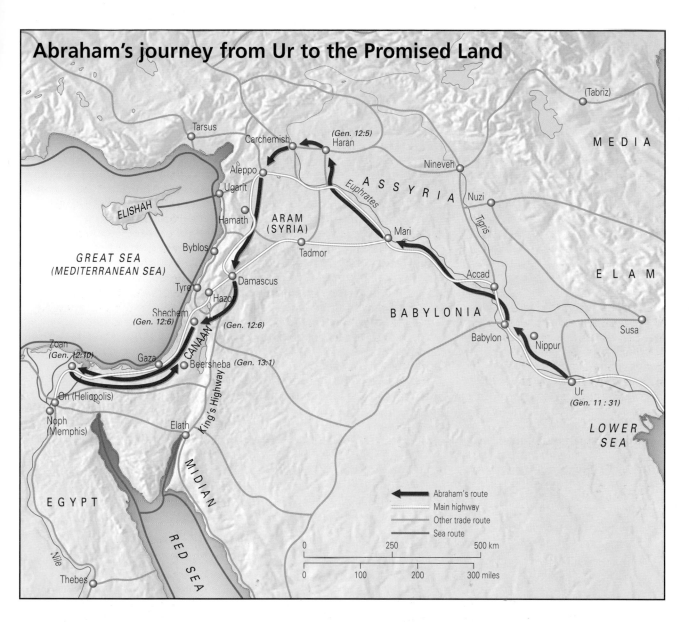

Abraham's journey from Ur to the Promised Land

given control over the Egyptian economy.

When, years later and in a great famine, Joseph's brothers came to Egypt to try to buy food, they had no idea that Joseph held their fate in his hands. Joseph's family were eventually reconciled with him, and he was able to see that God had used circumstances for good, even when some actions, such as those of his brothers, had been intended for bad. The whole family, including Jacob, finally went to live in Egypt.

A chosen people

1. *God chose both parents of the promised son.* Abraham had other sons, but it was only the son of Abraham and Sarah who was to be father of the chosen people. Much is said about women and their interests; Sarah, Isaac's wife, Rebekah, and Jacob's two main wives all have important roles in the story.

2. *God chose Abraham and Sarah's family, but this did not mean he was uninterested in other people.* We also learn about God's care for Hagar, the Egyptian slave whom Abraham and Sarah treated badly, and his care for Abraham's nephew Lot, who made some

bad decisions.

3. *The people God chose were not perfect;* they made many mistakes. But if they were willing to listen and learn there was always a way forward; God still wanted them to belong to him.

4. *God gave the chosen people the land of Canaan, but that did not mean he could look after them only there.* God was concerned with what was happening in the whole world, including Egypt, and his power was just as real in these other countries.

A new nation

Exodus, Numbers, Joshua, Judges, Ruth

For many years the Abraham clan lived as honoured guests of the Egyptians, since they were relatives of Joseph, who had saved Egypt from disaster. (In Egypt they became known as the people of Israel, the name that God gave Jacob.) They prospered in Egypt, and did not return to Canaan.

However, after many years, when Joseph had been forgotten, the Egyptians grew jealous of this immigrant community. The Israelites became slaves, used ruthlessly by Pharaoh to construct his magnificent buildings. Eventually, more than 300 years after Joseph's death, the Egyptians murdered a generation of Israelite boys at birth, to avoid any possible future rebellion. At this point God stepped in.

Moses saved from death
A determined mother, her daughter and a compassionate Egyptian princess were used by God to alter events. Israel was a male-dominated society, but women often played significant roles. These three women ensured that an Israelite baby boy, Moses, was saved from death, brought up in the palace and given an exclusive education. However, this made him rather arrogant, and if God was to use him, he needed to learn humility. Moses broke the Egyptian law, fled the country and spent 40 years in an isolated desert community.

Moses saves his people
At the age of 80, Moses reluctantly returned to Egypt, and eventually became one of Israel's greatest leaders. God used Moses to help his people escape slavery, through the Exodus from Egypt, and set up the legal and religious systems that were to provide the basis of their national life for centuries to come. It seemed that they were now ready to return to the Promised Land – and that Abraham's family could at last fulfil their destiny.

However, at the last moment the Israelites were too timid to go forward, and ended up wandering around the desert for another 40 years. By the time they entered the land of Canaan, led now by Moses' successor, Joshua, virtually all the adults who had left Egypt with Moses had died.

What were the ten plagues of Egypt?

Exodus 7–12

Moses warned Pharaoh of ten plagues on the land of Egypt. Since the Egyptian gods were thought to be bound up with the forces of nature, each disaster was an attack on their power.

1. Water to blood *Exodus 7:14-24*
The Nile turned to blood. Possibly red dirt or algae clogged the Nile and killed the fish, making the river the Egyptians regarded as the source of life smell of death. The first six plagues all seem to emerge from the Nile and demonstrate God's power over it.

2. Frogs *Exodus 8:1-15*
Frogs, a symbol of fertility, overran the land and when they died, polluted Egypt.

3. Gnats *Exodus 8:16-19*
A small stinging insect, such as the sand flea, is probably meant. Egypt's magicians could not repeat this miracle and told Pharaoh it was the work of God.

4. Flies *Exodus 8:20-32*
Swarms, possibly of biting swamp flies, infested Egypt. The diseases they bear may have been the source of the fifth and sixth plagues.

5. Death of cattle *Exodus 9:1-7*
Many believe that the plague that struck the cattle of Egypt was anthrax. The Israelite cattle were immune, showing that God distinguished between his people and their oppressors.

6. Boils *Exodus 9:8-12*
Probably skin anthrax, carried by the bites of the flies, which fed on the rotting frogs.

7. Hail *Exodus 9:13-35*
The storm ruined the barley and flax, but spared the land of Goshen, occupied by the Israelites.

8. Locusts *Exodus 10:1-20*
Locusts stripped the land of any remaining crops. Following the other plagues that devastated the economy of Egypt, this plague was disastrous.

9. Darkness *Exodus 10:21-29*
The sun, representing the Egyptian god Ka, was darkened for three days. Some suggest this was due to a khamsin, a fierce wind that fills the air with dirt. The text, however, indicates a deeper and more terrifying darkness.

10. Death of the firstborn
Exodus 11:1–12:36
This final plague took the firstborn of every Egyptian household, but left the Israelites untouched. This caused such terror that Pharaoh finally urged Moses to lead Israel out of his land to freedom. The gods of Egypt were shown to be powerless before the God of the Hebrews.

The Exodus from Egypt

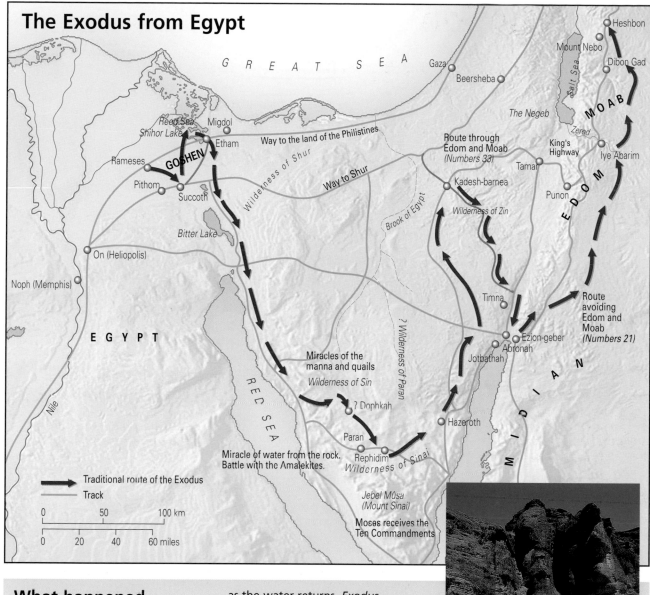

Map labels:
GREAT SEA · Heshbon · Mount Nebo · Dibon Gad · Gaza · Beersheba · The Negeb · Salt Sea · MOAB · Reed Sea · Shihor Lake · Migdol · Etham · Way to the land of the Philistines · Route through Edom and Moab (Numbers 33) · King's Highway · Iye Abarim · Rameses · GOSHEN · Way to Shur · Zered · Pithom · Succoth · Wilderness of Shur · Tamar · EDOM · Bitter Lake · Brook of Egypt · Kadesh-barnea · Wilderness of Zin · Punon · On (Heliopolis) · Noph (Memphis) · EGYPT · ? Wilderness of Paran · Timna · Route avoiding Edom and Moab (Numbers 21) · Ezion-geber · Abronah · Jotbathah · Miracles of the manna and quails · Wilderness of Sin · Hazeroth · Nile · ? Dophkah · RED SEA · MIDIAN · Paran · Miracle of water from the rock. Battle with the Amalekites. · Rephidim · Wilderness of Sinai · Jebel Mûsa (Mount Sinai) · Moses receives the Ten Commandments

Legend:
➤ Traditional route of the Exodus
— Track

0   50   100 km
0   20   40   60 miles

What happened to the Israelites during the Exodus?

1. The Israelites are told to leave Egypt by Pharaoh Rameses II. The years of slavery are over. *Exodus 12:29-36*

2. They travel to the region of the Bitter Lakes. *Exodus 12:37-39; 13:17–14:4*

3. Rameses changes his mind and pursues his escaped slaves. He traps the Israelites at the sea. *Exodus 14:5-12*

4. God tells Moses to hold out his stick over the sea. The waters are driven back and the people cross on dry land. The Egyptians are drowned as the water returns. *Exodus 14:13-31*

5. After three days they arrive at Marah – but the water is too bitter to drink. *Exodus 15:22-26*

6. God first provides manna and quails to eat. *Exodus 16*

7. God provides water from a rock. The Amalekites attack and are defeated. Moses' father-in-law advises Moses. *Exodus 17–18*

8. Israel receives the Law from God at Mount Sinai. *Exodus 19–32*

9. Miriam becomes leprous for her jealousy and rebellion against Moses. *Numbers 12:1-16*

10. Eleven days after leaving Mount Sinai, Moses sends twelve spies into Canaan. *Numbers 13:1-24*

Cliffs in the Negeb.

11. The spies return. Ten bring bad reports, leading the people to rebellion. They want a new leader to take them back to Egypt. *Numbers 13:5–14:10*

12. As punishment, God sends them to wander in the desert 40 years before entering Canaan. *Numbers 14:11-38*

From the Orthodox Monastery, can be seen the traditional site of the Israelite camp near Mount Sinai.

The giving of the Law

The most important event of the wilderness period took place at the foot of Mount Sinai, where Israel accepted a God-given code of Law and undertook to worship Yahweh (the more accurate form of the name 'Jehovah') and no other god. Moses played the key role in this event too, which marked the beginnings of monotheistic faith, a faith virtually unique in the ancient world, even though for some centuries idolatry continued to plague Israelite society. (See also 'The people of the Law' pages 166–167).

The golden calf

While Moses was on Mount Sinai, the Israelites created and began to worship a golden calf. The calf symbolised fertility and strength in Canaanite culture, and Canaanite gods were often depicted standing on the back of a bull or calf. The Israelite worship of a calf violates the second commandment, forbidding the worship of idols.

Quails to eat

The Israelites were provided with quail to eat in the desert. The quail, a small, plump migrating bird, often flies in swarms across Sinai en route to Europe from Sudan. They usually fly with the wind, and get driven to the ground if they encounter a cross-wind. As they become exhausted by their exertions, the quails are easy to catch. Observers in Sinai have on occasion seen them cover the ground, so dense are they.

Manna
The Israelites' other main food in the desert was manna, which they found on the ground each morning. It was white, looked like coriander and tasted of honey. Its nature has been much debated, but its provision was ultimately miraculous. It taught the Israelites how important it was that they trust God.
Exodus 16:13ff, Deuteronomy 8:3.16.

Into the Promised Land

The new nation was now in the Promised Land, but life was still not easy. Joshua was a good leader and achieved great successes, such as the defeat of the city strongholds of Jericho and Ai. The Israelites annexed large tracts of land throughout Canaan and re-committed themselves to serving God and living as his covenant people.

However, Joshua died before the new nation was fully established in its new land, and no national leader replaced him. The Israelites were not completely committed to serving God, and enemies within and outside the supposedly conquered territories posed major problems for them. The Israelite tribes were very conscious of their individual identity, but less confident about their allegiance to the nation, resulting in much inter-tribal conflict.

Highs and lows

The book of Judges records the highs and lows of these years, until the setting up of a monarchy eventually united the nation. The judges were regional rather than national leaders, and though they sometimes acted as legal advisers, they were normally military leaders.

The book of Judges is no collection of hero stories. Its narratives concern a varied group of men and women used by God to prevent Israel becoming absorbed into surrounding nations. The accounts make no attempt to hide the decline in standards since Moses and Joshua, or to justify the behaviour of the nation and its leaders.

Judges records, but does not praise, Jephthah's thoughtless vow, which led to the death of his daughter, and Samson's immoral lifestyle. Judges amounts to a sorry story of syncretism, disobedience and disloyalty, alongside a number of high points. In this book, the women come out slightly better than the men, and Deborah is the only major judge who did not fall from grace.

Reading between the lines

1. *God is sovereign*, but this does not remove human responsibility. A view of God's sovereignty which holds that nothing human beings do makes any difference is quite alien to Old Testament thought.

2. *God is righteous*; the people's disobedience and corruption does not alter that.

3. *God is in control* and can transform even apparently hopeless situations.

4. *God is patient* and does not easily give up.

5. *God starts from where people are* and leads them on from there.

6. *God uses all kinds of people*: gifted hot-heads such as Moses, well-meaning weaklings such as Gideon, wise counsellors such as Deborah and even uncouth louts such as Samson.

Ruth

Ruth was a Moabite woman living in the time of the Judges, and the main protagonist of the book of the same name. She married an Israelite who moved to Moab with his father, brother and mother, Naomi. When Naomi's two sons both died, she decided to return to Israel, and Ruth went with her. In Bethlehem, Ruth claimed the protection of Naomi's relative Boaz, who married her after she gleaned in his fields. Ruth is important in the history of Israel because she was the great-grandmother of David.

By tradition the book of Ruth is by Samuel, and it is set in the period of the Judges. Its story of Ruth's faithfulness in helping her mother-in-law, and God's faithfulness, in preserving a family line that led ultimately to Jesus, is a welcome respite from the violence and unfaithfulness of much of the book of Judges.

Invasion of Canaan

Ajalon
Beth-horon
Bethel
Ai
Jericho
? Gilgal
Plains of Moab
Gezer
Gibeon
Kiriath-Jearim
Jebus (Jerusalem)
Abel-shittim
Azekah
Jarmuth
Bethlehem
? Libnah
Lachish
Hebron
Eglon
Salt Sea
Debir

Dividing the land

Once the Israelites had entered Canaan, each tribe was given an area in which to settle, mostly west of the River Jordan. The tribe of Levi was given no land, but was allocated certain towns to live in. Six 'cities of refuge' were also named.

After the death of Joshua, judges such as Ehud, Gideon and Samson led the Israelites against the Philistines and other enemies.
Joshua 8:13-21; Judges

The 12 cities of refuge
Moses was told to set up six cities of refuge (Numbers 35:6-15), spread throughout the land. Three were located east of the River Jordan, at Bezer, Ramoth-gilead and Golan; three west of the Jordan at Kedesh, Shechem and Kiriath-arba (Hebron).

A city of refuge provided a safe place to which a person who had accidentally killed someone could flee and obtain asylum until a trial could be held. If subsequently found innocent, the fugitive was allowed to remain in the city of refuge, safe from the revenge of the victim's family and friends.

Altars

From earliest times, altars were set up where people could worship God. They were usually simple piles of stones, set up to remind them of God's presence, or as a kind of table where sacrifices could be offered. Before the priestly system originated, apparently anyone could build his or her own altar; but later the system became regulated and worship was centralised.

In Israel, altars were made of stone, with no carving on them, and they were not usually cut to shape. This was to show that God was in control, and could not be manipulated by human artistry. Later, altars became more complex and were sometimes overlaid with metal.

Probable boundary of tribe of Israel
Migration of the tribe of Dan
City of refuge

54

The judges

The twelve tribes of Israel

Reuben	Gad
Judah	Joseph
Dan	Levi
Naphtali	Issachar
Simeon	Asher
Zebulun	Benjamin

Worship site at Dan.

Who were the judges of Israel and their adversaries?

Judge	Actions	Years the judge led Israel / *Years of oppression*	Reference in book of Judges
Oppressor			
Cushan, king of Aram		*8*	*3:8*
Othniel	Freed Israel from Mesopotamian oppressors	40	*3:7-11*
Eglon, king of Moab		*18*	*3:14*
Ehud	Freed Israel from Moabite oppressors	80	*3:12-30*
Shamgar	Freed Israel from Philistine oppressors	10	*3:31*
Jabin, king of Canaan		*20*	*4:3*
Deborah	Deborah the only woman judge. With Barak, freed Israel from Canaanite oppressors	40	*4:4–5:31*
Midianites		*7*	*6:1*
Gideon	Sought a sign from God. Freed Israel from Midianite oppressors	40	*6:11–8:35*
Abimelech	*Terrorised the people as self-proclaimed king of Israel*	*3*	*9*
Tola		23	*10:1-2*
Jair		22	*10:3-5*
Ammonites		*18*	*10:7-9*
Jephthah	Freed Israel from Ammonite oppressors	6	*10:6–12:7*
Ibzan		7	*12:8-10*
Elon		10	*12:11-12*
Abdon		8	*12:13-15*
Philistines		*40*	*13:1*
Samson	Famous for his remarkable strength	20	*13–16*
Eli	High priest and judge	40	*1 Samuel 1:1–4:18*
Samuel	High priest and judge	21	*1 Samuel 1:11–13:15*
Joel/Abijah			*1 Samuel 8:1-2*

Kings to lead

1 & 2 Samuel, 1 & 2 Kings, 1 & 2 Chronicles

Samuel – prophet and judge – initiated the monarchy to maintain Israel's national identity and hold the country together. For about a hundred years the country functioned successfully as a united kingdom, but King Solomon's ruthless efficiency was detested by the northern tribes, and after his reign they broke away.

For the next 200 years two kingdoms, Israel in the north and Judah in the south, co-existed. They were sometimes at war, sometimes in alliance; sometimes seeking to live as God's covenant people, more often turning away from God and ignoring the demands of the Law and the covenant. In 722 B.C. the northern capital, Samaria, fell to the Assyrians, Israel was exiled and the northern kingdom ceased to exist.

Beyond this outline, the story revolves around people, their inter-relationships and their relationship with God. We learn about the lives of ordinary people, particularly in accounts of the work of Elijah and Elisha and in the writings of the prophets Amos, Hosea and Micah. However, most of the records focus on the rulers and how they used and abused their power.

Samuel
Samuel can be seen as the last of the judges or the first genuine national leader since Joshua. He was a prophet, priest and kingmaker, who succeeded in holding the people together and making them think about God. He did not cling to power himself, but handed over authority, first to Saul and then to David.

Saul
Saul, the first king of Israel, was chosen and called, but not faithful. He was little different from the judges, except that his leadership was officially recognised and more permanent. But Saul became more interested in his kingly status than in the task God gave him; he began to assume that he could overrule God's commands – and was therefore replaced.

David
Although David never sought the crown during Saul's lifetime, when Saul died in battle he was pleased to take it. After initial skirmishes with Saul's son Ishbosheth, David took over the entire kingdom. Though a good soldier and diplomat, a committed believer and an able poet, he had a number of serious failings. He controlled the kingdom but did not always control himself or his own family, and experienced major problems with his sons.

Solomon
Solomon was in many ways the most gifted king of Israel. He inherited his father David's poetic skills, was a gifted scholar and brought prosperity to the nation. However, he led a life alien to God's pattern of kingship in Israel. Deuteronomy 17 states that kings should avoid stock-piling wealth, dependence on military strength, idolatry, polygamy and oppressive rule; but Solomon's reign was characterised by all these.

Rehoboam
Solomon's son Rehoboam did not inherit his father's gifts, but followed his father's oppression of the people. It is not surprising that the northern tribes rejected his kingship.

The world at large
In addition to the regular feuding between northern Israel and southern Judah, Israel's relationships with surrounding nations were often strained.

In the north-west, Tyre (in modern Lebanon) was normally friendly towards Israel. In the north, Syria was growing more powerful, sometimes acting as an ally but more often as an enemy, devastating farms in border raids. East of Israel, Ammon, Moab and Edom caused the Jews problems, although after Solomon's reign

David defeated the Jebusite inhabitants and made Jerusalem his capital city.

But now your kingdom will not endure; the LORD has sought out a man after his own heart and appointed him leader of his people, because you have not kept the LORD's command.

1 Samuel 13:14

they were weaker than Israel and Judah, and easily contained. To the south, Egypt was declining in power, while Greece, to the west, was growing in influence: Homer was writing at this time, and the first Olympic Games took place at the time when the northern kingdom of Israel was disappearing. However, Greek influence had not yet reached so far east.

Assyria, to the north-east, beyond Ammon and Syria, was emerging as the dominant power in the region. The Assyrian Empire initiated magnificent architectural schemes, but was famously cruel, with military power the key to status.

Israel and Judah were situated on important trade routes between Egypt and Assyria, and particularly in the late ninth and early eighth centuries B.C., had great opportunities for economic growth. Assyria first dominated then destroyed Syria, and for a time Israel was left to her own devices. But this period of prosperity proved to be illusory, and Israel was in turn destroyed.

Israel: the northern kingdom

There were 19 kings of Israel, starting with Jeroboam. Although his reign began well, Jeroboam soon became more concerned to maintain power than to obey God. In the books of Kings, all 19 kings are

Reading between the lines

1. *A good beginning is no guarantee of continuing faithfulness.*

2. *God will not give up on his people –* but those who completely reject the covenant will be allowed to live with the consequences of their decision.

3. *Economic prosperity and disaster were both used to make the nation recognise their need for God;* but the people had to respond in obedience and faith. Prosperity is not in itself evidence that God approves of the nation's behaviour.

described as 'evil'; but these books were compiled in the south, and their assessments may not be unbiased.

Nevertheless, despite the ministry of such prophets as Elijah, Elisha, Amos and Hosea, and the existence of many true believers, Israel eventually ceased to be part of God's covenant people. 2 Kings 17 serves as an epitaph for the northern kingdom, making it clear that their demise was totally deserved.

Judah: the southern kingdom

During this same period there were twelve rulers in Judah – eleven kings and the notorious Queen Athaliah, who killed her own grandchildren to retain her throne. Seven kings, six of whom reigned for 25 years or more, are described as 'doing what was right in the eyes of the Lord' – though this does not mean their reigns were perfect, as the writings of the prophets Micah and Isaiah make clear.

Corruption, injustice and idolatry do not seem to have been much less common than in Israel. However, the 'good' kings did make some attempt to lead the people within the requirements of the covenant. Possibly this led God to be merciful to Judah, so that the kingdom lasted for a further hundred years before being conquered by Babylon.

The kingdoms of Israel and Judah

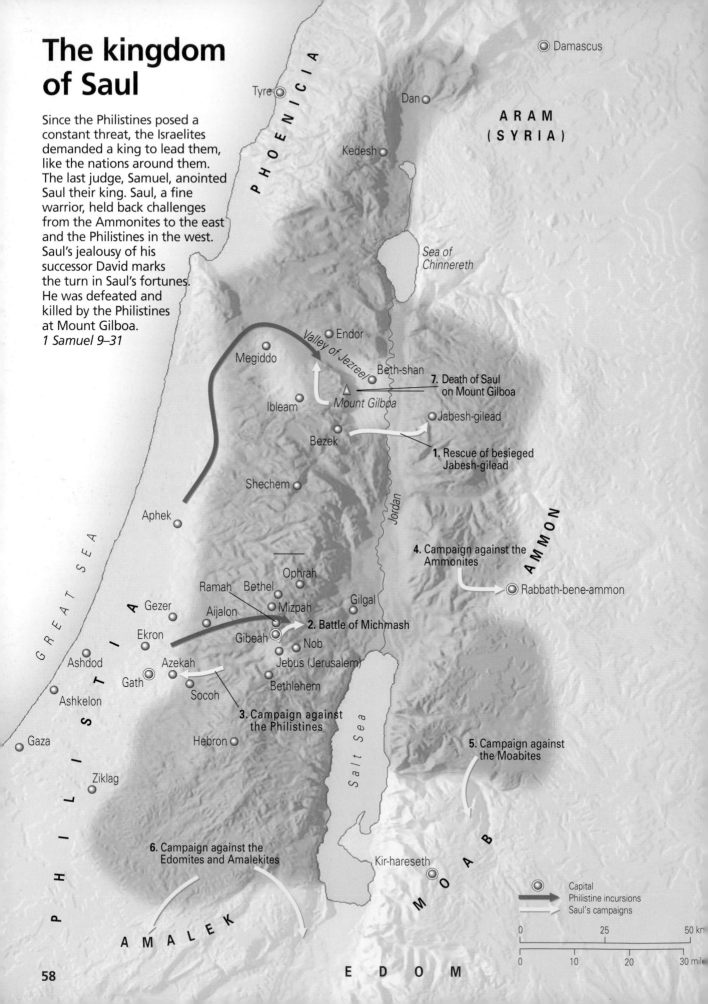

The kingdom of Saul

Since the Philistines posed a constant threat, the Israelites demanded a king to lead them, like the nations around them. The last judge, Samuel, anointed Saul their king. Saul, a fine warrior, held back challenges from the Ammonites to the east and the Philistines in the west. Saul's jealousy of his successor David marks the turn in Saul's fortunes. He was defeated and killed by the Philistines at Mount Gilboa.
1 Samuel 9–31

Damascus

PHOENICIA

Tyre

Dan

ARAM (SYRIA)

Kedesh

Sea of Chinnereth

Endor

Valley of Jezreel

Megiddo

Beth-shan

7. Death of Saul on Mount Gilboa

Mount Gilboa

Ibleam

Jabesh-gilead

Bezek

1. Rescue of besieged Jabesh-gilead

Shechem

Jordan

Aphek

AMMON

4. Campaign against the Ammonites

GREAT SEA

Rabbath-bene-ammon

Ophrah

Ramah   Bethel

Gilgal

Gezer

Mizpah

Aijalon

2. Battle of Michmash

Ekron

Gibeah

Nob

Ashdod

Azekah

Jebus (Jerusalem)

Gath

Socoh

Bethlehem

Ashkelon

3. Campaign against the Philistines

Salt Sea

5. Campaign against the Moabites

Gaza

Hebron

Ziklag

M O A B

6. Campaign against the Edomites and Amalekites

Kir-hareseth

P H I L I S T I A

| | Capital |
| Philistine incursions |
| Saul's campaigns |

A M A L E K

E D O M

0   25   50 km

0   10   20   30 miles

58

The united kingdom

Under King David and his son Solomon the kingdom prospered. David pushed back the frontiers of Israel to their farthest extent, conquering the Philistines, Moab, Edom, Ammon and the northern states, and leaving Solomon a peaceful and secure inheritance. David's empire stretched to the Euphrates in the north and Ezion-geber on the Gulf of Aqaba in the south, while the peoples of Edom, Moab, Ammon and Aram became his vassal states, and were forced to pay tribute. But David's most lasting achievement was his conversion of the newly captured Jerusalem into the state capital and national shrine.

2 Samuel, 1 Kings

Jerusalem in the time of David and Solomon

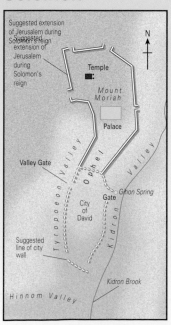

Suggested extension of Jerusalem during Solomon's reign
Suggested extension of Jerusalem during Solomon's reign

N

Temple

Mount Moriah

Palace

Valley Gate

Tyropoeon Valley

Ophel

Kidron Valley

Gihon Spring

Gate

City of David

Suggested line of city wall

Kidron Brook

Hinnom Valley

HAMATH

Cun
Lebo-hamath

Berothah

ARAM (SYRIA)

Damascus

GREAT SEA

PHOENICIA

Sidon

Ijon (Jaan)

Tyre
Usu
Dan

Kedesh

GESHUR

Acco
Chinnereth
Sea of Chinnereth

Dor

Megiddo

Ramoth-gilead

Taanach
Beth-shan

I S R A E L

Shechem

Jordan

Joppa

Jazer
AMMON

Gezer
Rabbath-bene-ammon

Ashdod
PHILISTIA
Jerusalem

Ashkelon
Gath

Medeba

Gaza
J U D A H
Hebron

Salt Sea

Aroer

Beersheba

King's Highway

M O A B

Zoar

Brook of Egypt

Tamar

E D O M

Kadesh-barnea

Territory of Judah and Israel
Vassal territory
Conquered territory

0   25   50   75 km

0   15   30   45 miles

Ezion-geber

Solomon's united kingdom

Solomon reigned for some 40 years (c.970–930 B.C.). The era of prosperity begun by David continued through his reign, during which Israel reached a peak of magnificence. Solomon's strengths were in administration, public works and diplomacy, and his reputation for wisdom became legendary.

Solomon divided his kingdom into twelve administrative districts, which facilitated a nation-wide building programme. Solomon developed a trade monopoly and exploited the natural resources of his empire, and also founded Israel's navy.
1 Kings, 2 Chronicles.

Solomon's Temple
Solomon's most famous achievement was the building of the Jerusalem Temple, of which nothing now remains.
(See pages 180–183)

The Queen of Sheba
Solomon's wisdom is celebrated by the story of the visit of the Queen of Sheba (2 Chronicles 9:1-12), who came to sample his learning. Sheba is often identified with modern Yemen, in the south-west corner of the Arabian peninsula. Since Solomon's new trading post at Ezion-geber may have threatened Sheba's trade, the queen's visit might also have been intended to build good relations with the emerging nation.

Boundary of Solomon's empire
Boundary of administrative district
Solomonic fortification or building project
United kingdom of Israel and Judah
Vassal kingdoms

The two kingdoms

1 & 2 Kings, 1 & 2 Chronicles

When the kingdom split into two, Solomon's son Rehoboam held on to Judah, plus Benjamin; this proved to be a small but stable political unit, called the kingdom of Judah. The northern part of Israel, which kept the name Israel, was bigger but never achieved political stability. After the first king, Jeroboam, scarcely any king or any dynasty was safe for long. Jeroboam's first tasks were to replace Jerusalem as capital and shrine city and to construct a new administration. The ancient shrines of Bethel and Dan were given new prominence. The first capital was Shechem, but later Samaria became the chief city.

During David's reign many Canaanites were absorbed into Israel and Judah, with the result that Canaanite religion, especially Baal-worship, became widely practised. Some of the prophets vigorously condemned this trend. It affected both kingdoms, but especially the northern one. In the ninth century, King Ahab's queen, Jezebel, determined to promote Baal-worship, and persecuted those prophets who opposed her plans. Elijah successfully opposed her (1 Kings 17–18). Ahab's dynasty was overthrown, the new king, Jehu, fiercely attacked Baal-worship, but it still continued. Hosea, in the eighth century, saw it as the chief religious problem of his day.

The ninth century also saw the rise of two military threats to Israel. One came from the neighbouring Aramean kingdom of Damascus, the other threat from the powerful kingdom of Assyria to the north-east. As early as Ahab's reign, in 853 B.C., several Palestinian states, including Israel and Damascus, formed an alliance to fight an invading Assyrian army. In the end Assyria destroyed the kingdom of Damascus, thus removing one threat to Israel, and for a time allowing Israel some peace and prosperity.

734 B.C. was a crisis year for Judah. The kings of Israel and Damascus joined forces and attacked Judah, besieging Jerusalem. The king of Judah, Ahaz, was advised by the prophet Isaiah to stand firm and take no action. Ahaz, however, took the unnecessary step of asking the Assyrians for help; that made Judah a vassal of Assyria and liable to pay a heavy annual tribute.

The end came for the kingdom of Israel in 722 B.C. Under her last king, Hoshea, Israel had foolishly rebelled against Assyria, after earlier submission, and the Assyrian armies devastated Israel and besieged Samaria, which fell after three years. Many citizens of Israel died, and many others were taken into exile (2 Kings 17). The traditional Israelite faith was not abandoned, but the large numbers of immigrants resulted in a mixed population, and the 'Samaritans', as they came to be called, were often despised and disliked by the Jews.

Judah: From Hezekiah to Zedekiah

Judah was not threatened by Assyria as early as Israel. But after King Ahaz became subject to the Assyrians (see above), the next king of Judah, Hezekiah, tried to reassert his independence. He can be praised for his religious reforms, but this political objective was impossible.

In consequence, in 701 B.C. Jerusalem suffered another siege, this time by the king of Assyria, Sennacherib. Hezekiah's kingdom was reduced by Sennacherib to less than half its previous size. Against all probabilities the city of Jerusalem was spared and Hezekiah retained his throne, though he had to submit again to Assyrian domination.

Thus Judah entered the seventh century B.C. alone (for Israel was now part of the Assyrian Empire) and subject to Assyria. It was during this period that Judah became increasingly idolatrous, and the long reign of Manasseh is denounced (2 Kings 21) for its evil practices.

The situation changed during the reign of Josiah (640–609 B.C.), whose reform programme resulted from the discovery of a 'book of the Law' in the Temple. During his reign the Assyrian Empire collapsed under attacks from the Medes and Babylonians. The Assyrian capital Nineveh fell in 612 B.C., an event hailed with joy by Nahum.

For ten years before Nineveh's fall, Josiah had been independent, able to carry out his own religious and political wishes. The prophet Jeremiah had nothing but praise for him (Jeremiah 22:15-16). However, his reign ended in tragedy. Judah had no hope of maintaining independence; the fall of Assyria meant that either Egypt or Babylon was certain to dominate Palestine. Egypt sent an army through Palestine in 609 B.C., which Josiah tried to prevent, only to die in battle (2 Kings 23:29-30).

Before long the Babylonians took control of the whole Palestinian area, led by Nebuchadnezzar, their most famous king (605–562 B.C.). The last kings of Judah never came to terms with Babylonian control. Jehoiachin rebelled, and the Babylonian army swiftly besieged Jerusalem in 597 B.C. Jehoiachin capitulated and was taken into exile in Babylon. His successor, Zedekiah, rebelled some years later, and Jerusalem suffered a longer and more disastrous siege. This ended in 587/86 B.C. with the destruction of the city and its Temple and with the deportation of all its leading citizens to Babylonia. Judah was no longer a kingdom and was partly depopulated. Many fled to Egypt, among them a reluctant Jeremiah, who throughout a long ministry had repeatedly warned against the political follies of Judah's kings.

Who were the kings and prophets of Judah and Israel?

Judah		Date BC	Israel		Assyria
King	**Prophet**		**King**	**Prophet**	
Rehoboam	Shemaiah	931	Jeroboam I	Ahijah	
Egypt invades Jerusalem					
Abijah	Iddo	913	*War with Judah*		
Asa	Azariah	911			
	Hanani	910	Nadab		
		909	Baasha	Jehu	
Allies with Syria against Baasha					
		886	Elah		
		885	Zimri		
		885	Tibni*		
		885	Omri		883-859 Ashurnasirpal II
			Samaria becomes capital		
		874	Ahab	Elijah, Micaiah	
Jehoshaphat	Jehu	870	*Allies with Judah against Syria*		
	Jahaziel	853	Ahaziah	Elisha	858-824 Shalmaneser III
	Eliezer	852	Jehoram Joram		
Jehoram Joram		848			
Ahaziah		841	Jehu		
Athaliah		841			
Jehoash Joash	Joel	835			
	Zechariah	814	Jehoahaz		
		798	Jehoash Joash		
Amaziah		796	*Fights Amaziah*		
		782	Jeroboam II	Jonah	782-773 Shalmaneser IV
Uzziah Azariah		767		Amos	
	Isaiah	753	Zechariah	Hosea	
Jotham regent		752	Shallum		
		752	Menahem		744-727 Tiglath-Pileser III
		742	Pekahiah		
			Pays tribute to Assyria		
Jotham		740	Pekah	Oded	
			Fights Assyria		
			Many deported		
Ahaz	Micah	732	Hoshea		
Tribute to Assyria			*Tribute to Assyria*		726-722 Shalmaneser V
		722	*Fall of Samaria*		721-705 Sargon II
Hezekiah		715			704-681 Sennacherib
Sennacherib invades		701			
Manasseh		687			680-669 Esarhaddon
Amon		642			
Josiah	Nahum	640			
Religious reform	Zephaniah				
	Habakkuk	612			*Nineveh falls*
Jehoahaz	Jeremiah	609			
Jehoiakim	Uriah	609			
		605			*Egypt loses battle of Carchemish*
Tribute to Egypt					
Jehoiachin		598			
Many deported to Babylon					
Zedekiah		597			
Fall of Jerusalem		587/86			

Israel and Judah during the reigns of Jeroboam II and Uzziah

Israel and Judah became powerful and wealthy nations during the reigns of Jeroboam II and Uzziah in the eighth century. Once again Israel and Judah gained control of the commercial highways in the region. Jeroboam reigned in Israel from c. 782 B.C. He recovered lands taken earlier by the Arameans of Damascus now that their power had been broken by the Assyrians. He established control over a large area of Aram (II Kings 14:25). The prophets Amos and Hosea condemned the internal moral and religious corruption and materialistic life-style.

Uzziah reigned in Judah from c. 767 B.C. He pushed back the frontier with the Philistines and recovered the territory of Edom which King David had conquered. The port of Ezion-geber was rebuilt, giving a renewed outlet to the Red Sea.

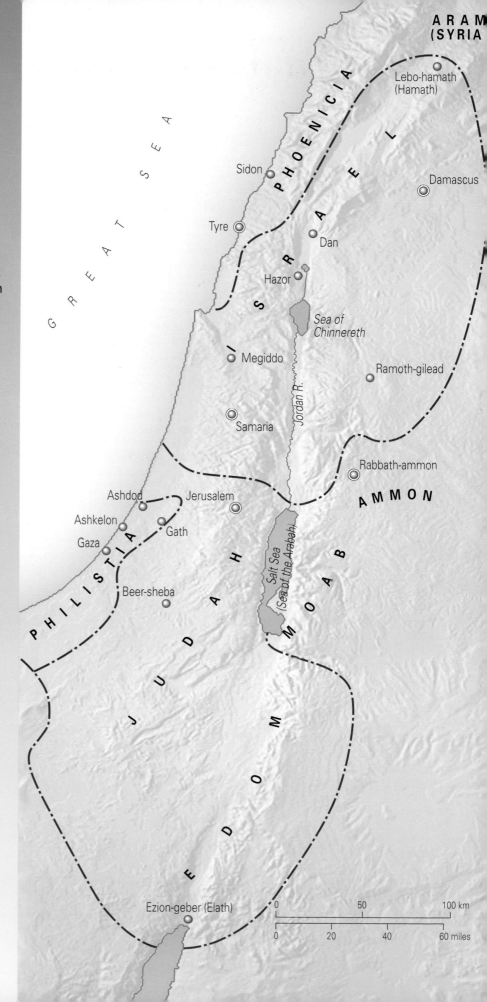

ARAM (SYRIA)

Lebo-hamath (Hamath)

PHOENICIA

Sidon

Damascus

I S R A E L

Tyre

Dan

Hazor

Sea of Chinnereth

Megiddo

Ramoth-gilead

Jordan R.

Samaria

Rabbath-ammon

AMMON

Ashdod

Jerusalem

Ashkelon

Gath

Gaza

PHILISTIA

Salt Sea (Sea of the Arabah)

MOAB

Beer-sheba

J U D A H

E D O M

Ezion-geber (Elath)

GREAT SEA

0   50   100 km

0   20   40   60 miles

Exile and return

2 Kings, 2 Chronicles, Jeremiah, Ezra, Nehemiah and Ezekiel

The Exile started with key workers and students being taken to Babylon on a scheme probably considered to benefit a poorer subsidiary nation. Then, as Judah continued to trouble Babylon, a large group, including the prophet Ezekiel, was exiled in 597 B.C., and a second large group followed after the destruction of Jerusalem in 587 B.C.

However, life was not all bad for the exiles in Babylon. They could practise trade, plant crops, mingle with the local population and even work in the Babylonian civil service. They were also allowed to maintain their own community and follow their own religion.

Ezekiel spent his first years as a prophet in Babylon trying to convince the people – who still hoped to return to Jerusalem – that exile was a deserved punishment from God. Once Jerusalem had been destroyed and they had lost hope, Ezekiel's message changed to one of encouragement and hope for the future. The Jews' God was a God of grace, who would show mercy to a penitent people and one day bring them back to their own land.

Babylon falls
Then, in a remarkably quick turn-about, Babylon was defeated by the Medo-Persians from the south. Persian influence rapidly stretched from Greece and Egypt in the west to India in the east, making it one of the world's most extensive empires.

The return
Almost immediately after coming to power in Babylon, the Persian ruler Cyrus instituted a policy of encouraging exiled communities to return home, taking with them their confiscated religious treasures and generous resettlement grants. Many of the exiles from Judah decided to remain in Babylon, but a committed group decided to return, and in 538 B.C. began to restore the nation.

Rebuilding the Temple
The returnees started well, rebuilding the altar in Jerusalem and laying foundations for the Temple; but the work was harder than they had expected. The land had been neglected, the people who had moved into the territory in the Jews' absence were hostile, and for several years harvests were poor. The Temple was eventually finished 17 years later, after the people had been challenged by the prophets Haggai and Zechariah. Although the community survived, and

Babylonian infantryman.

sought to live as God's covenant people, it was weak both economically and spiritually.

Rebuilding Jerusalem
Some 60 years later Ezra and Nehemiah, encouraged by later emperors, returned, giving the people new heart, and rebuilding the walls of Jerusalem. The capital city was restored, the economic system revived and religion renewed. It may not have been the triumphant return expected in Isaiah and elsewhere, but was nevertheless a remarkable achievement.

Sadly, fifth century B.C. Judah proved no better than her predecessors at taking advantage of new opportunities. Oppression of the poor and religious syncretism soon became rife. While religion became strong, it also became legalistic and introspective; ritual became more important than justice and mercy. It is perhaps not surprising that prophecy, which had formerly played such an important part in Israel's life, disappeared for four centuries – until John the Baptist emerged.

Glimmers of light
Old Testament history is seldom uplifting. However, through its pictures of human failure and disobedience we see glimmers of light. We read of faithful believers, and see a clear picture of the Creator God, who has made a covenant with his people: always there, always faithful, always just and with a plan that can bring human beings back into a relationship with himself.

The scene is set for the coming of Jesus. . . .

The three Jewish returns from Exile

	First return	Second return	Third return	
Scripture	Ezra 1	Ezra 2–6	Ezra 7–10	Nehemiah 1–2
Date	538 B.C.	525 B.C.	458 B.C.	445 B.C.
King of Persia	Cyrus the Great 559-530 B.C.	Cambyses 530-522 Darius 522-486	Artaxerxes I 465–425	Artaxerxes I
Leader of return		Zerubbabel	Ezra	Nehemiah
Leader's role		Governor	Priest	Governor
Number of returnees		49,897	1,774	Armed escort
Other leaders at the time		Joshua the priest Haggai, Zechariah	Nehemiah, Malachi	Ezra, Malachi
Result	Temple foundations laid Work stops	Work finished in 516	Law taught	Jerusalem's people separated from non-Jews Jerusalem's walls rebuilt

Rulers of the Persian Empire

Cyrus II 'the Great' 550–530
The conqueror of Babylon, Cyrus II reversed previous policy and returned exiled peoples to their homelands. By his decree, the Jews returned to Judea.
2 Chronicles 36:22, 23; Ezra 1–6; Isaiah 44:28; 45:1; Daniel 10:1

Cambyses II 530–522

Darius I 530–486
Darius I, a strong ruler, confirmed the decree of Cyrus II and ordered the Jerusalem Temple to be completed at Persian expense.
Ezra 5:3–6:15; Nehemiah 12:22; Haggai 1:1; Zechariah 1:1

Xerxes I 486–465
Xerxes I, probably Ahasuerus in the book of Esther, failed in two attempts to invade Greece.
Esther

Artaxerxes I 464–423 Nehemiah was cupbearer to Artaxerxes I, who granted his request and made him governor of Judea. During his rule the walls of Jerusalem were rebuilt.
Ezra 7:1, 21-26; Nehemiah 2:1-8

Xerxes II 425–424

Darius II 423–404

Artaxerxes II 404–359

Artaxerxes III 359–338

Arses 338–336

Darius III 336–331

All dates are approximate and B.C.

Relief of head of Darius I.

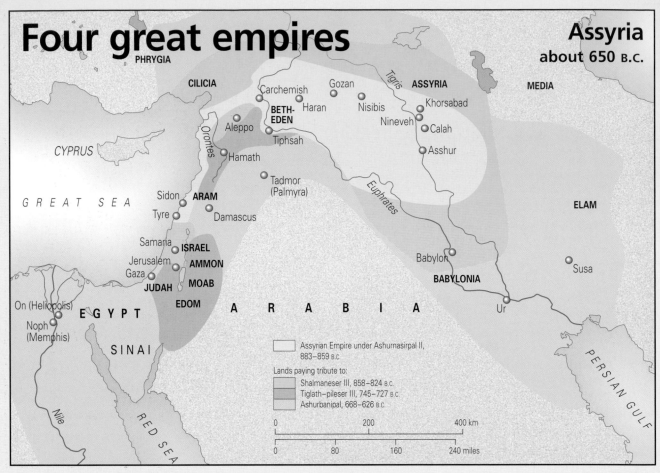

Four great empires

Assyria
about 650 B.C.

PHRYGIA

CILICIA

Carchemish · Gozan · ASSYRIA · MEDIA

BETH-EDEN · Haran · Nisibis · Khorsabad

Aleppo · Tiphsah · Nineveh · Calah

CYPRUS

Hamath · Asshur

GREAT SEA · Tadmor (Palmyra)

Sidon · ARAM · ELAM

Tyre · Damascus

Samaria · ISRAEL · Babylon · Susa

Jerusalem · AMMON · BABYLONIA

Gaza · JUDAH · MOAB · Ur

On (Heliopolis) · EGYPT · EDOM · A R A B I A

Noph (Memphis) · SINAI · PERSIAN GULF

Orontes · *Euphrates* · *Tigris* · *Nile*

RED SEA

Assyrian Empire under Ashurnasirpal II, 883–859 B.C.

Lands paying tribute to:
Shalmaneser III, 858–824 B.C.
Tiglath–pileser III, 745–727 B.C.
Ashurbanipal, 668–626 B.C.

0		200		400 km
0	80	160		240 miles

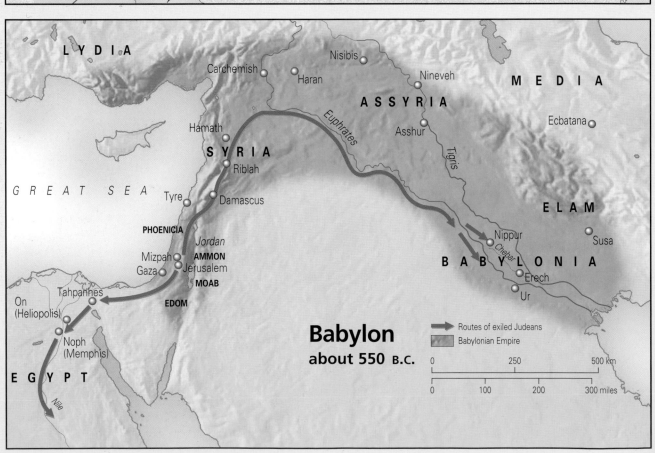

LYDIA · Nisibis · MEDIA

Carchemish · Haran · Nineveh · Ecbatana

ASSYRIA · Asshur

Hamath · *Euphrates* · *Tigris*

GREAT SEA · SYRIA · Riblah · ELAM

Tyre · Damascus · Nippur · Susa

PHOENICIA · *Jordan* · BABYLONIA

Mizpah · AMMON · *Chebar* · Erech

Gaza · Jerusalem · Ur

MOAB

Tahpanhes · EDOM

On (Heliopolis)

Noph (Memphis)

EGYPT

Nile

Babylon
about 550 B.C.

→ Routes of exiled Judeans
░ Babylonian Empire

0		250		500 km
0	100	200		300 miles

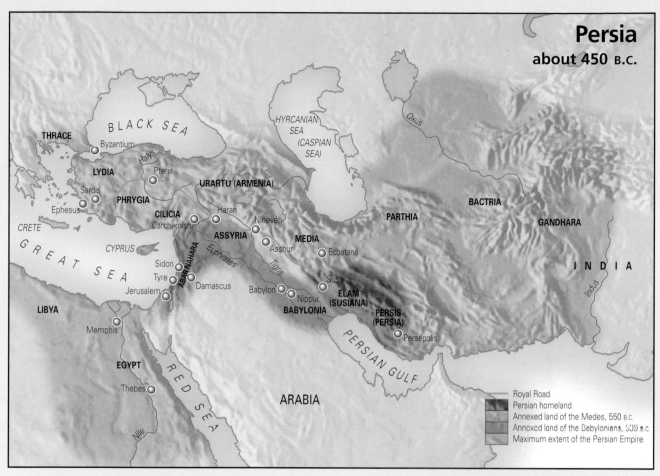

Persia
about 450 B.C.

THRACE
BLACK SEA
Byzantium
LYDIA
Halys
Pteria
Sardis
PHRYGIA
Ephesus
CRETE
GREAT SEA
CYPRUS
URARTU (ARMENIA)
Haran
CILICIA
Carchemish
Nineveh
ASSYRIA
Asshur
Sidon
Tyre
ABAR NAHARA
Euphrates
Tigris
Jerusalem
Damascus
Babylon
Nippur
LIBYA
BABYLONIA
MEDIA
Ecbatana
Susa
ELAM
(SUSIANA)
PERSIS
(PERSIA)
Persepolis
PARTHIA
BACTRIA
GANDHARA
INDIA
Indus
HYRCANIAN
SEA
(CASPIAN
SEA)
Oxus
Memphis
EGYPT
RED SEA
Thebes
Nile
ARABIA
PERSIAN GULF

Royal Road
Persian homeland
Annexed land of the Medes, 550 B.C.
Annexed land of the Babylonians, 539 B.C.
Maximum extent of the Persian Empire

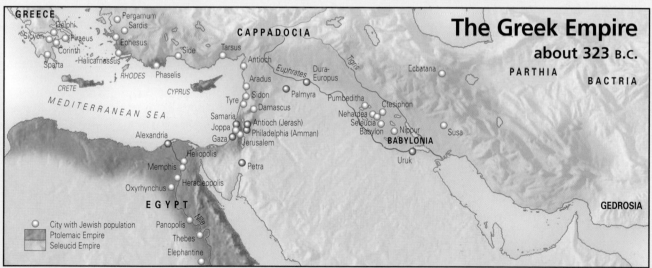

The Greek Empire
about 323 B.C.

GREECE
Pergamum
Sardis
Delphi
Sicyon
Piraeus
Corinth
Ephesus
Sparta
Halicarnassus
RHODES
Phaselis
CRETE
CYPRUS
MEDITERRANEAN SEA
CAPPADOCIA
Side
Tarsus
Antioch
Aradus
Tyre
Sidon
Damascus
Samaria
Joppa
Antioch (Jerash)
Gaza
Philadelphia (Amman)
Jerusalem
Alexandria
Heliopolis
Memphis
Oxyrhynchus
Heracleopolis
EGYPT
Panopolis
Thebes
Elephantine
Nile
Petra
Palmyra
Euphrates
Dura-Europus
Tigris
Pumbeditha
Nehardea
Seleucia
Babylon
Nippur
Uruk
BABYLONIA
Ctesiphon
Ecbatana
Susa
PARTHIA
BACTRIA
GEDROSIA

City with Jewish population
Ptolemaic Empire
Seleucid Empire

The **Assyrian Empire** reached its peak of power between 880 B.C. and 612 B.C. In 722 B.C. Assyria destroyed the northern kingdom, Israel, deporting its people; and subdued Judah, the southern kingdom.

The **Babylonians** took Nineveh, the Assyrian capital, in 612 B.C., and beat the Egyptians at Carchemish in 605 B.C.

In 586 B.C. Nebuchadnezzar destroyed Jerusalem and deported most of the people of Judah. So ended the kingdom of Judah.

In 539 B.C. Cyrus of **Persia** captured Babylon and took over the empire. Cyrus II encouraged his subject peoples to retain their religion and culture; in 538 B.C. the Jews were allowed to return to Judah to restore Jerusalem and rebuild the Temple.

Between 513 B.C. and 333 B.C. the Persians and Greeks struggled for supremacy in the Middle East. Finally Alexander the Great swept into Persia, conquering all in his path. At his death in 323 B.C. the huge **Greek Empire** was broken up; Palestine was now ruled by the Seleucid kings.

The methods of the prophets

One of the most important ways in which God spoke to Israel was through the prophets. These people – usually but not always men – had received a special calling from God. Some worked alone and some in groups, some were government officials and advisers of the king, others were critics of the government. Some were not concerned with government, but brought messages to ordinary people. Some spoke in very down-to-earth language, others used visions and obscure imagery.

Fortune-tellers?
We often think of prophets as those who told what was going to happen in the future – but that is not how the Old Testament prophets worked. In general the prophet's role was to help people understand what it meant to be the people of God in their particular circumstances. In many ways the prophets are better compared with business analysts than with fortune-tellers. Their messages were as varied as the circumstances in which their listeners found themselves, but the pattern is similar.

A variety of methods

Prophets could speak in parables and visions, judgement, salvation speeches, hymns, calls to battle, oracles of woe, triumphant proclamations and laments. However, although the prophets' methods varied, there were five main elements in their ministry:

1. **Analysing the current situation**. This could originate from thoughtful observation as well as from direct divine inspiration. The people needed to have a realistic picture of what was going on – and the prophet's role was 'to tell it as it was'. Often they denounced immorality, idolatry, injustice and oppression, while the people still regarded themselves as good and religious. In contrast, sometimes the people felt their position was so hopeless that the prophet's task was to help them to know the reality of God's sovereignty.

2. **Telling the people how God viewed their situation**. How did God regard their despair and disappointment? What did God think of their injustice and corruption? Did God share their joys? More often than not the people disobeyed God, rejecting his plans for them, and the prophets pronounced God's judgement on them.

3. **Initiating change**. The prophets wanted to change peoples' attitudes and behaviour. Having shown God's attitude towards a situation, the next step was to explain what God wanted the people to do about it: to repent, turn back to God, act against a

The non-writing prophets

Fifteen prophets – sixteen if we count Daniel, who was more a statesman – left books, and their writings make up almost one-third of the Old Testament. However, these were not the only people God used to prophesy. Many other prophets are mentioned in the Old Testament historical writings, and they too were ordinary people with strengths and weaknesses, joys and sorrows.

Non-writing prophets include:

• **Nathan** who played a significant role in the life of King David. He explained to David what God thought about the building of a Temple in Jerusalem, and set out the possibilities for David's dynasty, if his descendants acted with integrity. Nathan challenged David with God's view of his adultery, and later intervened to ensure that David was succeeded by Solomon rather than another of his sons.
• **Elijah** worked as a prophet in the northern

Elijah's successor as prophet of Israel, Elisha was renowned for his miracle-working ministry.

particular enemy or let justice enter their lives. These and similar messages played a major part in the prophets' oracles.

4. Foretelling the future. If the people heeded the prophets'

Miracles of Elijah and Elisha

Elijah

Fed by ravens (1 Kings 17:1-7)

Meal and oil for the widow of Zarephath (1 Kings 17:16)

Fire on the altar (1 Kings 17:38)

Taken in a whirlwind (2 Kings 2)

Elisha

River Jordan purified (2 Kings 2:19-22)

Mockers killed by bears (2 Kings 2:24)

Widow's oil multiplied (2 Kings 4:1-7)

Widow's son raised from dead (2 Kings 4:32-36)

Naaman's leprosy cured (2 Kings 5:10-14)

Axe-head restored (2 Kings 6:1-7)

Arameans struck with blindness (2 Kings 6:8-23)

Syrian army put to flight (2 Kings 7:6-7)

Sennacherib's army destroyed (2 Kings 19:35)

Hezekiah healed (2 Kings 20:1-7)

kingdom of Israel for about 50 years, challenging paganism during Ahab's reign, proclaiming God's sovereignty over Baal and his prophets and encouraging those who continued to serve God in difficult times.

• **Elisha** succeeded Elijah, beginning as the latter's personal servant, but ending up influencing the life of Israel and surrounding nations. Elisha was one of the few prophets whose ministry involved events regarded as miraculous.

• **Huldah** is one of the few women prophets we hear of. When King Josiah discovered the book of the Law, as he was restoring the Temple, he asked Huldah God's will in the matter. That it was a woman who was asked to pronounce on a matter of such significance was not apparently a problem for the officials or for the writer, who records the incident without comment.

message and followed God's path, then the future would be wonderful. The Old Testament includes many pictures of a glorious future, when Israel, enjoying prosperity and hope, stands as a model to the nations. However, if the Jews failed to heed the prophets' words, the future would be bleak; the Old Testament also has many pictures of the disaster and devastation that awaited them. The prophets referred to the future in order to influence behaviour in the present. Which of the possible futures lay ahead for Israel

depended on how, and how far, they responded to the messages of God sent through the prophets.

5. Telling the people what God was like. What was supremely important was God – and the people's relationship with him. God was real, God cared for them, they mattered to God. God would judge them – but he still loved them and they were his people.

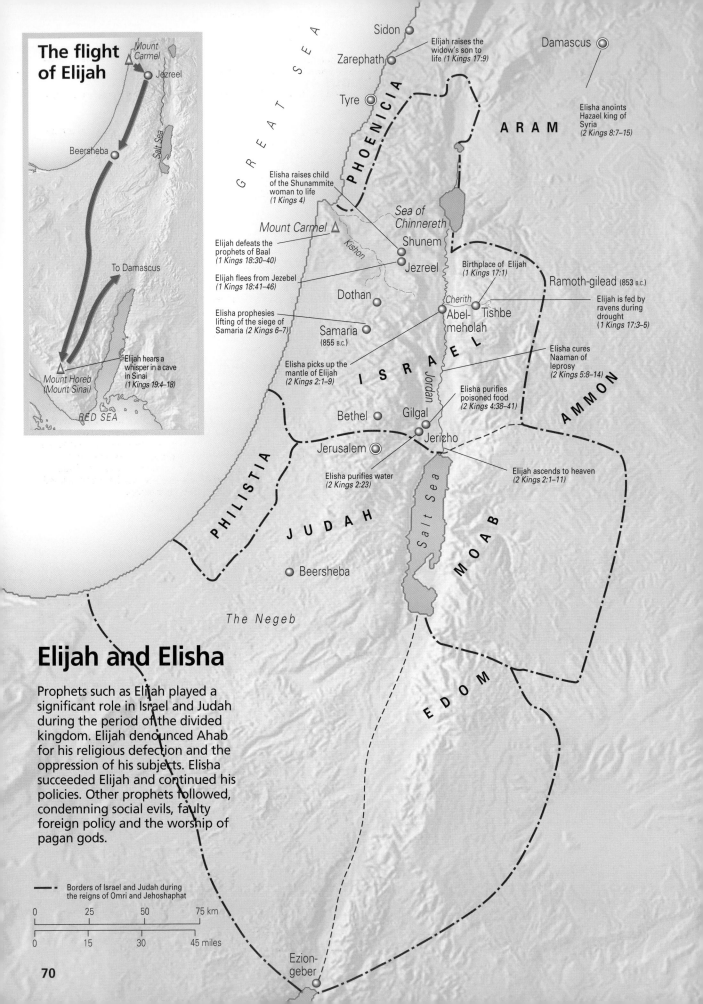

The flight of Elijah

Mount Carmel

Jezreel

Salt Sea

Beersheba

To Damascus

Elijah hears a whisper in a cave in Sinai (1 Kings 19:4–18)

Mount Horeb (Mount Sinai)

RED SEA

GREAT SEA

Sidon

Damascus

Zarephath

Elijah raises the widow's son to life (1 Kings 17:9)

Tyre

PHOENICIA

ARAM

Elisha anoints Hazael king of Syria (2 Kings 8:7–15)

Elisha raises child of the Shunammite woman to life (1 Kings 4)

Sea of Chinnereth

Mount Carmel △

Shunem

Elijah defeats the prophets of Baal (1 Kings 18:30–40)

Kishon

Jezreel

Birthplace of Elijah (1 Kings 17:1)

Ramoth-gilead (853 B.C.)

Elijah flees from Jezebel (1 Kings 18:41–46)

Dothan

Cherith

Tishbe

Elijah is fed by ravens during drought (1 Kings 17:3–5)

Abel-meholah

Elisha prophesies lifting of the siege of Samaria (2 Kings 6–7)

Samaria (855 B.C.)

I S R A E L

Jordan

Elisha cures Naaman of leprosy (2 Kings 5:8–14)

Elisha picks up the mantle of Elijah (2 Kings 2:1–9)

Elisha purifies poisoned food (2 Kings 4:38–41)

AMMON

Bethel

Gilgal

Jerusalem

Jericho

Elisha purifies water (2 Kings 2:23)

Elijah ascends to heaven (2 Kings 2:1–11)

Salt Sea

PHILISTIA

JUDAH

M O A B

Beersheba

The Negeb

E D O M

Elijah and Elisha

Prophets such as Elijah played a significant role in Israel and Judah during the period of the divided kingdom. Elijah denounced Ahab for his religious defection and the oppression of his subjects. Elisha succeeded Elijah and continued his policies. Other prophets followed, condemning social evils, faulty foreign policy and the worship of pagan gods.

Borders of Israel and Judah during the reigns of Omri and Jehoshaphat

| 0 | 25 | 50 | 75 km |

| 0 | 15 | 30 | 45 miles |

Ezion-geber

The message of the prophets

Isaiah—Malachi

Eighth century B.C.

Amos and Hosea, the only writing prophets from the northern kingdom, worked at this time, as did Isaiah and Micah in the southern kingdom. Isaiah addresses three separate situations, which we will look at separately.

Amos
Situation: Great prosperity and great corruption in the northern kingdom.
Message: God's judgement on injustice must be taken seriously.

Hosea
Situation: Great prosperity and great corruption in the northern kingdom.
Message: God loves the people deeply and is hurt by their idolatry and corruption. Because he takes them seriously, they will be judged.

Isaiah 1–39
Situation: The country was prosperous, profiting from problems in surrounding countries and enemies being occupied elsewhere. A big gap had opened up between rich and poor, and the judicial system benefited the rich at the expense of the poor.
Message: God is great and will judge injustice and oppression.

Isaiah 40–55
Situation: The Exile is assumed to have happened, judgement has fallen and Israel can now look ahead to a new future.
Message: God is great and will save. This section includes some of the greatest proclamations about God's nature in the Old Testament, looking forward to the coming of the Servant of God, the Messiah.

Isaiah 56–66
Situation: This looks further ahead to the situation after the return from Exile, when the nation was re-established. But there was disappointment that hopes for the future had not worked out as the people expected.
Message: God is great, even when life does not appear to be so great.

Micah
Situation: Great prosperity and great corruption in the southern kingdom.
Message: God will judge the people for their injustice and immorality; but for those who repent there is a great future and hope.

Up to the Exile

Four prophets – Nahum, Zephaniah, Habakkuk and Jeremiah – began work during the seventh century B.C. The dating for Obadiah, Jonah and Joel is less clear.

Nahum
Situation: Cruelty and sin in Nineveh, Assyria's capital.
Message: Judgement upon Nineveh.

Zephaniah
Situation: Sin and irreligion in Judah.
Message: Repent while there is still time.

Habakkuk
Situation: Corruption in Judah and the wickedness of her enemies.
Message: Amidst confusion and doubt, the reality of God remains.

Jeremiah
Situation: Babylon was attacking and Judah was about to be conquered.
Message: Be realistic about the situation. This is a well-deserved judgement from God, who will not intervene to save his people. Transform your lifestyle, accept punishment and wait in hope for God to bring salvation.

Obadiah
Situation: Trouble from enemies.
Message: Watch out, Edom! Israel's God is sovereign.

Jonah
Situation: Cruelty and sin in Nineveh, Assyria's capital city.
Message: Repent – or face destruction. God cares about the nations. Repentance is followed by mercy.

Joel
Situation: Life – and sin – continues.
Message: God will act. Calamity follows disobedience and blessing, righteousness.

The Exile – and beyond

Ezekiel
Situation: In Babylon during the exile.
Message: Accept your punishment, love God and hope for the future.

Haggai
Situation: Returned from Exile, the Temple has not been rebuilt.
Message: Put God first if you are to prosper.

Zechariah
Situation: Back from the Exile; but where was the glory?
Message: Visions, and God's coming Day.

Daniel
Situation: In Babylon
Message: Stories of honour and resistance, dreams and visions of the future.

Malachi
Situation: The ongoing struggle in Judah. The people believed but were uncommitted.
Message: Get your act together! If you do, you will be overwhelmed by blessings; if you don't, you will be overwhelmed by judgement.

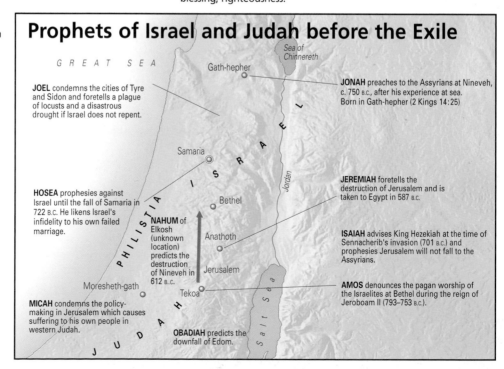

Prophets of Israel and Judah before the Exile

GREAT SEA

Sea of Chinnereth

Gath-hepher

JOEL condemns the cities of Tyre and Sidon and foretells a plague of locusts and a disastrous drought if Israel does not repent.

JONAH preaches to the Assyrians at Nineveh, c. 750 B.C., after his experience at sea. Born in Gath-hepher (2 Kings 14:25)

ISRAEL

Samaria

Jordan

HOSEA prophesies against Israel until the fall of Samaria in 722 B.C. He likens Israel's infidelity to his own failed marriage.

Bethel

JEREMIAH foretells the destruction of Jerusalem and is taken to Egypt in 587 B.C.

PHILISTIA

NAHUM of Elkosh (unknown location) predicts the destruction of Nineveh in 612 B.C.

Anathoth

ISAIAH advises King Hezekiah at the time of Sennacherib's invasion (701 B.C.) and prophesies Jerusalem will not fall to the Assyrians.

Jerusalem

Moresheth-gath

Tekoa

Salt Sea

AMOS denounces the pagan worship of the Israelites at Bethel during the reign of Jeroboam II (793–753 B.C.).

MICAH condemns the policy-making in Jerusalem which causes suffering to his own people in western Judah.

OBADIAH predicts the downfall of Edom.

JUDAH

Poetry and wisdom

Job, Psalms, Proverbs, Ecclesiastes and Song of Solomon

Poetry is not confined to one part of the Old Testament. Ceremonial poems and hymns are found in the historical books, while many of the prophets were also gifted poets, with songs and poems scattered throughout their writings. However, poetic material is most heavily concentrated in the book of Psalms.

Psalms contains an unclassified collection of 150 poems, originally on five separate scrolls. They include collections of psalms written by individuals, notably David; collections linked to specific places; psalms of a particular type, such as marching songs, used on annual trips to Jerusalem for the great feasts; and psalms that defy classification. The psalms appear to have been collected over a number of years, in much the same way as a church hymn-book might be put together today. The result is a fascinating collection of songs for every season, occasion and mood.

It is interesting to consider the situations in which the psalms were originally composed and used. Note that the categories used opposite overlap, and that a few psalms do not fit neatly into any category

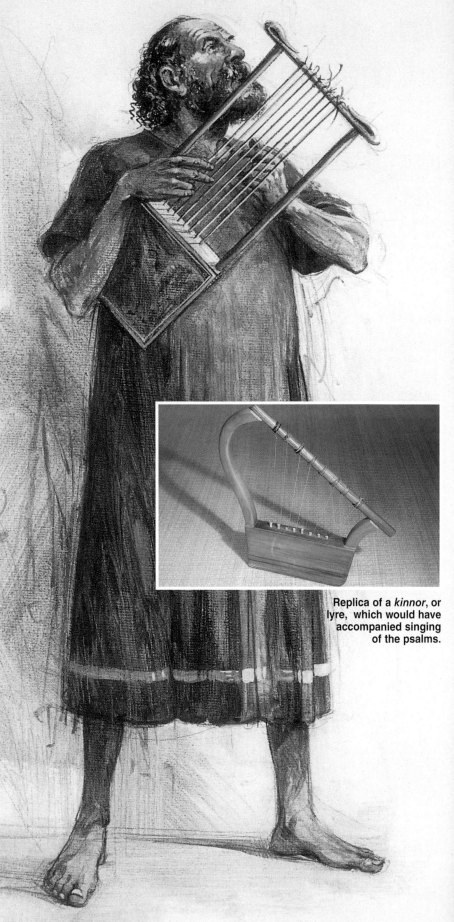

Replica of a *kinnor*, or lyre, which would have accompanied singing of the psalms.

Wisdom literature

Some psalms are known as wisdom poems, and are similar in content to such books as Proverbs, Ecclesiastes and Job. Old Testament wisdom literature is essentially a collection of commonsense observations about life. The wisdom thinker is not seeking to display his cleverness, but to work out what life is about.

Proverbs
The search for knowledge
Collections of 'have you noticed this' statements about how life *is* lived, aimed at working out how it *should be* lived. Proverbs reflects on hard work and laziness, pride and humility, friendship, discipline, speech, money and family life.

Job
The search for answers
Job is of course about suffering – but the underlying question is not so much, 'Why does suffering happen?' but, 'How should I react when suffering happens?'

Ecclesiastes
The search for meaning
How do we make sense of a world that at times appears meaningless?

1. Psalms of praise and thanksgiving
Some of these are clearly written for public worship and are intended to be sung by a congregation. Others are written in the light of some circumstance or incident, by or on behalf of a particular person or family.

Some psalms reflect on God and praise him for his majesty, compassion, justice or love, while others reflect on the wonder of creation and the created world. There are also harvest hymns, hymns for other festivals, and hymns recounting Israel's history and how God has constantly acted on the nation's behalf.
'*I will bless the LORD at all times. His praise shall continually be in my mouth*' Psalm 34:1.

2. Psalms of lament or complaint
The book of Psalms is often seen as the hymn-book of ancient Israel, yet although praise psalms form a large group, the largest group is of psalms of lament. Like the praise psalms, some relate to the whole community and were probably sung or recited when the people came together, while others are linked to individual circumstances. These psalms make it clear the writer is not happy – with his or her circumstances, his or her self, or often with God. They express, in vivid and emotive language, grief, confusion, misery and anger.

The psalmist may be persecuted, reflecting sadly on his or her own sin, depressed or simply perplexed. The lament psalms have in common a desire to express to God how the psalmist is feeling. There is no hint that the psalmists felt there were things too awful to talk about in God's presence.
'*Oh my God, I cry by day, but you do not answer; and by night, but find no rest*' Psalm 22:2.

The previous two categories overlap. Some psalms begin with despair and, as the writer thinks about God or comes into the Temple to meet fellow-Israelites, gradually come to terms with it and introduce a note of hope. Others begin with hope and decline into despair. There was always a psalm that helped the Israelites express how they were feeling. Faith in Israel's God did not have to include pretence.
'*My heart is in anguish within me, the terrors of death have fallen upon me . . . . But I call upon God and the LORD will save me*' Psalm 55:4, 16.

3. Other psalms
Smaller groups of psalms include:

Royal psalms – written by a kind of national poet, celebrating such occasions as the enthronement of a new king or a royal marriage.

Teaching psalms – where lessons about faith and belief are expressed in poetic form.

Nationalistic psalms – to encourage the people in the face of danger from enemies.

Psalms of intercession – asking God's help for the nation or for individuals.

Philosophical psalms – reflecting on difficult questions, such as why the wicked prosper, and why the righteous suffer.

Jews visiting Jerusalem for the festivals would have this view from the Mount of Olives.

Between the Testaments

From the Persians to the Greeks

The Old Testament historical story ends with Ezra and Nehemiah. We know very little in detail about Jewish affairs until about 200 B.C. The best information we have is the outline of history presented in Daniel 11.

The major event of this period was the fall of the Persian Empire to Alexander the Great (336–323 B.C.), whose home was Macedon (northern Greece), and who inaugurated an era of Greek rule throughout the eastern Mediterranean region and far beyond. He created an enormous empire, which embraced most of the diaspora Jews as well as those in Judea. Both Egypt and the former Babylonia came under his control, as well as the whole of Palestine.

Greek culture very soon became dominant throughout the eastern Mediterranean – the fact that the whole of the New Testament is written in Greek demonstrates this clearly. Greek ideas, philosophy, and customs were soon widespread. (This process is known as Hellenisation.) Many Greek ways of thinking were absorbed by subject peoples such as the Jews.

After Alexander's death in 323 B.C., his empire broke up into several smaller empires. The Greek general who became king of Egypt was named Ptolemy, and it was his Ptolemaic Empire which governed Judea for the next century. After the Exile the high priesthood had become the most important political position in Judea, subject to the foreign governor.

The neighbouring Greek Empire to the north centred on Syria; it is known as the Seleucid kingdom, after its first ruler, Seleucus. They quarrelled over the ownership of Palestine, and a Seleucid king, Antiochus III, defeated the armies of Egypt in 198 B.C. and took possession of Palestine.

The Maccabean Revolt

When Antiochus III conquered Judea in 198 B.C., the high priest was Simon II, who is praised in Ecclesiasticus 50; he gained important privileges for the Jews from the Seleucid authorities. A generation later, the Seleucid king Antiochus IV saw no reason why he should not make his own appointments to the high priesthood, which he considered primarily a political office, and so brought to an abrupt end eight centuries of Zadokite high priests.

Devout Jews were outraged at this interference in their religious affairs, but worse was to follow. In 168 B.C., angered by unrest in Jerusalem and frustrated in an attempt to invade Egypt, Antiochus made a violent attack on Jewish practices. He plundered the Temple, erected an altar there to a pagan god, and banned Jewish customs. The pagan altar was called by the Jews 'the Abomination of Desolation' (Daniel 11:31). Many devout Jews died for their faith (1 Maccabees 1).

A notable family known as Hasmonean or Maccabean, now sprang to prominence. An elderly priest named Mattathias sparked off a revolt. He had five sons, one of whom, Judas Maccabeus, soon became the leader of the rebels (1 Maccabees 2). He died in battle in 160 B.C., but his able brothers Jonathan (till 142 B.C.) and Simon (till 135 B.C.) continued the struggle. The Seleucid Empire was weakened by internal divisions, and eventually the Jews gained virtual independence. As early as 164 BC they were able to cleanse and rededicate the Temple.

Not all Jews were devout, and an influential party had hoped to encourage Hellenisation, opposed by those known as the Hasidim, 'the Devout'. The latter supported Judas in his fight to cleanse the Temple and to regain their right to practise their ancestral religion, but were not ambitious for political independence. There were thus various groupings among the Jews, which presently gave rise to the parties and sects well known by New Testament times – Pharisees, Sadducees and others.

Judas Maccabeus never held an official position, but his brother Jonathan was made high priest in 152 B.C. by a Seleucid king. Jonathan's family was priestly but not Zadokite, and this breach of sacred tradition scandalised some Jews.

Simon not only held on to the high priesthood but made sure that it would remain in his family (see 1 Maccabees 14:41). His successors went on to add the title of king to that of high priest. By now Judea was independent of the Seleucids, whose own kingdom was increasingly divided; the power of the future belonged to the Romans. Meanwhile the Hasmonean rulers were able to enlarge their realm at others' expense, taking control of such regions as Idumea to the south and Galilee to the north.

If the early Hasmoneans were patriots, their successors were worldly and violent men, especially Alexander Jannaeus (103–76 B.C.), who quarrelled with the pious Pharisees and executed hundreds of them. The period ended in civil war, with two Hasmonean brothers fighting for supremacy. The Romans stepped in and in 63 B.C. took control of the whole region; from now on they would organise affairs in Judea as they saw fit. The Roman general who marched into Judea was Pompey the Great.

Palestine under the Maccabees

The Seleucid kings were hated by the Jews for imposing Greek ('Hellenistic') culture and religion. Led first by Judas Maccabeus (166–160 B.C.), the Jews drove the Greeks out of Jerusalem and founded a new dynasty, the Hasmoneans. Probably the most triumphant moment came in 164 B.C. when, after its defilement by the Seleucids, the Temple was purified and restored, and sacrifices began to be offered again, inaugurating the Jewish festival of Hanukkah, or Dedication (see John 10:22). Alexander Jannaeus (103–76 B.C.) completed the conquest of almost the whole of Israel.
1 and 2 Maccabees

Tyre

Antiochia

PHOENICIA

Gischala

Seleucia

Ptolemais

Sea of Galilee

Gabara

Hippos

Sepphoris

Dium

Geba

Mount Tabor △

Philoteria

Abila

GALILEE

Gadara

Dora

GILEAD

Strato's Tower

Scythopolis

Pella

SAMARIA

Samaria

Jordan

Shechem △

Gerasa

Apollonia

Mount Gerizim

PEREA

Joppa

Arimathea

Philadelphia

Lydda

JUDEA

Jamnia

Emmaus

Jericho

Samaga

Azotus

Jerusalem

Medeba

Ascalon

MEDITERRANEAN SEA

PARALIA

Beth-zur

Anthedon

Marisa

Dead Sea

Gaza

Hebron

Orda

IDUMEA

En-gedi

MOAB

Gerar

Raphia

Beersheba

Malatha

Zoar

Rhinocorura

NABATEA

Independent Judea after Jonathan's campaigns, 142 B.C.
Land conquered by Simon, 142-135 B.C.
John Hyrcanus I, 128-104 B.C.
Aristobulus I, 104-103 B.C.
Alexander Jannaeus, 103-76 B.C.
Boundary of Hasmonean kingdom, 76 B.C.
Hellenistic city

| 0 | | 25 | | 50 km |
| 0 | 10 | 20 | 30 miles |

What does the Old Testament Apocrypha consist of?

The Apocrypha is a collection of books and additions to Old Testament books written between 300 B.C. and A.D. 100. These books were not accepted by the Jews as part of the Hebrew Scriptures. They were, however, included in the Septuagint (the Greek translation of the Hebrew Bible). The books of the Apocrypha are interesting, and valuable as historical documents, and range from narrative history to pious fiction. Most Protestants acknowledge the literary value and historical significance of the Apocrypha, but do not view it as possessing spiritual authority. Roman Catholics and some Eastern Orthodox Churches recognise most of the Apocryphal writings as Scripture (see page 11).

1 Esdras
An historical account, paralleling Chronicles, Ezra and Nehemiah, of the return of the Jews from Babylonian captivity.

2 Esdras (4 Ezra)
Visions and revelations of early Jewish rabbis.

Tobit
A didactic fiction about Tobit's trials in eighth century B.C. Nineveh.

Judith
The fictional exploits of a Jewish heroine, Judith, who assassinated the Assyrian general Holofernes.

Additions to Esther (also known as The Rest of Esther)
Five additions which give a more religious emphasis to the book of Esther.

The Wisdom of Solomon
A first-century B.C. exhortation to wisdom.

Ecclesiasticus also known as the Wisdom of Sirach/Ben Sira
A collection of the writings of Joshua ben-Sera (c.180 B.C.) giving his advice for a successful life – combining personal piety with practical wisdom.

Baruch
This book was allegedly written by Baruch, a friend of Jeremiah, and was meant as an encouragement to Jews in the Babylonian Exile of 597 B.C.

The Letter of Jeremiah
An attack on idolatry in the form of a letter from Jeremiah, often added to the book of Baruch.

The Song of the Three Holy Children
A hymn of praise sung by Shadrach, Meshach and Abednego in the fiery furnace described in Daniel.

The Story of Susanna
The story of a virtuous woman who was falsely accused of adultery and defended by Daniel.

Bel and the Dragon
A folkloric story written to ridicule idolatry.

The Prayer of Manasseh
The prayer of the idolatrous king Manasseh, begging for forgiveness, as referred to in 2 Chronicles 33:11-19.

1 Maccabees
The struggle of Jews against Hellenistic rulers (175–134 B.C.), particularly the battle with Antiochus Epiphanes.

2 Maccabees
A narrative of the Maccabean revolt.

3 Maccabees
An account of Jewish life under Ptolemy IV (221–204 B.C.).

4 Maccabees
A tract about the rule of reason over passion.

Psalm 151

Assyrian relief showing a defeated city being pillaged.

Part of a Greek text of the Bible.

Introducing the New Testament

Jesus – the reason for it all

The New Testament exists only because of Jesus of Nazareth. Though he wrote nothing himself, he caused the New Testament – a collection of writings of such extraordinary quality that they have shaped world history, and continue deeply to affect the lives of those who read them.

Yet, strangely, less than half of the New Testament (47 per cent) is directly concerned with the life and teaching of Jesus. The rest is taken up with descriptions of his effect on people after his death. Although the Gospels record his powerful impact on some individuals, his life actually ended in apparent failure.

But after his death that all changed. Suddenly there were thousands of disciples, and within a few years even the opponents of this new Jesus-movement recognised that it had 'turned the world upside-down' (Acts 17:6).

The resurrection

Why this sudden change? The New Testament hinges around it, focusing the reason for it on Jesus' resurrection from death. This is central to the literary phenomenon we call 'the New Testament'. For suddenly Jesus became the content of the message, rather than the source of it. Unlike other disciples of great teachers, the first Christian apostles, who wrote the New Testament, did not think of themselves as passers-on of tradition – the stories of his life and records of his teaching. Instead, they were proclaimers of the Saviour, who by his death and resurrection had opened heaven to all.

It was not that the memories of Jesus' life were unimportant: the very presence of the Gospels in the New Testament shows how

A typical artist's impression of Jesus of Nazareth. But who was Jesus? What was he really like?

vital they were for the first Christians. But the remaining 53 per cent of the New Testament, beginning with Acts, arises primarily from this conviction about his resurrection and its significance. The early confessions of faith in (for instance) Philippians 2:6-11 or 1 Timothy 3:16 summarise the message beautifully.

So who was Jesus?

By its very structure, the New Testament compels its readers to decide whether they accept the apostolic confession of Jesus as Saviour and Lord. But that decision is not the only challenge issued by the New Testament. Those who make the confession

are still faced with the challenge of history: Who was Jesus?

In 1892 Martin Kähler, Professor of Theology at Leipzig, published a highly influential lecture entitled 'The so-called historical Jesus and the real, biblical Christ'. Worried by nineteenth-century attempts to write a psychological biography of Jesus, and thus to make him 'ordinary' and perhaps more acceptable, Kähler argued that we must see that the 'real' Jesus (German: *geschichtlich*) is not a reconstructed figure, understood through the channels of historical research. He is simply the Jesus attested by the New Testament – the Saviour and Lord.

Kähler's distinction is certainly attractive to Christians faced with awkward questions such as, 'How can we be sure that Jesus really was as the New Testament portrays him?' It would be nice to reply, 'I disallow the question – because my faith rests not on what Jesus *was*, but on what he is, the "biblical Christ".'

An unavoidable question

The difficulty is that the central New Testament confession is in the past tense: it is a confession that 'Christ died for our sins according to the Scriptures, that he was buried, and that he was raised again on the third day . . .' (1 Corinthians 15:3-4). It explains the historical event of his death ('for our sins'). It claims that the hype about his resurrection is not illusory but points to another real historical event of staggering significance. It then builds present-tense confession ('Jesus is Lord', 1 Corinthians 12:3) and future-tense confession ('He will come again', 1 Thessalonians 5:2) on this historical basis.

A rabbi from Bible times. Jesus was not a typical rabbi.

A tomb with a roll-away stone. The New Testament hinges on Jesus' resurrection.

So Christians cannot avoid the challenge of the historical question, 'Did it really happen? Was Jesus really like that?', even though their faith may actually rest upon a living experience of the Holy Spirit in the present.

Current scholarship emphasises three things about Jesus:

1. *Jesus' Jewishness*
In many ways we cannot understand Jesus without understanding the Jewish world in which he lived and ministered. And this is not just a matter of his cultural environment (the customs, religion and politics of his day), but also of his theological thought-world. He clearly lived out of the Old Testament (as we call it), quoting and applying it as rabbis always did.

2. *Jesus' newness*
But at the same time Jesus was not a typical rabbi, nor indeed a typical Jew. He did not engage in normal debate with other rabbis, but taught on his own authority, and claimed that the Scriptures had been fulfilled through him uniquely (e.g. Matthew 5:17; Luke 4:21). People saw him as some kind of new leader – but what exactly? It is fascinating that his contemporaries asked the same questions about him as people today: Is he some kind of prophet? What kind, exactly? Is he a political deliverer? Or just a healer, using divine, or demonic, powers? Or is he no more than a sage, a wise man, with some good ideas – or perhaps with bad, deceptive ideas? What does he mean by calling himself 'the Son of Man' – or is he talking about someone else? Can he be 'the Christ'? Jesus was so puzzlingly unusual that it is perfectly possible that he predicted his own death and resurrection, as the Gospels suggest. His disciples simply failed to grasp what he meant (e.g. Mark 9:9-10).

3. *Jesus' messianic awareness*
This debate about the newness of Jesus shades over into what Jesus believed about himself. Scholars are now in broad agreement that, in some sense, he must have thought of himself as a Messiah-figure. But in what sense? Here agreement ends. He seems to have been willing to accept the title 'Christ' (Mark 8:29-30), but what did he understand by this term? Modern questions and puzzles are paralleled by the variety of different interpretations of him in the New Testament – amounting to a fascinating, kaleidoscopic presentation of one of the most powerful and intriguing people of all time.

Comparative lengths of New Testament books

Matthew
Mark
Luke
John
Acts
Romans
1 & 2 Corinthians
Galatians
Ephesians
Philippians
Colossians
1 & 2 Thessalonians
1 & 2 Timothy
Titus
Philemon
Hebrews
James
1 & 2 Peter
1, 2 & 3 John
Jude
Revelation

He was manifested
in the flesh,
vindicated in the Spirit,
seen by angels,
preached among the nations,
believed in the world, taken up in glory.
1 Timothy 3:16

Jesus' life

Jesus was born in Bethlehem, in Judea, probably in 5 B.C. He lived most of his life in Galilee, became an itinerant preacher and healer in his mid-thirties, but was quickly executed for political sedition at the age of about 38. He left no writings and a small group of about 120 followers.

Hardly the stuff of religious revolution. How did this beginning produce such a world-changing result? We need to seek the real, inner quality of this life, by interrogating all the New Testament witnesses. We start by thinking about the basic facts.

Three crowded years

Jesus lived in obscurity in Nazareth, a village in Galilee, until he began his public ministry, probably in A.D. 30. The story really begins in the previous year, as dated by Luke (Luke 3:1-2), when Jesus' cousin John 'the Baptist' started a brief career as a prophet. Huge crowds flocked to hear him (Matthew 3:5), among them Jesus, whose baptism by John in the Jordan river marks the beginning of his ministry in all four Gospels.

The most likely broad chronology of Jesus' ministry is provided by John's Gospel, in which three Passovers are mentioned (including the Passover at which he was executed). The date of his death can fairly securely be fixed in April A.D. 33: so from some time in mid-A.D. 30 until then, he travelled around Galilee, Samaria and Judea (then under Roman rule). Occasionally he ventured outside traditional Jewish territory (Matthew 15:21; 16:13), but basically he confined himself to 'the lost sheep of the house of Israel', as he put it (Matthew 10:6). He had remarkable powers of healing, which created a huge response. But all the Gospels agree that it was his teaching which captivated people, conveying a powerful sense of the mysterious significance of his own person.

Jesus' message

According to Matthew, Jesus' proclamation was the same as

A quiet stretch of the River Jordan, near the Sea of Galilee.

John the Baptist's: 'Repent, for the kingdom of heaven has come near!' (Matthew 3:2; 4:17). But in fact Jesus put a different spin on this message, compared with John. 'The kingdom of God' (or 'of heaven') was a potent idea for Jews, expressing their sense that their real king was God, and fuelling their expectation that one day God himself would come to deliver them from alien rule, and establish them again as his chosen people. So 'the kingdom of God is near!' was a message loaded with political freight – and revolutionary fervour.

Both John and Jesus tried to dampen down political excitement. John emphasised the personal response of repentance, and he kept away from Jerusalem where all messianic revolution-aries would press their cause. In addition, he pointed people away from himself to 'one coming after me' (Matthew 3:11), with whom the kingdom would really arrive. Similarly, Jesus refused openly to proclaim himself as the Messiah, and avoided political arguments. Asked whether he supported Roman taxation (the hottest issue of all), he re-routed the question

Cave beneath the modern Chapel of the Annunciation, Nazareth.

Galilee in the time of Jesus

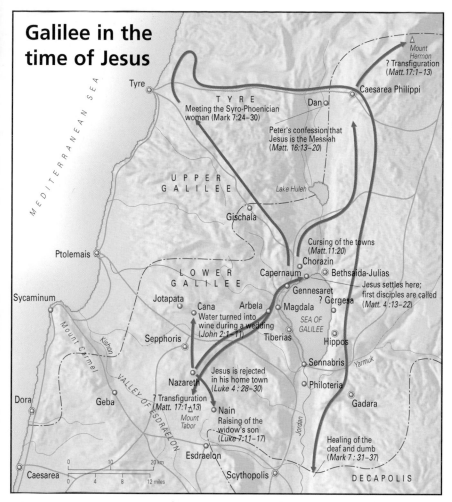

Map labels:
- MEDITERRANEAN SEA
- Tyre
- Mount Hermon
- ? Transfiguration (*Matt. 17:1–13*)
- Caesarea Philippi
- TYRE
- Dan
- Meeting the Syro-Phoenician woman (Mark 7:24–30)
- Peter's confession that Jesus is the Messiah (*Matt. 16:13–20*)
- UPPER GALILEE
- Lake Huleh
- Gischala
- Ptolemais
- Cursing of the towns (*Matt. 11:20*)
- Chorazin
- LOWER GALILEE
- Capernaum
- Bethsaida-Julias
- Gennesaret
- ? Gergesa
- Jesus settles here; first disciples are called (*Matt. 4:13–22*)
- Sycaminum
- Jotapata
- Cana
- Arbela
- Magdala
- SEA OF GALILEE
- Water turned into wine during a wedding (*John 2:1–11*)
- Sepphoris
- Tiberias
- Hippos
- Sennabris
- Yarmuk
- Mount Carmel
- Kishon
- VALLEY OF ESDRAELON
- Nazareth
- Jesus is rejected in his home town (*Luke 4:28–30*)
- Philoteria
- Dora
- Geba
- ? Transfiguration (*Matt. 17:1–13*)
- Mount Tabor
- Nain
- Raising of the widow's son (*Luke 7:11–17*)
- Gadara
- Jordan
- Esdraelon
- Caesarea
- Scythopolis
- Healing of the deaf and dumb (*Mark 7:31–37*)
- DECAPOLIS
- 0 10 20 km / 0 4 8 12 miles

Star of Bethlehem

The best candidate for the famous 'star of Bethlehem' described in Matthew 2 is a comet, recorded by Chinese astronomers, which appeared in the eastern sky in March, 5 B.C., and remained visible for about 70 days, moving slowly towards the south.

(Research by Prof. Colin Humphreys of Cambridge University: *Tyndale Bulletin* 43 1992, 31–56)

around duty to God (Luke 20:21-26). He broke religious taboos in reaching out to the outcast and 'untouchables', and proclaimed a kingdom in which the poor are blessed and the self-righteous condemned.

More than a prophet
But there came a moment, probably in April A.D. 32, when an excited Passover crowd wanted to make Jesus king (John 6:15). Jesus refused to precipitate an uprising. For he preached a kingdom of God which in one sense had come already (see e.g. Luke 17:20-21). And this is where we must consider that mysterious quality, that 'extra' that set Jesus apart from John and all other prophets – a quality that people found very hard to define, but which led the first Christians to feel that in Jesus they had met God in a unique way. Whereas John told his disciples to fast in order to

prepare for the kingdom, Jesus and his disciples feasted in celebration of its arrival (Mark 2:18-20). The sick were healed in fulfilment of the Scriptures which promised the presence of God with his people (Matthew 11:2-6; Isaiah 35:4-6). Jesus forgave sins with divine authority – and people felt forgiven (Mark 2:1-12; Luke 7:36-50). He taught 'with authority, not like the teachers of the law' (Matthew 7:29).

What gave Jesus these qualities? Was it simply the power of a unique personality? Or – the view that began to appeal to the religious authorities – was he able to exert demonic control over people (Luke 11:15; John 8:48)? In addition, the authorities began to feel threatened, as Jesus started to criticise them directly in the last year of his ministry (see Matthew 23; John 8:42-47).

Death and resurrection
In this increasingly tense situation, Jesus began to predict his own death – but the Gospels are united in recording that he also predicted his resurrection, and that he spoke of his death as 'for others', 'a ransom for many' (Mark 10:45; John 6:51; Luke 18:31-34). Is this just later Christian thinking, read back on to his lips? In the search for the origin of the Christian view that Jesus' death was planned by God as a means of salvation, the best candidate is still that Jesus himself began to speak of his death in this way – and expected his own resurrection, in fulfilment of the same Scriptures that had already been fulfilled in part through his ministry.

He demanded, and received, a tremendous response from his disciples (Mark 10:28-31). And when the conviction of his resurrection grew, this response became the heart – as we shall see – of all authentic Christian worship and living.

The political background of Jesus' life

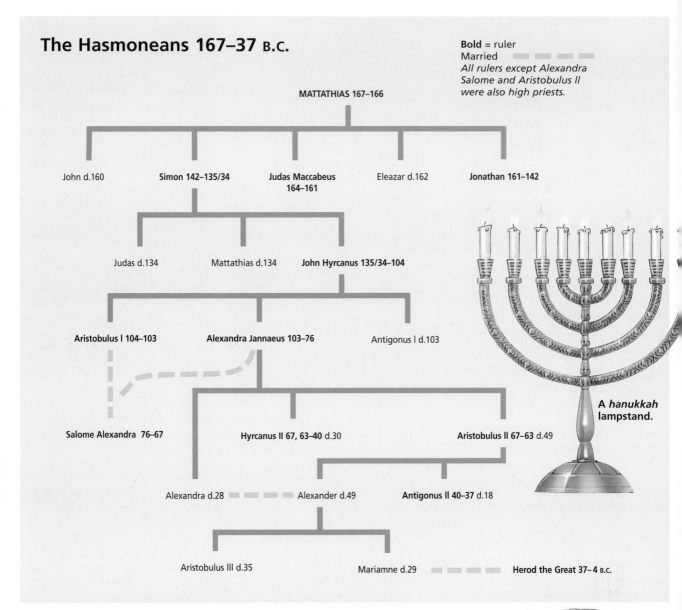

The Hasmoneans 167–37 B.C.

Bold = ruler
Married ▬ ▬ ▬ ▬
All rulers except Alexandra Salome and Aristobulus II were also high priests.

MATTATHIAS 167–166

John d.160 — **Simon 142–135/34** — **Judas Maccabeus 164–161** — Eleazar d.162 — **Jonathan 161–142**

Judas d.134 — Mattathias d.134 — **John Hyrcanus 135/34–104**

Aristobulus I 104–103 — **Alexandra Jannaeus 103–76** — Antigonus I d.103

Salome Alexandra 76–67 — **Hyrcanus II 67, 63–40** d.30 — **Aristobulus II 67–63** d.49

Alexandra d.28 ▬ ▬ ▬ Alexander d.49 — **Antigonus II 40–37** d.18

Aristobulus III d.35 — Mariamne d.29 ▬ ▬ ▬ **Herod the Great 37–4 B.C.**

A *hanukkah* lampstand.

Roman official posts in New Testament times

Caesar	Family name of Julius Caesar taken by Augustus and used as a title for the emperor from that time. *Luke 2:1; 3:1*
Proconsul	Governor of a province administered by the Roman Senate. *Acts 13:7; 18:12*
Procurator	Imperial financial agent in a Senate province, or governor of a minor province under an imperial legate. *Matthew 27:11; Acts 23:24; 24:27*
Tribune	High-ranking military officer in charge of up to 1,000 men. *Acts 21:31*
Centurion	Officer in charge of 100 men. *Mark 15:39; Acts 10:1*

Roman coin of Tiberius

Who were the Roman emperors of Bible times?

Name	Reign	Christian events	Bible reference
Julius	49–44 B.C.		
Augustus	27 B.C.–A.D. 14	Birth of Jesus	*Luke 2:1*
Tiberius	A.D. 14–37	Ministry and death of Jesus	*Luke 3:1*
Caligula	A.D. 37–41		
Claudius	A.D. 41–54	Jews expelled from Rome	*Acts 11:28; 18:2*
Nero	A.D. 54–68	Trial of Paul Persecution at Rome	*Acts 25:10–12; 27:24*
Galba	A.D. 68–69		
Otho	A.D. 69		
Vitellius	A.D. 69		
Vespasian	A.D. 69–79	Jerusalem destroyed	
Titus	A.D. 79–81		
Domitian	A.D. 81–96	?Persecution	
Nerva	A.D. 96–98		
Trajan	A.D. 98–117		
Hadrian	A.D. 117–138		

Dating

The first Christian calendar, dividing history into B.C. (before Christ) and A.D. (*anno domini*, 'in the year of our Lord') was worked out by a monk in the sixth century A.D. But it has now been discovered that he was about five years out in his calculations, so Jesus was born about 5 B.C. – not A.D. 1 – towards the end of the reign of Herod the Great.

Star in the Grotto in the Church of the Nativity, Bethlehem.

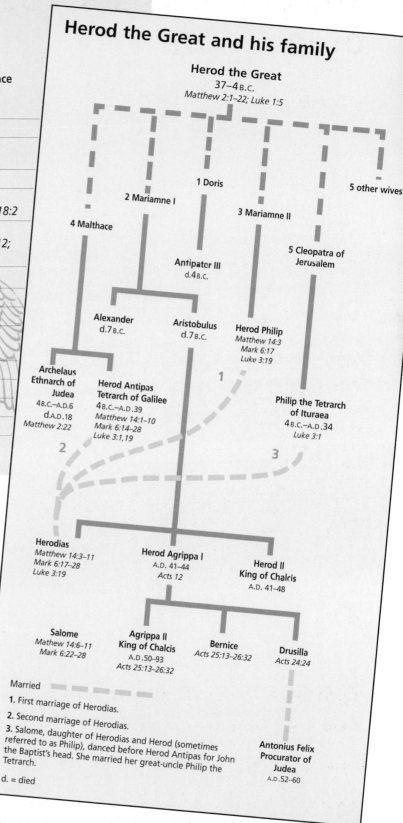

Herod the Great and his family

Herod the Great
37–4 B.C.
Matthew 2:1–22; Luke 1:5

1 Doris

2 Mariamne I

3 Mariamne II

5 other wives

4 Malthace

5 Cleopatra of Jerusalem

Antipater III
d.4 B.C.

Alexander
d.7 B.C.

Aristobulus
d.7 B.C.

Herod Philip
Matthew 14:3
Mark 6:17
Luke 3:19

Archelaus Ethnarch of Judea
4 B.C.–A.D. 6
d.A.D. 18
Matthew 2:22

Herod Antipas Tetrarch of Galilee
4 B.C.–A.D. 39
Matthew 14:1–10
Mark 6:14–28
Luke 3:1,19

Philip the Tetrarch of Ituraea
4 B.C.–A.D. 34
Luke 3:1

Herodias
Matthew 14:3–11
Mark 6:17–28
Luke 3:19

Herod Agrippa I
A.D. 41–44
Acts 12

Herod II King of Chalcis
A.D. 41–48

Salome
Mathew 14:6–11
Mark 6:22–28

Agrippa II King of Chalcis
A.D. 50–93
Acts 25:13–26:32

Bernice
Acts 25:13–26:32

Drusilla
Acts 24:24

Antonius Felix Procurator of Judea
A.D. 52–60

Married

1. First marriage of Herodias.
2. Second marriage of Herodias.
3. Salome, daughter of Herodias and Herod (sometimes referred to as Philip), danced before Herod Antipas for John the Baptist's head. She married her great-uncle Philip the Tetrarch.

d. = died

ATLANTIC

OCEAN

BRITANNIA

GERMANIA
INFERIOR

Rhine

BELGICA

Danube

LUGDUNENSIS

GERMANIA
SUPERIOR

RAETIA

NORICUM

AQUITANIA

ALPES POENINAE

PANNONIA

NARBONENSIS

DALMAT

LUSITANIA

TARRACONENSIS

ALPES
COTTIAE

ALPES
MARITIMAE

Salo

Rome

CORSICA

ITALIA

BAETICA

SARDINIA

EPIR

MAURETANIA

Carthage

SICILIA

Syracuse

AFRICA

M E D I

☐ Roman Empire in 14 A.D.

☐ Client state

─·─ Boundary of province

── Roman Empire at its greatest extent in 116 A.D.

── Roman road

0	250	500 km

0	100	200	300 miles

The Roman Empire

CASPIAN SEA

DACIA

BLACK SEA

OESIA

THRACIA

ARMENIA

BITHYNIA AND PONTUS

Nicomedia

ACEDONIA

CAPPADOCIA

Thessalonica

ASSYRIA

ASIA

Tigris

GALATIA

MESOPOTAMIA

Corinth

CILICIA

Ephesus

Athens

Antioch

ACHAEA

SYRIA

Euphrates

LYCIA AND PAMPHYLIA

CRETE

CYPRUS

RANEAN SEA

JUDEA

Jerusalem

Cyrene

Alexandria

ARABIA NABATEA

CYRENAICA

AEGYPTUS

Nile

RED SEA

The Gospels

The four Gospels are the centrepiece of the New Testament – indeed, of the Christian faith. Without them Christianity could not have developed as it did, for as a religion it depends absolutely on the historical claim that Jesus of Nazareth lived, taught, acted, died and rose from death at a particular time and place, and that these events show him to be Son of God and Saviour.

So Christianity exposes itself to the fundamental challenge:

• *Are the Gospels reliable?* They clearly purport to be historical accounts of the life of Jesus, but does the claim stand critical scrutiny? This question quickly involves another:

• *What exactly are the Gospels?* We need to judge them on their own terms, and not ask them to conform to our requirements. And this in turn makes us ask:

• *Why are there four Gospels – and how should we understand the relationship between them?* At first sight, both the overlaps and differences between them set a question-mark against their reliability.

What are the Gospels?
We start with the second question. In recent years a scholarly consensus (led by Dr Richard Burridge) has grown that the Gospels are examples of a genre, or type of writing, known as the '*Bios*' (Greek for 'life'). The Graeco-Roman '*Bios*' was typically a work of short to medium length (fitting on to one papyrus roll), concentrating on an individual of special significance, whose story would be told through typical incidents revealing his or her character, drawing moral lessons to be learned, and focusing on the birth and death of the person concerned.

This immediately suggests that we should not ask the Gospels to provide a comprehensive biography of Jesus, minutely documenting the details of his life. Not 'biography', but '*bios*' – a broad-brush presentation – of the person through typical incidents that enable us to understand him.

Why four Gospels?
A widely-given answer is that each Gospel was associated with an important Christian centre, or with one of the leading apostles. Hence initially (this view suggests) each Gospel was only written for a limited circle – a single church or maybe a group of churches – to address their particular needs.

Recently this theory has been attacked by a group of scholars led by Prof. Richard Bauckham He points out that there was extensive contact between the earliest Christian groups, and that it is highly unlikely that the Gospel-writers, as authors of a '*Bios*', were trying to meet needs just in their own churches. And ancient book-production was very haphazard. Authors could not prescribe who might receive a copy or make further copies for friends.

Filling in the gaps
If Bauckham's picture is right, then the Gospel-writers almost certainly had contact with each other, and tried deliberately to supplement each other. This has long been recognised in the case of Mark. Mark is the shortest Gospel, and about 95 per cent of his content is reproduced in Matthew and Luke, which are both much longer. It looks very much as if Mark was the first to

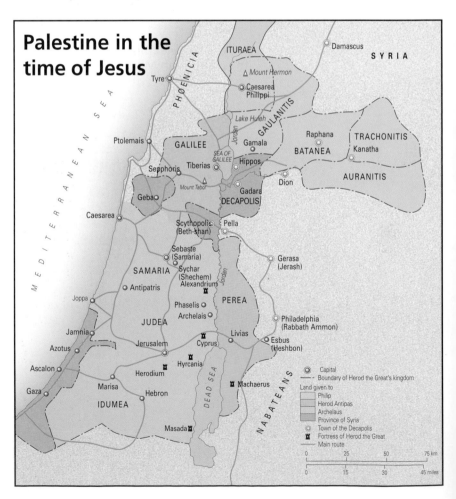

Palestine in the time of Jesus

... since I myself have carefully investigated everything from the beginning, it seemed good also to me to write an orderly account ... so that you may know the certainty of the things you have been taught.

Luke 1:3-4

be written, and then Matthew and Luke both used Mark, adding further extensive material. Scholars can't decide whether Matthew knew Luke, or vice versa, or whether they were written independently. John has so little material in common with the others that it looks as if he knew all three, and deliberately tried to widen the picture they paint – using other traditions, and telling the story very differently.

So it seems as though the Gospel-writers each knew that the other Gospels were inadequate, and sought to extend the picture. The first Christians recognised this by refusing to choose between them, and accepting all four together as providing a composite identikit of Jesus of Nazareth.

How accurate is this identikit?

The Gospels first circulated under the gaze of eyewitnesses of Jesus' ministry. Luke claims that his Gospel rests upon extensive research among 'eyewitnesses and servants of the word' – that is (probably), those charged with remembering the 'word' of Jesus (Luke 1:1-4). Within the parameters of the 'Bios' genre, Luke has striven for accuracy. The differences between the Gospels underline the impression of a figure of such towering significance that any attempt to capture him in words is bound to be inadequate. But there is no need to doubt the broad reliability of these accounts.

Mark

An early tradition connects Mark's Gospel with Peter (see 1 Peter 5:13), and it is likely that Mark represents the collection of stories and traditions which Peter used in his long ministry. But Mark has woven them together into a crisp and vivid presentation of Jesus, emphasising his power as a healer, his preaching (although Mark doesn't record much of it), the opposition he provoked, the puzzlement he caused even among his disciples, and their difficulty in deciding who or what he was. Mark emphasises Jesus' expectation of his own death, his call to sacrificial discipleship embracing suffering like his, and his pronouncement of judgement on the Temple and the leaders of Israel. He tells the story of Jesus' last week in great detail. The resurrection is not directly described, and Mark's story does not end so much as break off, as though Mark wanted to convey an impression of incompleteness.

Outline of Mark

1:1-15	The scene is set
1:16–3:6	Jesus' initial ministry in Galilee
3:7–4:34	Jesus the teacher
4:35–6:6	Jesus the healer
6:7–9:1	On a wider stage: Jesus the Messiah
9:2–10:45	The heart of discipleship: Jesus the leader
10:46–13:37	Jesus the Son of David, the Master of the House
14:1–15:47	Jesus the new covenant sacrifice
16:1-8	The new start

The Church of the Holy Sepulchre, Jerusalem, probable site of Jesus' death and burial.

Anyone who wants to follow me must pick up a cross and carry it behind me. If you want to save your life, you will lose it. If you lose your life for my sake and the gospel, you will save it.

Mark 8:34-35

Four Gospels . . . one life

Jesus' life
A simple harmonisation of the Gospels

	Matthew	Mark	Luke	John
Jesus' birth and childhood 4/5 B.C.				
Jesus' genealogy	1:1-17		3:23-38	
Jesus' birth is foretold	1:18-25		1:26-38	
Jesus is born	2:1-12		2:1-39	
Jesus' childhood and visit to Temple			2:40-52	
Jesus prepares for his public ministry A.D. 29				
Jesus is baptised	3:13-17	1:9-11	3:21-22	
Jesus is tempted in the wilderness	4:1-11	1:12-13	4:1-13	
Jesus' ministry begins				
John points to Jesus				1:19-34
John's disciples attracted				1:35-51
The first miracle: water into wine				2:1-11
'You must be born again'				3:1-21
Jesus in Galilee				
Jesus arrives in Galilee	4:12-17	1:14	4:14	4:43-45
Jesus calls the first of the Twelve	4:18-22	1:16-20	5:1-11	
Many miracles	8:1-17	1:40–2:12	5:12-26	
The Sermon on the Mount	5:1–7:29		6:20-49	
Jesus speaks in parables	13:1-53	4:1-34	8:4-18	
A series of miracles	8:23–9:8, 18-26	4:35–5:43	8:22-56	
Jesus affirmed as Christ and Son of God	16:13-26	8:27–9:1	9:18-27	
Jesus is transfigured	16:27–17:13	9:2-13	9:28-36	
Jesus predicts his death and resurrection	17:22-23	9:31-32	9:43-45	
Jesus' last Galilean ministry	17:24–18:35	9:33-50	9:46-50	7:1-9
Jesus in Judea and Perea				
Jesus' journey to Jerusalem	19:1-2	10:1	9:51-62	7:10
Jesus claims deity				8:12-59
Jesus the good Shepherd				10:1-21
Parable of the good Samaritan			10:25-37	
Jesus in Mary and Martha's home			10:38-42	
Jesus teaches a prayer			11:1-13	
Jesus raises Lazarus				11:1-44
Jesus travels towards Jerusalem				
The rich young ruler	19:16-30	10:17-31	18:18-30	
Jesus predicts his death	20:17-19	10:32-34	18:31-34	
Jesus arrives at Bethany				11:55–12:11

Jesus' last week, death and resurrection – see pages 102-104

Who wrote the New Testament?

Name	Nationality	Occupation	Writings	How he died
Matthew	Jewish	Tax-collector	Gospel of Matthew	By tradition martyred in Ethiopia
Mark	Jewish		Gospel of Mark	By tradition martyred
Luke	Greek	Physician	Gospel of Luke Acts	By tradition martyred in Greece
John	Jewish	Fisherman	Gospel of John 1, 2 & 3 John Revelation	Banished to Patmos; natural death
Paul	Jewish	Pharisee/ Tentmaker	Romans 1 & 2 Corinthians Galatians Ephesians Philippians Colossians 1 & 2 Thessalonians 1 & 2 Timothy, Titus Philemon	By tradition martyred in Rome by Nero
James	Jewish		James	By tradition martyred
Peter	Jewish	Fisherman	1 & 2 Peter	By tradition crucified upside-down in Rome by Nero
Jude	Jewish		Jude	By tradition martyred
Author unknown	Jewish		Hebrews	

Who are the Marys of the New Testament?

Mary, mother of Jesus
The Jewish woman from Nazareth whom God chose to give birth to his Son. Married to Joseph, she was a descendant of David. Mary stood at the foot of the cross when Jesus was killed.
Matthew 1:18-25; Luke 1:26-45; John 19:25-27; Acts 1:14

Mary of Bethany
With her sister Martha and brother Lazarus, a close friend of Jesus, whose feet she anointed with perfume.
Luke 10:38-42; John 11:1-45; 12:1-3; compare Matthew 26:7; Mark 14:3

Mary, mother of James and Joseph (Joses)
A Galilean woman who, after being healed, followed Jesus and supported his ministry financially.
Matthew 27:56; 28:1; Mark 15:40, 41, 47

Mary Magdalene
Another Galilean woman whom Jesus healed, and who helped to support Jesus' ministry.
Matthew 27:56, 61; 28:1; Mark 15:40, 47; 16:1, 9; Luke 8:2; John 20:1, 2, 11-18

Mary, mother of John Mark
A relative of Barnabas; her home was a gathering place for the Jerusalem church.
Acts 12:12, 13; Colossians 4:10

Mary of Rome
A woman commended by Paul.
Romans 16:6

New Testament Apocrypha

A number of books, dating from the second century to the Middle Ages, were not finally accepted into the canon of Scripture, and are known as New Testament apocrypha. Like the books of the New Testament proper, some are in the form of gospels, some letters, some Acts, some apocalypses. But they differ markedly in content from the canonical books: for instance the apocryphal gospels focus on parts of Jesus' life (for instance his infancy) and have little interest in his adult ministry. Some are bizarre or offensive, some heretical and some contain 'secret knowledge' . Although the apocryphal New Testament books may contain some genuine words of Jesus, it is almost impossible to distinguish them from the added and worthless material.

Examples of New Testament apocrypha include:

Gospel of Hebrews: which records Jesus' resurrection appearance to James

Gospel of Peter: which heightens the miraculous in the accounts of the death and resurrection of Jesus

Gospel of Thomas: which has many sayings similar to those in the Synoptic Gospels, but with an added Gnostic flavour

Acts of Peter: which tells how Peter defeated Simon Magus (Acts 8) and Paul founded the Roman church.

Matthew

Matthew's Gospel is very different from Mark's, although he incorporates nearly the whole of Mark (about 92 per cent). When he uses Mark's material, he usually condenses it, telling the stories with less detail (and thus less vividly). His Gospel is about 60 per cent longer than Mark, with a wealth of new material.

Who wrote the first Gospel – and when?
The ascription to Matthew, one of Jesus' disciples (also called 'Levi': Matthew 9:9; 10:3; Mark 2:14) goes back to the early second century, and there is little reason to doubt it.

The second question is harder to answer. Jesus' prediction in chapter 24 of the destruction of the Temple drops no hints that it has already happened. If it had, we might have expected that the connection made there between that dreadful event and 'the coming of the Son of Man' would be qualified in some way – for the Temple was destroyed by the Romans in A.D. 70, but this was not followed by the cosmic appearance of the Son of Man as 24:29 suggests. So in all likelihood Matthew's Gospel was published before A.D. 70.

Why was Matthew written?
Matthew's Jewishness (his interest in the fulfilment of Scripture, for instance – see below) has suggested to some that he was writing for Jewish Christians, perhaps for a specific group troubled by a difficult relationship with the synagogue. At first, most Jewish Christians continued to worship in their local synagogue. But as the first century progressed, relationships became increasingly strained, especially as the number of Gentile Christians multiplied, and Jewish Christians felt more and more pressure to live in fellowship with them. If they did so, they could no longer obey the traditional Jewish food and purity laws.

So in many places there came a 'parting of the ways', to use the understated phrase by which scholars describe a painful severing of relationships between Jews and Christians. For instance, the ways parted in Jerusalem when the Jewish Christians there obeyed Jesus' command in Matthew 24:15-16 and fled across the Jordan when the Romans advanced to attack. They did not stay to defend Jerusalem alongside their fellow-Jews.

Prof. Graham Stanton suggests that the trauma surrounding this parting of the ways prompted Matthew to write for his group of churches. He wanted to show how Jesus fulfils the Law (e.g. 5:17), how he too was rejected by his fellow-Jews, how he criticised the Jewish leadership and especially accused them of wrongly interpreting the Law (chapters 5 and 23), and how he called his followers to respond with love towards their enemies (5:43ff) and to reach out positively to the Gentile world in his name (10:18; 28:18-20).

On the other hand, as we saw on page 86, Richard Bauckham cautions us against finding local

This early synagogue at Capernaum stands over the synagogue that Jesus knew. Jesus made the lakeside town of Capernaum his headquarters during his Galilean ministry.

A Pharisee at prayer, with prayer shawl and phylacteries.

purposes for the Gospels. Such suggestions generally only relate to parts of the Gospel. So maybe we should give weight just to the comparison with Mark: Matthew simply wanted to enlarge Mark's picture of Jesus, especially by adding records of his actual teaching.

Matthew's special interests

Here is a summary of the four emphases that distinguish Matthew from the other Gospels:

• *The fulfilment of the Old Testament*. On twelve occasions Matthew notes that this or that took place 'in order to fulfil what was written by the prophet . . .' In addition, he records Jesus' saying that 'I have not come to abolish the law and the prophets, but to fulfil them' (5:17). The genealogy with which he begins emphasises Jesus' position as 'Son of David' – the Messiah who comes laden with Old Testament promise.

• *Jesus as teacher.* Matthew includes five solid blocks of teaching from Jesus, most notably the 'Sermon on the Mount' (chapters 5–7; also chapters 10, 13, 18 and 23–25). This probably reflects a concern with teaching and discipling new converts. Matthew has written his Gospel so that the story has a kind of topical structure – see the plan alongside.

• *Outreach to the Gentile world*. The appearance in chapter 2 of the 'wise men' – astrologers – from the East signals Matthew's conviction that this 'King of the Jews' is set to rule the whole world. This conviction is given concrete shape at the other end of the Gospel, when Jesus claims authority over heaven and earth and commissions his disciples to 'make disciples of all nations' (28:18-19). In between we meet significant individuals such as the Roman centurion whose faith is greater than any Jew's (8:5-13), we see 'the Son of Man' sitting on the throne to judge all nations (25:31ff), and we hear Jesus' famous 'mission discourse' (chapter 10).

• *Issues of church peace and discipline*. Matthew's emphasis on practical discipleship shades over into a concern with conflict-management and discipline within the Church. This appears especially in chapter 18 (where he alone uses the word 'church', 18:17, compare 16:18), but we can discern this interest in other passages also, like 5:21-26 and 7:1-5.

'Do you understand this?' Jesus asked. 'Yes,' they replied. 'So,' said Jesus, 'every scribe trained for the kingdom of heaven is like a householder who uses both new and old treasures.'
Matthew 13:51-52

Matthew's interest in the Old Testament

A survey of Matthew's 'fulfilment' passages conveys the strength of his concern to show how the Old Testament was fulfilled through Jesus.
Matthew 1:22; 2:15; 2:17; 2:23; 4:14; 8:17; 12:17; 13:14; 13:35; 21:4; 26:56; 27:9

Jesus' words and deeds

Miracles of Jesus

Healing of individuals

Healing of individuals	Matthew	Mark	Luke	John
Son of government official				4:46-54
Sick man at a pool				5:1-15
Man in synagogue		1:21-28	4:31-37	
Man with skin-disease	8:1-4	1:40-45	5:12-14	
Roman officer's servant	8:5-13		7:1-10	
Dead son of a widow			7:11-15	
Peter's mother-in-law	8:14-15	1:29-31	4:38-39	
An uncontrollable man	8:28-34	5:1-20	8:26-39	
Paralysed man	9:1-7	2:1-12	5:17-26	
Woman with severe bleeding	9:20-22	5:25-34	8:43-48	
Dead girl	9:18-26	5:21-43	8:40-56	
Dumb man	9:32-34			
Man with a paralysed hand	12:9-14	3:1-6	6:6-11	
Blind and dumb man	12:22		11:14	
Canaanite woman's daughter	15:21-28	7:24-30		
Deaf and dumb man		7:31-37		
Blind man at Bethsaida		8:22-26		
Boy with epilepsy	17:14-18	9:14-29	9:37-43	
Blind Bartimaeus	20:29-34	10:46-52	18:35-43	
Woman with a bad back			13:10-17	
Sick man			14:1-6	
Man born blind				9:1-41
Dead friend named Lazarus				11:1-44
Slave's ear			22:47-51	

Healing of groups

Healing of groups	Matthew	Mark	Luke	John
Crowd in Capernaum	8:16-17	1:32-34	4:40-41	
Two blind men	9:27-31			
Crowd by Lake Galilee		3:7-12		
Crowd on the hillside by Lake Galilee	15:29-31			
Ten men			17:11-19	

Control over laws of nature

Control over laws of nature	Matthew	Mark	Luke	John
Water changed into wine				2:1-11
Catch of fish			5:1-11	
Jesus calms a storm	8:23-27	4:35-41	8:22-25	
Crowds: over 5,000 people fed	14:13-21	6:32-44	9:10-17	6:1-13
Jesus walks on the water	14:22-33	6:45-52		6:16-21
Crowds: over 4,000 people fed	15:32-38	8:1-10		
A fish and the payment of taxes	17:24-27			
Fig tree withers away	21:18-22	11:12-14, 20-24		
Another catch of fish				21:1-11

92

Where do we find miracles in the Bible?

Most of the miracles in the Bible are clustered around a few people and events:

- **Moses** and the beginnings of the people of Israel

- **Elijah** and **Elisha** and the beginnings of the line of prophets who recalled their people to their covenant (agreement) with God

- **Jesus** and the beginning of the new Israel

- The **apostles** and the founding of the Christian Church

People raised from the dead

Zarephath widow's son
1 Kings 17:17-24

Shunammite woman's son
2 Kings 4:32-37

Man whose body touched Elisha's bones
2 Kings 13:20-21

People at Jesus' death
Matthew 27:52-53

Son of the widow of Nain
Luke 7:11-15

Jairus' daughter
Luke 8:41-42, 49-55

Lazarus
John 11:1-44

Dorcas
Acts 9:36-42

Eutychus
Acts 20:9-10

Parables and illustrations of Jesus

	Matthew	Mark	Luke	John
About nature and farm life				
Birds and flowers	6:25-34	12:22-31		
A tree and its fruit	7:15-20		6:43-45	
The sower	13:1-9, 18-23	4:1-9, 13-20	8:4-8, 11-15	
Growing seed		4:26-29		
Unfruitful fig tree			13:6-9	
Weeds	13:24-30, 36-43			
Mustard seed	13:31-32	4:30-32	13:18,19	
Lost sheep	18:10-14		15:1-7	
Workers in the vineyard	20:1-16			
Tenants in the vineyard	21:33-46	12:1-12	20:9-19	
Fig tree	24:32-35	13:28-31	21:29-33	
Sheep and goats	25:31-46			
Harvest time			4:35-38	
The shepherd			10:1-18	
Grain of wheat			12:20-26	
The vine			15:1-17	
About familiar things in Bible times				
Water			4:5-14	
			7:37-39	
Salt	5:13			
Light	5:14-16	4:21, 22	8:16-18	12:35-36
Bread				6:25-35
House builders	7:24-27		6:46-49	
Patching clothes	9:16	2:21	5:36	
New wine	9:17	2:22	5:37-39	
Yeast	13:33		13:20-21	
The pearl	13:45-46			
The fishing net	13:47-50			
Lost coin			15:8-10	
About everyday life				
Unwilling children	11:16-19		7:31-35	
New truths and old	13:51-52			
Forgiveness	18:21-35			
Two sons	21:28-32			
The wedding feast	22:1-14		14:15-24	
Ten girls at a wedding	25:1-13			
Servants	25:14-30		19:11-27	
Debts and debtors			7:41-47	
Good Samaritan			10:25-37	
Friend in need			11:5-13	
Rich fool			12:16-21	
Watchful servants		13:33-37	12:35-40	
Humility and hospitality			14:7-14	
Cost of discipleship			14:25-33	
Lost son			15:11-32	
Shrewd manager			16:1-13	
Rich man and Lazarus			16:19-31	
A servant's duty			17:7-10	
The persistent widow			18:1-8	
Pharisee and tax-collector			18:9-14	

Parables

Parables are stories based on everyday life. They teach a particular truth.
There are different types of parables:

• **short sayings,** for example: 'You are like light for the whole world' *Matthew 5:14*.
• **longer sayings,** for example: 'No one uses a piece of new cloth to patch up an old coat, because the new patch will shrink and tear off some of the old cloth, making an even bigger hole' *Mark 2:21*.
• **complete stories,** for example: the man sowing corn *Luke 8:4-8*.

Jesus' parables divided the listeners into two groups: those who wanted to understand and those who were unwilling or uninterested. To those who wanted understanding they were a means of learning more.

There are no parables in John's Gospel but John does record Jesus using common things and everyday life to point to truths about God and God's world.

Jesus met the Samaritan woman at the well.

Who was Jesus of Nazareth?

Who did Jesus think he was?
Who did those around him think he was?
Who *was* Jesus of Nazareth?
To answer these questions, let us look at four titles that have been applied to him.

A wandering rabbi

In many respects Jesus was very much like the rabbis of his period, who roamed around, accompanied by disciples, dispensing advice and debating interpretations of the Law. But they tended to come from one of the recognised rabbinic schools, and to be sought out by disciples who would attach themselves to them. By contrast, in spite of Jesus' ability to speak with authority (Mark 1:22 and parallels), he appears to have had no such formal training, and is the one who took the initiative to gather his inner circle of twelve disciples around him.

Messiah/Christ

By the time that the apostle Paul was writing, 20 years after Jesus' life, he was using the term *Christos* (which is simply the Greek word for *Messiah*) as a title for Jesus, as if it were his surname. But at the time of Jesus, *Messiah* would have had very different connotations. Jewish hopes and expectations regarding the arrival of a Messiah were complex and varied, but there was a significant stream of thought that hoped for the arrival of a great leader from the line of King David, who would come and deliver military victory over the occupying Roman powers and herald a new age of freedom and prosperity for Israel.

Jesus fulfils some, but not all, of these expectations. He came from David's line, he restored many to wholeness, he chose twelve disciples in a clear allusion to the

Relief of Jesus praying in Gethsemane.

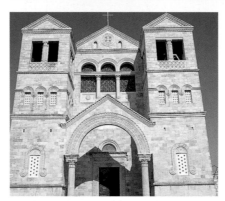

The Church of the Transfiguration, Mount Tabor.

twelve tribes of Israel, and he entered Jerusalem riding on a donkey in fulfilment of Zechariah 9:9. Yet, he had no intention of bringing about a military uprising, and, when one of his disciples acknowledged him as Messiah, he told him to hush it up (Mark 8:30 and parallels).

Some scholars claim that Jesus had no Messianic pretensions at all, and that all references to his being Messiah are later inventions of the early Church. But it would make no sense for the Church to give him that title, if he hadn't made some reference to it himself; for, by not bringing about military victory and by dying an ignominious death, he had ultimately failed to meet the

popular expectation of a Messiah.

So why did Jesus seem so reluctant to make the claim to be Messiah? This could be for a number of reasons:
1. There would be great political danger in making such a claim openly, for the occupying powers would be very sensitive to someone making claims to be a saviour of the nation. (Although there is a degree of doubt regarding the exact wording of Jesus' statements at this trials, it is surely no coincidence that it is when Jesus is under arrest and knows that he is about to die that he is most open about his identity.)
2. Because Jesus' idea of a suffering Messiah was so different from popular conceptions, it would have led to misunderstanding.
3. There was a tradition that one could not claim to be Messiah until one had accomplished the Messiah's task. In Jesus' case, this was not until after he had died.

Son of God

At the time, the term *son of God* was sometimes used to refer to particularly special people or heavenly beings. Paul and other later New Testament writers spoke

of *the* Son of God to refer to Jesus in a special relationship to God. Jesus never used the term himself, but the Gospels clearly record many references to Jesus' unique sonship.

Most significantly, on two occasions a voice from heaven described him to be 'my beloved son'. The first was at the beginning of his ministry, at his baptism (Mark 1:11 and parallels), and the second was at the extraordinary event known as the Transfiguration (Mark 9:7 and parallels). At this event, the disciples who were with Jesus saw his clothes become dazzling white, as he appeared to be joined by Moses and Elijah before being enveloped by a cloud. Jesus was also happy to talk about God as 'my Father' (e.g. Matthew 11:27), and even referred to him by the familiar term, *abba*, whose closest translation is *dad* or *daddy*.

Son of Man

This was Jesus' favoured way of talking about himself. Some scholars, such as Geza Vermes, see it as just another way of saying 'I' or 'a man like me'. While there may be some truth in this in some instances, there must be more, given the heavenly associations of the term in Daniel 7 and some of the inter-testamental writings. Whatever its origins, it certainly helped Jesus to identify himself with humankind.

Artist's impression of rabbi displaying the Torah in a synagogue. Notice the women in the separate gallery.

Luke

Luke's Gospel is the longest of the four – in fact, the longest single work in the New Testament. It forms a two-volume work with the Acts of the Apostles, ascribed to Paul's travelling companion Luke from the earliest years of the Church.

Luke also incorporates much of Mark's Gospel, but less than Matthew – about 55 per cent of it, contributing about 30 per cent of his material. But unlike Matthew, Luke has 'bunched' the material he has in common with Mark: it appears (broadly) in chapters 5–6, 8–9, 18 and 19–22. In the middle of Luke's Gospel is a long section (9:51–18:14) which has no parallels in Mark, and not many in Matthew. It has been called Luke's Travel Narrative, for at the start of this section Jesus 'set his face to go to Jerusalem' (9:51), and from then onward is on the move, gradually travelling south from Galilee for the final show-down in Judea.

Luke's purpose

Luke himself refers to 'many' who had produced written accounts of Jesus before him (1:1). In comparison with these 'many', Luke sets out to produce 'an orderly account' for his patron, Theophilus, based on his own careful research (1:3). He gives us the impression that confusion reigned supreme – prompting his desire to provide Theophilus with a definitive account (1:4).

Theophilus

Some have argued that Theophilus is an imaginary figure, and point to the meaning of his name, 'lover of God'. But in all likelihood he was real, perhaps a wealthy, newly converted (and confused?) Christian who supported Luke through his period of research. Maybe he lived in Caesarea Philippi, for it appears that Luke was with Paul for at least part of his two-year imprisonment there (Acts 27:1), and this would have been an excellent base from which to research the Gospel.

Luke with Acts

It is important to read the Gospel and Acts together, for they have many themes in common and an over-arching structure that unites them. For instance, Luke's birth narrative (unique to him) contains the figure of Simeon, an old Jew 'looking forward to the consolation of Israel' (Luke 2:25), who recognises the baby Jesus as the Messiah and prophesies that he will bring salvation to 'all peoples, a light for revelation to the Gentiles, and for glory to your people Israel' (2:31f). This prophecy looks forward to the end of the book of Acts, where the gospel has reached Rome, the

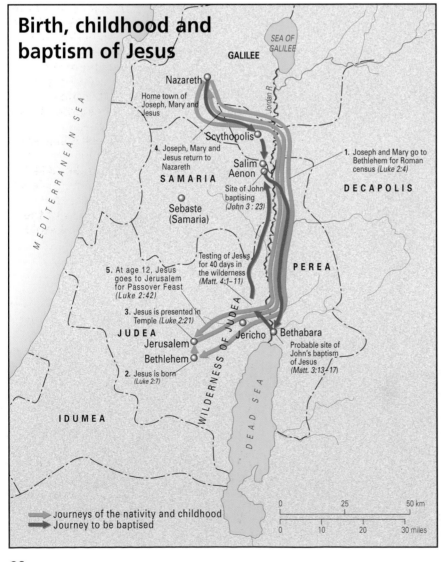

Birth, childhood and baptism of Jesus

SEA OF GALILEE

GALILEE

MEDITERRANEAN SEA

Jordan R.

Nazareth
Home town of Joseph, Mary and Jesus

Scythopolis

4. Joseph, Mary and Jesus return to Nazareth

Salim
Aenon
Site of John baptising (John 3:23)

1. Joseph and Mary go to Bethlehem for Roman census (Luke 2:4)

SAMARIA

DECAPOLIS

Sebaste (Samaria)

Testing of Jesus for 40 days in the wilderness (Matt. 4:1–11)

PEREA

5. At age 12, Jesus goes to Jerusalem for Passover Feast (Luke 2:42)

3. Jesus is presented in Temple (Luke 2:21)

JUDEA
Jerusalem
Bethlehem

WILDERNESS OF JUDEA

Jericho

Bethabara
Probable site of John's baptism of Jesus (Matt. 3:13–17)

2. Jesus is born (Luke 2:7)

DEAD SEA

IDUMEA

Journeys of the nativity and childhood
Journey to be baptised

| 0 | 25 | 50 km |
| 0 | 10 | 20 | 30 miles |

> Sovereign Lord, as you have promised, you now dismiss your servant in peace. For my eyes have seen your salvation, which you prepared in the sight of all people, a light for revelation to the Gentiles and for glory to your people Israel.
>
> Luke 2:29-32

Luke's themes and interests

There are many, including:

• The Holy Spirit. Luke emphasises the re-birth of prophecy at the time of Jesus' birth (e.g. 1:41; 1:67), and the power of the Spirit resting on Jesus (1:35; 3:22; 4:14), and this anticipates his great interest in the Spirit in Acts.

• Poverty and riches. Much material signals Luke's interest in the deceptiveness of wealth, and the blessings of poverty, especially the voluntary poverty to which Jesus calls his disciples (e.g. 1:53; 6:20-26; 12:13-21; 14:33; 16:19-31; 19:1-10 etc.). This theme, too, is developed in Acts.

• Women. The prominent role played by women in the Acts story is anticipated in the Gospel as we see Jesus treating women very differently from the norm in Jewish culture: e.g. 7:36-50; 8:1-3. And Luke follows this through by emphasising the female players: Mary, Elizabeth, Anna (2:36-38), the widow of Nain (7:11-17), Martha and Mary (10:38-42),

the 'daughter of Abraham' bound by Satan (13:10-17 – the only known occasion on which this female equivalent of 'son of Abraham' is used).

• Social outcasts. Jesus' ministry to social outcasts is a feature in all the Gospels, but Luke takes special delight in it. Whether it's poor shepherds (2:8ff), a rich tax-collector (19:1-10, 18:9-14), an apostate waster (15:11-32), unclean Samaritans (17:11-19, 10:29-37), a prostitute (7:36-50), or a crucified terrorist (23:39-43), Luke loves to show the doors of the kingdom being thrown wide for them.

• Prayer. Where his story runs parallel to Matthew and Mark, Luke adds a reference to prayer on no fewer than eleven occasions. He emphasises Jesus' private prayer (5:16; 6:12; 9:18), especially at vital moments (3:21; 9:28), and makes his example inspiring (11:1), not to say awesome (22:40-46).

centre of the empire, and we hear Paul's comment that 'this salvation of God has been sent to the Gentiles' (Acts 28:28). Luke's message is that Israel finds her salvation and 'glory' in and through the salvation of the Gentiles by faith in Christ, and not in rivalry or separation. Luke probably wrote primarily for Gentile readers such as Theophilus. His Greek is cultured and vivid, although he deliberately employs the style of Septuagint (Old Testament) Greek in his opening chapters, to underline the Jewishness of the start of this powerful, well-told story.

Outline of Luke:	
1:1-4	Literary preface
1:5–2:52	The story begins: two wonderful births
3:1–4:13	The turning-point in history, the birth of the New Age
4:14–9:50	Jesus' Galilean ministry, in fulfilment of Isaiah 61:1-2 (see 4:18-19)
9:51–19:28	Jesus en route for Jerusalem: the new lifestyle of the kingdom
19:29–21:38	In Jerusalem, ministry in the Temple

Luke stresses Jesus' ministry to outcasts such as poor shepherds.

Opening the book, he found the place where it is written,
'The Spirit of the Lord is upon me!'
Luke 4:17-18

Jesus in Galilee

Jesus spent much of his ministry preaching and healing in Galilee. Although this Roman province was largely Jewish, many non-Jews also settled there. The Galileans, with a dialect of their own, were despised by many Jews from Jerusalem.

• In Jesus' time, many towns clustered around the **Sea of Galilee**. It was while sailing across the lake that Jesus calmed a sudden storm (Mark 4:35-41).

• Jesus came to live in **Capernaum** (Matthew 4:13), and cured a Roman officer's slave (Matthew 8:5-13), a leper (Matthew 8:2-4), Peter's mother-in-law (Matthew 8:14-15), a man with an evil spirit (Mark 1:21-26) and a paralysed man (Mark 2:1-12). Jesus preached in the Capernaum synagogue (Mark 1:21), called Matthew (Matthew 9:9) and paid the Temple tax here (Matthew 17:24), and denounced the town for its lack of faith (Matthew 11:23).

• In **Chorazin**, Jesus performed miracles, and later denounced the people for their lack of faith (Matthew 11:21)

• Jesus also visited **Bethsaida,** where he restored the sight of a blind man (Mark 8:22), and withdrew for a time of rest (Luke 9:10).

• At **Magdala**, Jesus was dining with Simon the Pharisee, when Mary anointed him (Luke 7:36-8:2).

• **Tabgha** may be the place where the risen Christ met the disciples and ate with them (John 21:1-14).

• The **Mount of Beatitudes** is the hill where, by tradition, Jesus taught the Sermon on the Mount (Matthew 5:1–7:29).

Above: The Sea of Galilee from near the site of Gergesa.

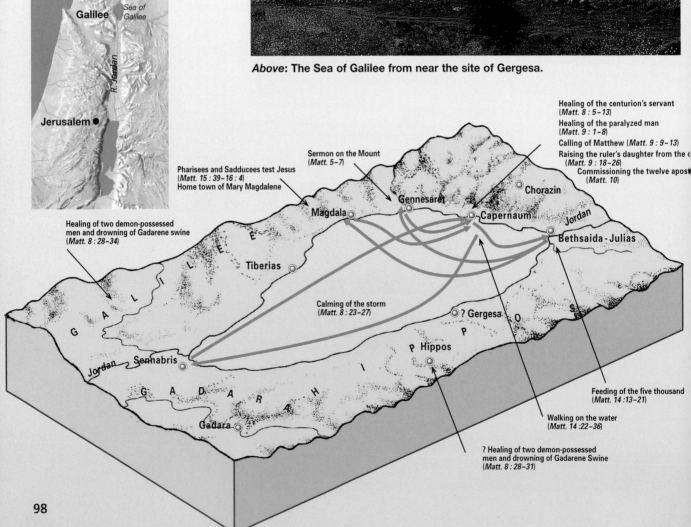

Galilee

Sea of Galilee

R. Jordan

Jerusalem ●

Healing of the centurion's servant
(*Matt. 8 : 5–13*)
Healing of the paralyzed man
(*Matt. 9 : 1–8*)
Calling of Matthew (*Matt. 9 : 9–13*)
Raising the ruler's daughter from the d
(*Matt. 9 : 18–26*)
Commissioning the twelve apost
(*Matt. 10*)

Sermon on the Mount
(*Matt. 5–7*)

Pharisees and Sadducees test Jesus
(*Matt. 15 : 39–16 : 4*)
Home town of Mary Magdalene

Healing of two demon-possessed
men and drowning of Gadarene swine
(*Matt. 8 : 28–34*)

Chorazin

Gennesáret

Magdala

Capernaum

Jordan

Bethsaida - Julias

Tiberias

G A L I L E E

Calming of the storm
(*Matt. 8 : 23–27*)

? Gergesa

P Hippos

Jordan

Sennabris

G A D A R A

Gadara

Feeding of the five thousand
(*Matt. 14 :13–21*)

Walking on the water
(*Matt. 14 :22–36*)

? Healing of two demon-possessed
men and drowning of Gadarene Swine
(*Matt. 8 : 28–31*)

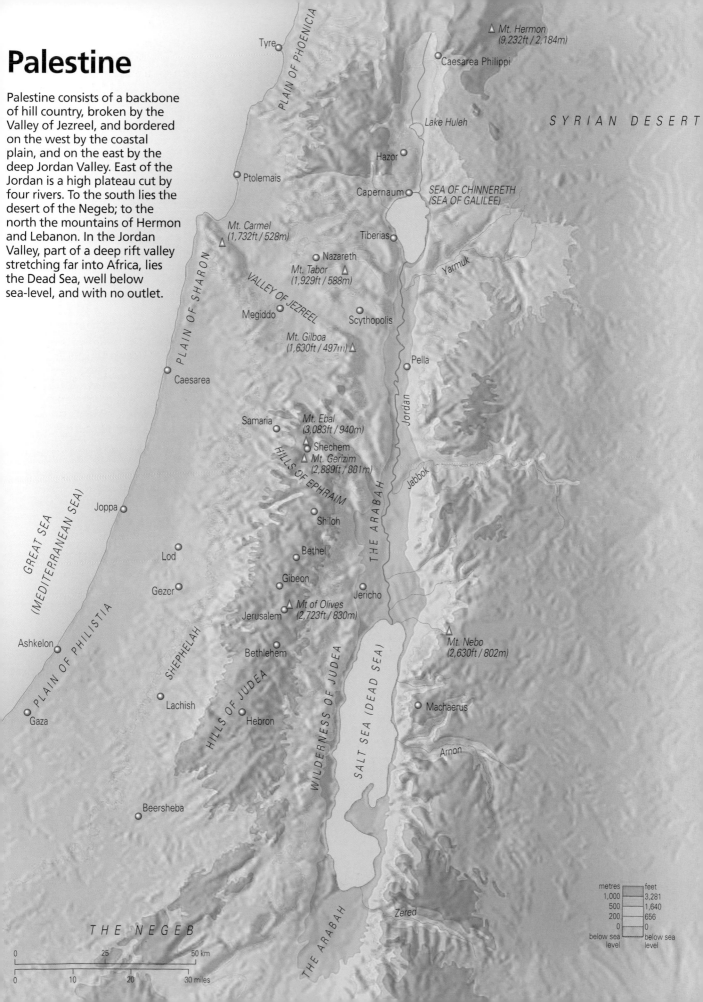

Palestine

Palestine consists of a backbone of hill country, broken by the Valley of Jezreel, and bordered on the west by the coastal plain, and on the east by the deep Jordan Valley. East of the Jordan is a high plateau cut by four rivers. To the south lies the desert of the Negeb; to the north the mountains of Hermon and Lebanon. In the Jordan Valley, part of a deep rift valley stretching far into Africa, lies the Dead Sea, well below sea-level, and with no outlet.

Tyre

PLAIN OF PHOENICIA

△ Mt. Hermon
(9,232ft / 2,184m)

Caesarea Philippi

Lake Huleh

SYRIAN DESERT

Hazor

Ptolemais

Capernaum

SEA OF CHINNERETH
(SEA OF GALILEE)

Mt. Carmel
(1,732ft / 528m)
△

Tiberias

Nazareth

Mt. Tabor
(1,929ft / 588m)

Yarmuk

VALLEY OF JEZREEL

PLAIN OF SHARON

Megiddo

Scythopolis

Mt. Gilboa
(1,630ft / 497m) △

Pella

Caesarea

Jordan

Samaria

Mt. Ebal
(3,083ft / 940m)
△ Shechem
△ Mt. Gerizim
(2,889ft / 881m)

HILLS OF EPHRAIM

Jabbok

GREAT SEA
(MEDITERRANEAN SEA)

Joppa

Shiloh

Lod

Bethel

THE ARABAH

Gibeon

Gezer

Jericho

Mt of Olives
(2,723ft / 830m)

Jerusalem △

PLAIN OF PHILISTIA

Ashkelon

Bethlehem

Mt. Nebo
(2,630ft / 802m)
△

Lachish

SHEPHELAH

HILLS OF JUDEA

Hebron

WILDERNESS OF JUDEA

SALT SEA (DEAD SEA)

Machaerus

Gaza

Arnon

Beersheba

THE NEGEB

THE ARABAH

Zered

metres | feet
1,000 | 3,281
500 | 1,640
200 | 656
0 | 0
below sea level | below sea level

0 _____ 25 _____ 50 km
0 __ 10 __ 20 __ 30 miles

John

'John last of all, conscious that the "bodily" facts had been made clear in the [synoptic] Gospels, was urged by his companions and, divinely moved by the Spirit, composed a "spiritual" Gospel.' These words come from the end of the second century, from the pen of Clement of Alexandria. And in modern scholarship Clement's description of John as 'a spiritual Gospel' has seemed to summarise John's apparent interest in the meaning of Jesus' life, rather than in the facts of it. For instance, John includes long 'discourses', unparalleled in the synoptics, in which Jesus makes powerful and dramatic claims for himself (e.g. 5:19-47; 6:35-58; 10:1-39). Whereas in the synoptics Jesus is reluctant to call himself 'Messiah' or 'Son of God' in public (e.g. Mark 8:29-30), he does not hesitate in John!

John's aim

But even a quick reading reveals that John is not unaware of a distinction between 'the facts' and 'the meaning'. He includes hosts of narrative details, for instance, of time and place and it is he who gives us the tradition that Jesus' ministry lasted for over two years, including at least three Passovers. The Gospel presents itself as eyewitness testimony to the incarnation of the Word (1:14). In this respect, John is no different from the synoptics: as a '*Bios*', his Gospel aims to present the historical Jesus so that readers may understand him.

John and the synoptics

Why then is John so different from the synoptics? This is a most important question – the credibility of the Gospels as reliable guides depends upon it. The earliest answer was given by second-century Gnostic Christians, who fell in love with John because it seemed to contain special, secret traditions of Jesus which supported their mystical approach to the faith. They believed that John had drawn on separate traditions, unknown or unused by the other evangelists.

This view of John was revived in the twentieth century, especially by Prof. C. H. Dodd, who argued that John wrote independently of the synoptic Gospels, drawing on Jesus-traditions associated with Judea rather than with Galilee. There may well be truth in this,

Coin of the Roman Emperor Augustus (31 B.C.–A.D. 14), who was emperor at the time of the birth of Jesus of Nazareth (Luke 3:1).

but it is noteworthy that in John, even when Jesus is in Galilee, the stories barely coincide. John gives us the wedding at Cana (2:1-11), to which there is no synoptic parallel; the royal official (4:46-54), which has some elements in common with the centurion-story in Luke 7:1-10 but may be a different story altogether; and the feeding of the 5,000 followed by the stilling of the storm, which occur together in Matthew and Mark as in John (Mark 6:34-52; John 6:1-21), but which John expands with the 'Bread of Life' discourse (6:22-59). John is aware of a wider ministry in Galilee (7:1), but seems deliberately to have used material not in the synoptics.

A tiled café sign in modern Cana. John gives us the wedding at Cana (2:1-11), to which there is no synoptic parallel.

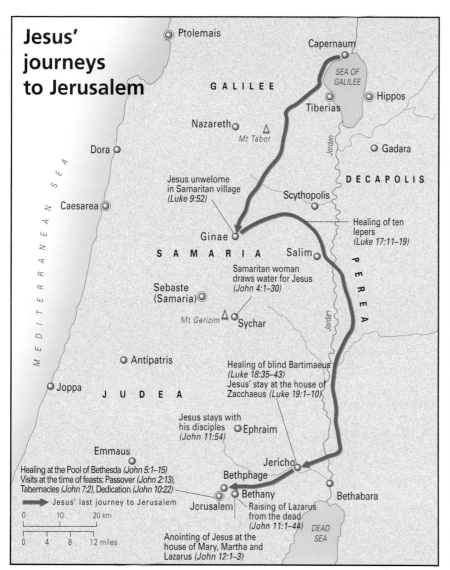

Jesus' journeys to Jerusalem

- Ptolemais
- Capernaum
- SEA OF GALILEE
- GALILEE
- Hippos
- Tiberias
- Nazareth
- Mt Tabor
- Dora
- Gadara
- DECAPOLIS
- Caesarea
- Jesus unwelome in Samaritan village (Luke 9:52)
- Scythopolis
- Healing of ten lepers (Luke 17:11–19)
- Ginae
- Salim
- SAMARIA
- Samaritan woman draws water for Jesus (John 4:1–30)
- Sebaste (Samaria)
- PEREA
- Mt Gerizim
- Sychar
- Antipatris
- Healing of blind Bartimaeus (Luke 18:35–43)
- Jesus' stay at the house of Zacchaeus (Luke 19:1–10)
- Joppa
- JUDEA
- Jesus stays with his disciples (John 11:54)
- Ephraim
- Emmaus
- Jericho
- Healing at the Pool of Bethesda (John 5:1–15)
- Visits at the time of feasts: Passover (John 2:13), Tabernacles (John 7:2), Dedication (John 10:22)
- Bethphage
- → Jesus' last journey to Jerusalem
- 0   10   20 km
- 0   4   8   12 miles
- Bethany
- Bethabara
- Jerusalem
- Raising of Lazarus from the dead (John 11:1–44)
- DEAD SEA
- Anointing of Jesus at the house of Mary, Martha and Lazarus (John 12:1–3)
- MEDITERRANEAN SEA
- Jordan

An outline of John:

1:1-18	The Prologue: the Word of God becomes flesh
1:19–2:12	The Word revealed to Israel in the testimony of others
2:13–4:54	The Word revealed as Saviour of Israel, Samaria – and the world (Passover)
5:1–6:71	The Word as the Giver of Life (Tabernacles, Passover)
7:1–10:21	The Word and human reaction: faith and dispute (Tabernacles)
10:22–11:54	The Word as the Restorer of Israel (Dedication)
11:55–13:30	The Word prepares for Passover, to lay down his life
13:31–17:26	The Word looks forward to the life of the Church
18:1–20:31	The death and resurrection of the Word
21:1-25	The Word commissions the Church

Deliberately? This involves a subtle and balanced judgement. In the light of what we know about the Jesus-traditions in the early Church, is it more likely that John deliberately, or accidentally, ended up so different? The large amount of material in common between the synoptics supports the view that the stories of Jesus' short ministry quickly became standardised around a fairly limited corpus of shared memories. And so the balance of probability tips towards the deliberate supplementation of the synoptics by someone who was aware of much extra material not caught up into the synoptic tradition. In particular, he used 'controversy' material – traditions of Jesus' arguments with Jewish scholars in Jerusalem, in which he

had been much more open about his claims than he usually was with the ordinary people.

John's readership

What governed John's choice? Recent scholarship has underlined his Jewishness – revealed in his interest in the Temple and the Jewish festivals (around which he structures the Gospel), in the Old Testament and its right interpretation, and in his use of 'wisdom' ideas, of Moses-traditions, of the 'I am he' sayings in Isaiah 40–55, and of the imagery of light, water, bread, and sheep associated with the Law and with Israel. While clearly directed at a wide audience – for instance, explaining Jewish customs and terms for Gentile readers – it could well be that

John wrote especially for Jews in the aftermath of the destruction of the Temple and Jerusalem in A.D. 70, wanting to present Jesus as the answer to their loss and their need.

Many recent writers, such as Prof. Alan Culpepper, have underlined the literary artistry of John's Gospel, its quality and power as a story. It retains this power across time and culture, one of the great classics of world literature.

These things have been written so that you might believe that Jesus is the Messiah, the Son of God, and so that you might have life through faith in him.
John 20:31

Jesus' last week

	Matthew	Mark	Luke	John
Sunday (Palm Sunday)				
Jesus enters Jerusalem in triumph	21:1-9	11:1-10	19:28-44	12:12-19
Jesus visits Temple and returns to Bethany	21:10-17	11:11	19:45-46	
Monday				
Jesus curses an unfruitful fig tree	21:18-19	11:12-14		
Jesus cleanses the Temple court		11:15-19	19:45-48	
Tuesday				
Jesus explains the withered fig tree	21:20-22	11:20-26		
Jesus' authority is questioned	21:23-27	11:27-33	20:1-8	
Jesus teaches in the Temple	21:28–22:45	12:1-37	20:9-44	
Jesus condemns the scribes and Pharisees	23:1-36	12:37-40	20:45-47	
Jesus points out the widow's gift		12:41-44	21:1-4	
Jesus predicts the destruction of the Temple and the end of the world	24:1-44	13:1-37	21:5-36	
Wednesday				
Jewish leaders conspire against Jesus	26:1-5	14:1-2	22:1-2	
Jesus anointed at Bethany	26:6-13	14:3-9		
Judas agrees to betray Jesus	26:14-16	14:10-11	22:3-6	
Thursday (Maundy Thursday)				
Jesus prepares to celebrate Passover	26:17-19	14:12-16	22:7-13	
The Last Supper	26:20-29	14:17-25	22:14-38	13:1-38
Jesus and disciples withdraw to Gethsemane	26:30-46	14:26-42	22:39-46	18:1
Jesus betrayed and arrested	26:47-56	14:43-52	22:47-53	18:2-12
Jesus tried before Annas				18:12-14, 19-23
Jesus before Caiaphas and the Sanhedrin; Peter's denial	26:57-75	14:53-72	22:54-71	18:15-18, 24-27
Friday (Good Friday)				
Jesus tried before Pilate; Judas' suicide	27:1-10	15:1-5	23:1-5	18:28-38
Jesus sent to Herod			23:6-16	
Pilate imposes sentence of death	27:15-26	15:6-15	23:17-25	18:39–19:16
Jesus scourged and led to Golgotha	27:27-32	15:15-21		19:16, 17
Jesus' crucifixion and death	27:33-56	15:22-41	23:33-49	19:18-30
Jesus is buried	27:57-61	15:42-47	23:50-56	19:31-42
Saturday				
The tomb is guarded	27:62-66			
Sunday (Easter)				
The empty tomb and the risen Christ	28:1-20	16:1-8	24:1-53	20:1–21:25

Jerusalem – Jesus' last week

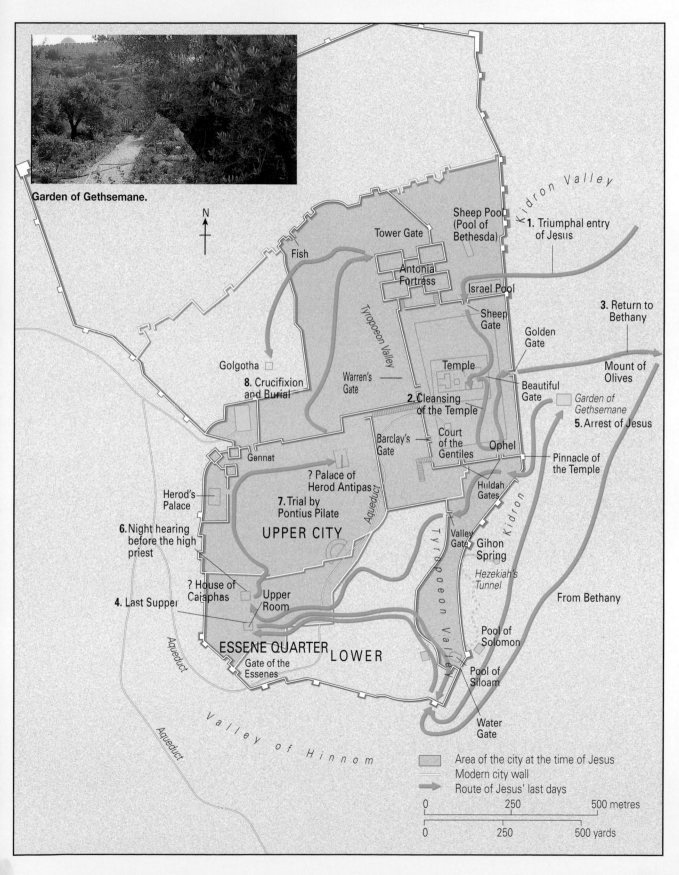

Garden of Gethsemane.

N

Kidron Valley

Sheep Pool (Pool of Bethesda)

1. Triumphal entry of Jesus

Tower Gate

Fish

Antonia Fortress

Israel Pool

3. Return to Bethany

Sheep Gate

Golden Gate

Tyropoeon Valley

Temple

Mount of Olives

Golgotha

Warren's Gate

8. Crucifixion and Burial

Beautiful Gate

Garden of Gethsemane

2. Cleansing of the Temple

5. Arrest of Jesus

Barclay's Gate

Court of the Gentiles

Ophel

Gennat

Pinnacle of the Temple

? Palace of Herod Antipas

Huldah Gates

Herod's Palace

7. Trial by Pontius Pilate

Aqueduct

UPPER CITY

Valley Gate

Gihon Spring

Hezekiah's Tunnel

From Bethany

6. Night hearing before the high priest

Tyropoeon Valley

? House of Caiaphas

Upper Room

4. Last Supper

Pool of Solomon

Kidron

ESSENE QUARTER LOWER

Pool of Siloam

Aqueduct

Gate of the Essenes

Aqueduct

Water Gate

Valley of Hinnom

Area of the city at the time of Jesus

Modern city wall

Route of Jesus' last days

| 0 | 250 | 500 metres |
| 0 | 250 | 500 yards |

Jesus' resurrection appearances

The Gospels do not describe the resurrection itself, but they recount the meetings of many different people with the risen Christ. Many reliable witnesses claimed to have seen Jesus alive after his death (1 Corinthians 15:3-8).

Mary Magdalene.

The following people all met the risen Christ:

1. Mary Magdalene (John 20:11-18).

2. Simon Peter (Luke 24:34).

3. The two disciples on the road to Emmaus (Luke 24:13-22).

4. The disciples – apart from Thomas (John 20:19-23).

5. The disciples – including Thomas (John 20:24-29).

6. Mary Magdalene and 'the other Mary' (Matthew 28:1-10).

7. The apostles in Galilee (Matthew 28:16-17).

8. Seven disciples by the Sea of Tiberias (John 21:1-14).

9. More than five hundred of his followers (1 Corinthians15:6).

10. James (1 Corinthians 15:7).

11. His disciples (Acts 1:4-9).

12. Paul (Acts 9:1-9).

The Garden Tomb, Jerusalem, is probably similar to the tomb in which Jesus was buried.

Jesus ascends to heaven

40 days after his resurrection Jesus ascended to heaven. In the period since his resurrection, Jesus had appeared many times to his disciples, teaching them and preparing them for his departure.

As his disciples watched, Jesus rose bodily from the Mount of Olives until he was hidden by a cloud (Mark 16:19; Luke 24:50, 51; Acts 1:9-11).

The ascension of Jesus
• symbolises his raising to '[God's] right hand in the heavenly realms' (Ephesians 1:20-22).

• signifies Christ's completed work of redemption (Hebrews 10:11-14)

• is linked with the sending of the Holy Spirit (John 15:26–16:16)

• implicitly promises Christ's bodily return (Acts 1:11).

The resurrection and ascension of Jesus

Map labels:
Ptolemais
Capernaum
Miraculous catch of fish (John 21:7–14)
Sea of Galilee
MEDITERRANEAN SEA
Tiberias
Nazareth
GALILEE
Jordan
Caesarea
Scythopolis
Sebaste (Samaria)
SAMARIA
Appearance to two disciples on the road to Emmaus (Luke 24:36)
Resurrection (John 20:1–9)
Appearance to Mary Magdalene in the garden (John 20:10–18)
Doubt of Thomas (John 20:24–31)
Appearance to his disciples in locked room (John 20:19–23)
Jericho
Emmaus
Roads
Jerusalem
Bethany
Mount of Olives
Ascension (Luke 24:50–53)
Jordan
Dead Sea
JUDEA
0   10   20 km
0   4   8   12 miles

The good news travels

After the coming of the Holy Spirit on the day of Pentecost, the believers in Jerusalem began to preach boldly and increased in numbers daily (Acts 2:1-47). The Jewish leaders tried to stop them, but in fact helped the young movement to spread (Acts 4:1-31).

Stephen, a leader of the church in Jerusalem, was accused of blasphemy and the Jews had him stoned to death (Acts 6:1–8:2). Believers in Jerusalem were persecuted, and many fled – south into Judea, north to Samaria, and west to the coast and even as far as Cyprus (Acts 8:1-3; 11:19). Many of the apostles also left Jerusalem and preached elsewhere. Philip, Peter and John all made conversions in Samaria (Acts 8), a 'no-go' area for religious (or 'strict') Jews.

Philip set out for Gaza, baptising an official from Ethiopia, before moving on to preach in the coastal towns (Acts 8:26-40).

Peter travelled to Caesarea, after having been shown in a vision that he should take the gospel to the Gentiles (Acts 10:1-48). As the persecution of Christians by Jews in Jerusalem became more evident so Jewish Christians dispersed northwards. They had reached as far as Antioch, third largest city in the Roman Empire, by the time Paul embarked on his missionary journeys (Acts 13).

Paul's journey to Damascus
Some time after Stephen's death, while Paul (then Saul) was still a Pharisee, he got permission from the Temple authorities to go to Damascus to search out Christians (Acts 9:1-2). It was on the way there that he received his blinding vision of the risen Christ. After regaining his sight in Damascus with the help of Ananias in Straight Street, Paul became a Christian and was himself forced to flee for his life back to Jerusalem (Acts 9:23-26). He was soon in danger again, from Hellenist Jews, and departed for his home town of Tarsus via Caesarea.

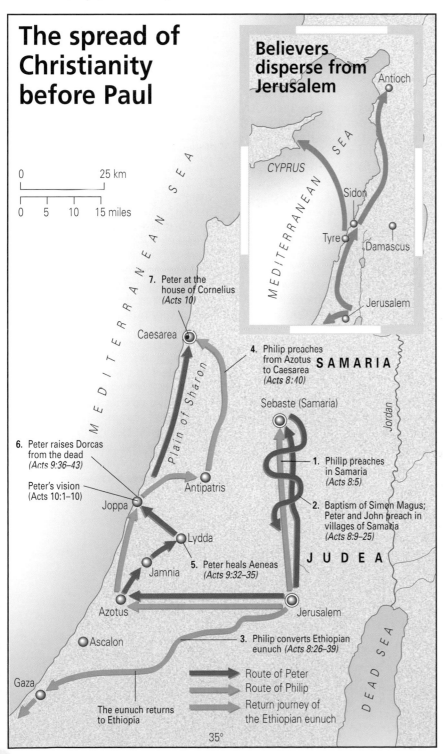

The spread of Christianity before Paul

Believers disperse from Jerusalem

0   25 km
0   5   10   15 miles

MEDITERRANEAN SEA

CYPRUS

Antioch

Sidon

Tyre

Damascus

Jerusalem

7. Peter at the house of Cornelius (Acts 10)

Caesarea

4. Philip preaches from Azotus to Caesarea (Acts 8:40)

SAMARIA

Sebaste (Samaria)

Plain of Sharon

Jordan

6. Peter raises Dorcas from the dead (Acts 9:36–43)

Peter's vision (Acts 10:1–10)

Joppa

Antipatris

1. Philip preaches in Samaria (Acts 8:5)

2. Baptism of Simon Magus; Peter and John preach in villages of Samaria (Acts 8:9–25)

Lydda

Jamnia

5. Peter heals Aeneas (Acts 9:32–35)

J U D E A

Azotus

Jerusalem

Ascalon

3. Philip converts Ethiopian eunuch (Acts 8:26–39)

DEAD SEA

Gaza

The eunuch returns to Ethiopia

Route of Peter
Route of Philip
Return journey of the Ethiopian eunuch

35°

The Acts of the Apostles

Luke's second volume, Acts, is the second longest document in the New Testament. Like his Gospel, it is structured around a journey. Parallel to Jesus' journey to Jerusalem is Paul's journey to Rome. Both journeys carry God's plan of salvation with them – salvation won at great personal cost (although of course Luke does not present Paul as a Saviour like Jesus).

Paul's commission
At Paul's conversion, the Lord appoints him as 'an instrument . . . to bring my name before Gentiles and kings, and before the people of Israel' (9:15). He becomes the centre of the story from chapter 13 onwards, as we see the gospel spreading westward through Paul's ministry, until he reaches Rome (as a prisoner) in chapter 28. But Israel is never forgotten – throughout the story Paul's priority is to contact Jews first. But Luke's great passion is to display the universal relevance and power of the gospel, as foreshadowed at the start of the story, in Acts 1:8.

Luke's participation
Luke himself becomes a participant in the second half of the book. In 16:10, in the middle of Paul's second missionary journey, a 'we' suddenly appears in the narrative, and the author apparently accompanies Paul on the following journey to Philippi. The 'we' ceases when Paul leaves Philippi (16:40), only to reappear when Paul returns there in 20:5. The author then accompanies Paul to Jerusalem (21:17), disappears during the events related in chapters 22–26, but reappears for Paul's final journey to Rome (27:1–28:16).

The author thus subtly gives us confidence in the reliability of the narrative. It is clear, for instance, that he took great pains to note the details of the sea-journey and shipwreck in Acts 27 (one of the 'we' passages). Because this fits so well with his comment in Luke 1:3 about careful research, we gain confidence in the whole story.

Luke's purpose
But Luke was writing as an ancient, not a modern, historian. So he does not provide answers to some of the questions that interest us. What, for instance, happened to the other apostles listed in Acts 1:13? How many of the 3,000 converted at Pentecost were from the places listed in 2:9? Did they then establish churches 'back home'? How did the gospel spread east from Jerusalem? What in fact were the dates of the landmark events – Paul's conversion, the murder of James, the Apostolic Council? Asking questions like these reveals that Luke's purpose was not to provide an overall survey of the first three decades of church history, but to give a demonstration of the power and potential of the gospel in action, and of its growth from Jewish infant to world-wide adolescent.

Relief on a Roman gravestone, Philippi, scene of Paul's imprisonment (Acts 17).

Built into the story – and arising from this purpose – are various theological issues, discussion of which Luke skilfully weaves into his narrative. We pick out three:

• *Church growth and the plan of God.* Luke wanted to show God at work through the story, because he believed that the gospel was God's means of salvation for all (4:12). But at the same time he had a very human story to tell, including many mistakes, disagreements and setbacks. On the one hand, God had already appointed the 'times and seasons' by which the kingdom would come (1:7), so that the growth of the Church was inevitable and irresistible (5:38-39). But on the other hand, the gospel encoun-

All Pharisees respected labour and hard work, and had to have a trade. Tentmaking was Paul's trade.

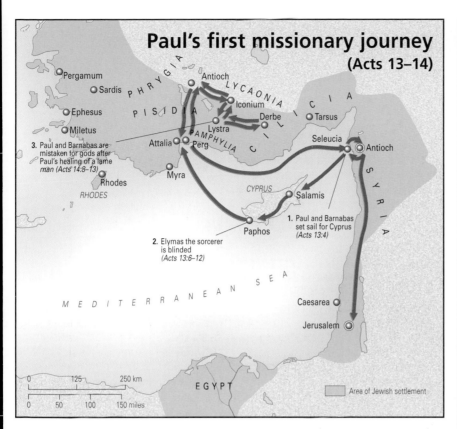

Paul's first missionary journey
(Acts 13–14)

- Pergamum
- Sardis
- Ephesus
- Miletus
- Rhodes / RHODES
- Antioch
- Iconium
- Derbe
- Tarsus
- Lystra
- Attalia / Perg
- Seleucia
- Antioch
- Salamis
- Paphos
- Myra
- Caesarea
- Jerusalem

PHRYGIA — PISIDIA — LYCAONIA — CILICIA — PAMPHYLIA — SYRIA — CYPRUS

MEDITERRANEAN SEA

EGYPT

3. Paul and Barnabas are mistaken for gods after Paul's healing of a lame man (Acts 14:8–13)

1. Paul and Barnabas set sail for Cyprus (Acts 13:4)

2. Elymas the sorcerer is blinded (Acts 13:6–12)

0 125 250 km
0 50 100 150 miles

Area of Jewish settlement

tered strong opposition, and that opposition was actually essential to the story, because Jesus' crucifixion had been both God's plan and an act of dreadful wickedness (see 2:23; 3:13-15; 4:10).

So Luke shows God thoroughly

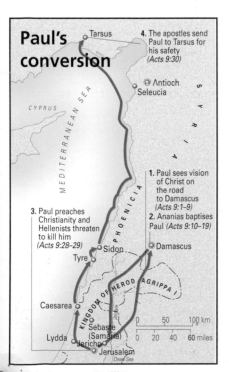

Paul's conversion

- Tarsus
- Antioch / Seleucia
- CYPRUS
- Damascus
- Sidon
- Tyre
- Caesarea
- Sebaste (Samaria)
- Lydda
- Jericho
- Jerusalem / Dead Sea

MEDITERRANEAN SEA — PHOENICIA — SYRIA — KINGDOM OF HEROD AGRIPPA I

4. The apostles send Paul to Tarsus for his safety (Acts 9:30)

1. Paul sees vision of Christ on the road to Damascus (Acts 9:1–9)

2. Ananias baptises Paul (Acts 9:10–19)

3. Paul preaches Christianity and Hellenists threaten to kill him (Acts 9:28–29)

0 50 100 km
0 20 40 60 miles

involved in a messy story, preparing Saul even as Stephen is stoned, releasing Peter from prison after James' death, bringing good out of Paul and Barnabas' argument, and getting the gospel to Rome, but by a most tortuous and difficult route. Having been stoned at Lystra, Paul tells the Christians there, 'It is necessary for us to enter God's Kingdom through many tribulations' (14:22: for Luke, 'necessary' points to God's plan).

• *The relation between Jews and Gentiles before God*. The gospel starts life Jewish. But must Gentiles become Jews in order to benefit from it? Luke shows the Christians wrestling with this, and his own answer is clear: certainly not! He follows the first Jewish Pentecost (chapter 2) with another in Samaria (chapter 8) and another for Gentiles (chapter 10), thus showing that the Spirit treats all equally.

• *The fulfilment of prophecy*. Luke is describing something completely new in the history of Israel. Never since the election of Abraham has anything happened like this. So he is eager to show

that these events are not novel, as well as new, but are the proper fulfilment of Israel's covenant with God. He makes this case chiefly in the speeches which are such an important feature of Acts: see 2:16-36; 3:21-23; 4:11; 7:2-53; 8:32-35; 13:16-47; 15:13-21; 28:25-28. This has to be a powerful and essential case, if Jews and Gentiles alike are to be convinced.

> You will receive power when the Holy Spirit has come upon you; and you will be my witnesses in Jerusalem, in all Judea and Samaria, and to the ends of the earth.
> Acts 1:8

Paul's early letters

The date of Galatians
The dating of Paul's letters is uncertain, and the date of Galatians particularly so. Galatians may not be one of 'Paul's early letters'. However, on balance, it is *probably* his earliest surviving letter, written to the churches he visited on his first missionary journey (Acts 13–14), during the period mentioned in Acts 15:35.

Faith or law?
We learn much about Paul, and what made him tick, from Galatians. He was deeply concerned that his converts were abandoning 'the gospel of Christ' (1:7) by agreeing to be circumcised – under pressure from 'the circumcision group' (2:12). These were Jewish Christians like those referred to in Acts 15:1, who taught (as summarised there): 'Unless you are circumcised following Moses' custom, you cannot be saved.' They seem to have followed Paul around his new Galatian churches, adding this requirement to the gospel that he had taught.

Paul was furious! 'You foolish Galatians! Who has bewitched you?'(3:1). Passionately he argues that circumcision is a sign of a wholly different kind of relationship with God – a relationship based on law and requirement, rather than on faith and grace (3:11-12; 5:3-6). His own experience on the Damascus Road is vital here (1:13-16): at that moment he 'died to the law' (2:19), for he discovered, to his horror, that his zeal for the Law had led him to 'persecute the church of God' (1:13). And since the Messiah had to die, the Law could not be God's answer to sin, as he had thought: 'If righteousness could be gained through the law, Christ died for

nothing!' (2:21, cf. 3:21f).

So the thought that his Galatians might turn to the Law for salvation felt to Paul like rejecting Christ and joining his enemies. He recounts how he stood out in public against Peter himself, when the latter 'wobbled' under pressure from 'the circumcision group' (2:11-16). How did you receive the Spirit? he pointedly asks the Galatians: by obeying the Law, or by believing in Jesus? (3:2).

1 and 2 Thessalonians
1 Thessalonians is probably Paul's second letter – written from Athens, not long after the campaign in Thessalonica recorded in Acts 17:1-10. 2 Thessalonians followed, probably within months. Many scholars believe that 2 Thessalonians is not by Paul, because of its different teaching about the second coming of Christ (compare 1 Thessalonians 4:13–5:11 with 2 Thessalonians 2:1-12). But Paul is tackling different problems in the two letters, and drawing on different aspects of his teaching to do so. In the first letter he deals with the Thessalonians' concern about the premature death of some believers; in the second, with the strange view that the *parousia* (second coming) of Christ had already occurred.

Opposition in Thessalonica
The gospel met immediate opposition in Thessalonica. Some of the first Jewish converts were grabbed by a rioting crowd and dragged before the city authorities, charged with sedition against Rome. Paul and Silas had to escape from the city under cover of night.

What caused this opposition? It is clear that first Paul himself, and then his Thessalonian converts, felt the sting of the same passionate

persecution which he himself had launched at the church. The reasons may have been different, but the fundamental motivation was the same: 'zeal for the law'.

Why Paul provoked such hatred we can see, for instance, in 1 Thessalonians 1:4-5. Paul calls the Thessalonians 'brothers loved by God', and says, 'We recognise your election, because our gospel

Outlines of early letters

Galatians

1:1-10	The single gospel of Christ
1:11–2:21	The single gospel: received, agreed, and defended
3:1–4:31	The single gospel: promised beforehand to Abraham
5:1–6:10	The single gospel: practical consequences
6:11-18	The heart of the single gospel: the cross of Christ

1 Thessalonians

1:1–3:13	Looking back – the gospel in Thessalonica
1:2-10	The people who received it
2:1-12	The apostle who preached it
2:13-16	The enemies who opposed it
2:17–3:10	The messenger who encouraged it
3:11-13	Paul's prayer for them now
4:1-12	In the present – living a holy life
4:13–5:11	Looking ahead – to the coming of the Lord
5:12-28	Living now in the light of the End

2 Thessalonians

1:1-12	The shape of the Christian life
2:1-12	The 'rebellion' and the coming of Jesus
2:13–3:5	Belonging to Jesus in the meantime
3:6-18	Business as usual?

Fact file: Paul

34 A.D.	Converted on the Damascus Road
37	First visit to Jerusalem (*Galatians 1:18, Acts 9:26-30*). Returns to Tarsus
47-48	Ministers in Antioch (*Acts 11:25-26*)
48	Second visit to Jerusalem (*Galatians 2:1-10; Acts 11:30*)
49	First missionary journey – to the Galatian churches (*Acts 13–14*)
49	Apostolic Council in Jerusalem (*Acts 15*)
50	Writes Galatians Second missionary journey begins (*Acts 15:36*) Ministers in Thessalonica, arrives in Corinth (*Acts 18:1*)
50-51	Writes 1 and 2 Thessalonians

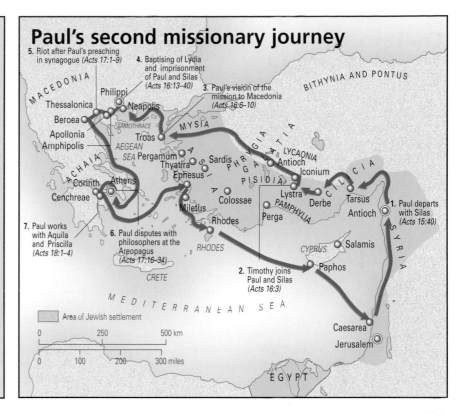

Paul's second missionary journey

5. Riot after Paul's preaching in synagogue (*Acts 17:1–9*)
4. Baptising of Lydia and imprisonment of Paul and Silas (*Acts 16:13–40*)
3. Paul's vision of the mission to Macedonia (*Acts 16:6–10*)
1. Paul departs with Silas (*Acts 15:40*)
7. Paul works with Aquila and Priscilla (*Acts 18:1–4*)
6. Paul disputes with philosophers at the Areopagus (*Acts 17:16–34*)
2. Timothy joins Paul and Silas (*Acts 16:3*)

Area of Jewish settlement

0   250   500 km
0   100   200   300 miles

came to you . . . with power.' The terms 'loved' and 'election' are both technical terms, special to Israel's relationship with God. Paul applies them without hesitation to these Gentile Thessalonians because he really believed, as he says in Galatians 3:28-29, that the old covenant-distinction between Israel and the Gentiles had been abolished, and Gentiles had become 'the seed of Abraham' through faith in Christ. Similarly in 1 Thessalonians 2:13 Paul insists that his message is 'the word of God' – a description which ought to be reserved for the sacred Scriptures of Israel! No wonder the 'zealous for the law' tried to stop him. They could not accept such a denial of Israel's special status.

Paul – missionary pastor

These three letters give us unique insight into Paul the missionary, pastor and theologian. He felt commissioned by God himself to preach a unique gospel, which he believed he had received direct from Christ on the Damascus Road (Galatians 1:12). But if Galatians makes him seem rather fierce, 1 Thessalonians is full of moving expressions of love and concern for his converts. And in both the Thessalonian letters we see the motivating conviction behind his missionary zeal – the belief that Christ would return soon as Saviour and Judge of all.

Remains of the Roman aqueduct at Antioch, Asia Minor.

> We know that a person does not gain acceptance with God by the works of the law, but only through faith in Jesus Christ!
> Galatians 2:16

Paul and Corinth

Remains of the ancient Temple of Apollo, Corinth.

Paul's two letters to the church at Corinth provide powerful insight into Paul the person, and into his teaching on a wide range of topics: not just the big 'theological' topics like Christ, the Law, the cross and atonement, the Holy Spirit, resurrection, and final judgement, but also many practical issues such as church discipline, sex and marriage, relation to pagan society, the Eucharist, the use of 'spiritual gifts', love and unity, giving, and attitudes towards suffering. Woven into this great mix is the constant thread of Paul's own relationship with the church in Corinth.

Conflict in Corinth

The opposition seems to have started soon after Paul left Corinth. He had ministered there for 18 months or more (Acts 18:11,18), before returning to his home church in Antioch. But soon he was off again – his third missionary journey – and before long settled in Ephesus for a ministry of over two years (Acts 19:8,10). 1 Corinthians was probably written in his second year there (1 Corinthians 16:8-9). But by then he had already written to the church at least once, for in 1 Corinthians 5:9-11 he refers to an earlier letter which they had misunderstood.

2 Corinthians was written with much emotion from Macedonia (Acts 20:1; 2 Corinthians 7:5). Paul had left Ephesus and travelled north, deciding not to visit Corinth, because an earlier visit (not recorded in Acts) had been so 'painful', both to him and to the Corinthians (2:1; 13:2). Instead, he had written 'out of much distress and anguish of heart' (2:4), and then waited anxiously for Titus to return with their reply. Eventually Titus met Paul in Macedonia with good news (7:7-16). In response, Paul dashed off 2 Corinthians, vivid, passionate, disorganised, sparkling in style and in theology – his most personal and revealing letter.

Troubles in the church

What was the problem? In 1 Corinthians Paul compiles a sad catalogue, although he pointedly starts with warm encouragement (1:4-9). There was grave immorality, which for some reason they were happy to accept (5:1-2). Some of the wealthier Christians had been taking each other to court over grievances (6:1-8). Some church members had been using prostitutes, while others had been renouncing sex altogether, even within marriage (6:12-20; 7:1ff). There was also disagreement – and hurt consciences – over whether it was right to eat meat which had been offered in temples and then sold in the market (chapters 8–10), and Paul was deeply concerned about their worship services, especially the conduct of some women (11:2-16), the divisions between rich and poor apparent at the Eucharist (11:17-34), and their over-use of the gift of tongues (chapter 14). If this were not bad enough, the church had divided into factions claiming favourite teachers (1:12), and some were denying the bodily resurrection of Christ (15:12).

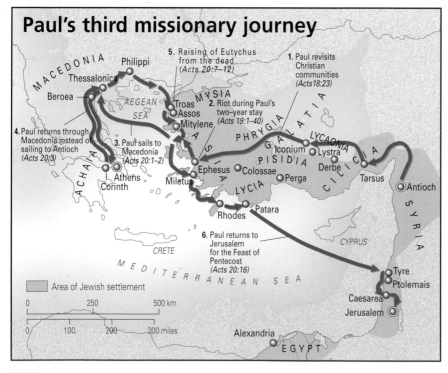

Paul's third missionary journey

1. Paul revisits Christian communities (Acts 18:23)
2. Riot during Paul's two-year stay (Acts 19:1-40)
3. Paul sails to Macedonia (Acts 20:1-2)
4. Paul returns through Macedonia instead of sailing to Antioch (Acts 20:3)
5. Raising of Eutychus from the dead (Acts 20:7-12)
6. Paul returns to Jerusalem for the Feast of Pentecost (Acts 20:16)

MACEDONIA — Philippi, Thessalonica, Beroea
AEGEAN SEA
MYSIA — Troas, Assos, Mitylene
ASIA
PHRYGIA
GALATIA
LYCAONIA — Iconium, Lystra, Derbe
PISIDIA
Ephesus, Colossae, Perga
CILICIA — Tarsus
ACHAIA — Athens, Corinth
Miletus
LYCIA — Patara
Rhodes
ANTIOCH
SYRIA
CRETE
CYPRUS
MEDITERRANEAN SEA
Tyre, Ptolemais
Caesarea
Jerusalem
Alexandria
EGYPT

Area of Jewish settlement

0   250   500 km
0   100   200   300 miles

Attacks on Paul

By the time we get to 2 Corinthians, Paul is aware of accusations made against him personally: that he lacks the decisiveness expected of a Spirit-filled person (1:15-22), that he does not have 'letters of recommendation' from other churches (3:1-3), that he is a poor and unimpressive speaker (10:1,10), that he cannot produce a proper list of miracles and visions to qualify as a true apostle (12:10-12, cf. 1 Corinthians 4:8-13), that he pretended not to receive money from them but was actually feathering his own nest (12:14-18).

Paul's patience and love in the face of all this is truly moving, and deeply instructive for our understanding of him as a person and the conduct of his apostleship. He does not mince his words, yet leaves the Corinthians in no doubt about his concern and care for them.

The source of the problems

Paul tackles the problems theologically – that is, by taking his readers back to the fundamental principles of christology, ecclesiology, anthropology and eschatology offended by their behaviour. This reveals that the rag-bag of problems in Corinth may have had a common basis. Some were claiming to be 'wise' (1 Corinthians 3:18), to have 'knowledge' (1 Corinthians 8:1), to be 'rich' (1 Corinthians 4:8, cf. 2 Corinthians 8:9) and 'spiritual' (1 Corinthians 3:1). They spoke the language of angels (1 Corinthians 13:1), performed miracles, and believed that they had already experienced the resurrection. ('There is no resurrection' in 1 Corinthians 15:12 means 'there is no future bodily resurrection'.) As 'spiritual', they discounted the significance of the body – and so either indulged it with prostitutes or renounced sex completely, and had no objections to eating meat sacrificed to idols. 'Everything's allowed!' was their slogan (1 Corinthians 6:12). Thinking about themselves in this way, it was easy to make distinctions

between themselves and the less 'wise', and thus to create factions in the church.

Correcting the errors

Paul affirms their spiritual enthusiasm and experience, but not their arrogance or bad theology. He insists that Christ rose from the dead physically, that our resurrection is also physical, and future, that our bodies are spiritually significant as 'limbs of Christ', that the 'wise' and the 'spiritual' do not divide into factions, that the Church is a unity as the Body of Christ, indwelt as a whole by the liberating Spirit of God, that he himself was appointed by God to bring the gospel to Corinth, that weakness and suffering (rather than supercharged victory) are the norms for the Christian life . . . etc., etc.! The richness of these two letters cannot adequately be summarised.

Outlines of Corinthians

1 Corinthians

1:1-9	Greetings and thanksgiving
1:10–3:23	The unity of the Church around the message of the cross
4:1-21	Paul's self-defence
5:1–6:20	The Church and the world: the necessary distance
7:1-40	Christians, sex and marriage
8:1–11:1	Food sacrificed to idols: willingness to give up one's rights for others
11:2-34	Worshipping rightly in Christ
12:1–14:40	The Body of Christ – one in love and in mutual ministry
15:1-58	The resurrection – Christ's and ours
16:1-24	Wider fellowship: giving to others, greetings from others

2 Corinthians

1:1-11	Paul's sufferings for Christ and for the Corinthians
1:12–2:13	Paul and the Corinthians: pain, forgiveness and longing
2:14–7:4	Life in Christ: freedom in suffering, the gospel in weakness, hope in the face of death, genuine love
7:5-16	Titus' news and Paul's response
8:1–9:15	Wider fellowship: giving to Paul's collection project
10:1–12:21	Paul, the 'super-apostles' and the issue of boasting
13:1-14	Final warnings, and greetings

Fact file: Paul

50–52	Ministers in Corinth. Returns to Antioch (*Acts 18:22*)
53	Starts third missionary journey. Begins ministry in Ephesus (*Acts 18:23–19:1*)
54	Writes 1 Corinthians
54/55	'Painful' visit to Corinth (*2 Corinthians 2:1*)
55	Leaves Ephesus. 'Severe' letter to Corinth (*2 Corinthians 2:4*) Ministers in Troas and Macedonia. Writes 2 Corinthians. Arrives in Corinth for the winter (*Acts 20:3*)

Who is weak, and I do not feel weak? Who stumbles into sin, and I do not burn with concern?
2 Corinthians 11:29

Paul and Rome

Paul's letter to the Romans is his longest and most influential. Martin Luther regarded Romans and the Gospel of John as 'the chief pillars of the New Testament', containing 'the purest gospel'. He gave Romans this accolade because it contains the clearest exposition of Paul's doctrine of justification by faith, which Luther regarded as the heart of the Christian message. Whereas Paul's other letters are related to problems in the churches addressed, Romans is more like a detached summary of his gospel (1:16), perhaps sent to Rome because he wanted to introduce himself to them, so that they would willingly support him (1:13; 15:22-24).

Paul's manifesto
However, Romans is not 'the gospel in abstract'. It is rooted in Paul's missionary work. Günther Bornkamm has called it 'Paul's Last Will and Testament', because he suggests that Paul wrote it consciously at a turning-point in his life. After finishing his ministry in the east (15:19, 23), he is now undertaking a dangerous journey to Jerusalem. He does not know whether he will survive it (15:30-31). So he sends to the Roman church, which he hopes to visit, a summary of the gospel for which he has fought, 'the power of God for salvation' for Jews and Gentiles alike (1:16).

There is much drama, therefore, just under the surface. We catch echoes of the arguments, sometimes intense, through which Paul has come. And 'justification by faith' is at the heart of it. In Galatians Paul argues his case directly and passionately. In Romans he reflects on the argument, draws wider implications, and spells out the consequences – but still passionately.

Fact file: Paul

56	Writes to Rome from Corinth Travels to Jerusalem Riot, arrest and hearing before Felix (*Acts 20–24*)
56–58	In prison without trial in Caesarea (*Acts 24:27*)
58	Hearings before Festus and Agrippa (*Acts 25–26*) Sea journey and shipwreck on Malta (*Acts 27:1–28:10*)
59	Arrives in Rome

Justification by faith
The essence of the argument concerns the relation between Christ and God's covenant with Israel. For many Jewish Christians, the covenant was the foundation of all relationship with God. It was 'for ever' – enshrined in the promises given to Abraham and sealed by the giving of the Law through Moses. It followed, therefore, that the blessings brought by the Messiah were available only within the covenant – to Jews, first and foremost, but also to Gentiles who committed themselves to the God of Israel through circumcision.

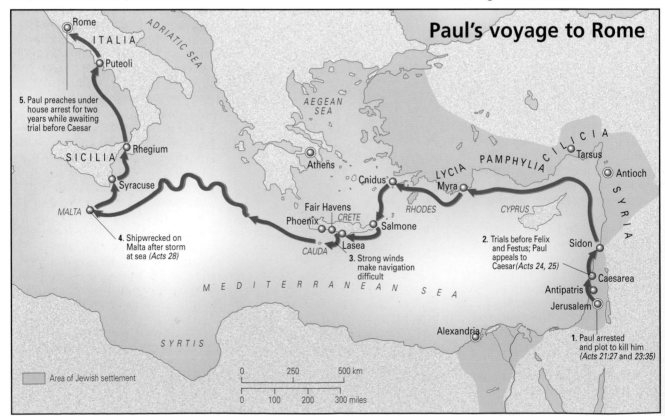

Paul's voyage to Rome

Rome
ITALIA
ADRIATIC SEA
Puteoli

5. Paul preaches under house arrest for two years while awaiting trial before Caesar

Rhegium
SICILIA
Syracuse
MALTA

4. Shipwrecked on Malta after storm at sea (*Acts 28*)

AEGEAN SEA

Athens
Cnidus
Fair Havens
Phoenix CRETE Salmone
Lasea
CAUDA

3. Strong winds make navigation difficult

RHODES

LYCIA
Myra
PAMPHYLIA
CILICIA
Tarsus
Antioch
CYPRUS
SYRIA

2. Trials before Felix and Festus; Paul appeals to Caesar (*Acts 24, 25*)

Sidon
Caesarea
Antipatris
Jerusalem

1. Paul arrested and plot to kill him (*Acts 21:27* and *23:35*)

MEDITERRANEAN SEA

Alexandria

SYRTIS

☐ Area of Jewish settlement

0   250   500 km
0   100   200   300 miles

The Forum, ancient Rome.

Paul's answer

Paul refused to accept this impressive argument. In a nutshell, he says:

1. The covenant with Israel was never designed to bring blessing exclusively to those within it, but was meant to bring blessing to the Gentile world. Paul uses Old Testament quotations to make this point (2:22-24; 4:16-17; 9:25-26; 10:12-13, 20; 15:8-12).

2. Neither was the covenant ever a guarantee of salvation. In fact, it promised judgement on the disobedient, as much as blessing on the circumcised (2:25-29; 9:27-29; 11:7-10, 20). Only Christ brings a guarantee of salvation (8:31-39),

Bust of the Emperor Nero.

and he came not just to fulfil the promises to Abraham, but to meet the need of the world caused by the sin of Adam (5:12-21).

3. Jesus brings salvation, through his atoning death, to all who believe, Jew or Gentile (3:21-31), because all have exactly the same need of deliverance from the power of sin (1:18-32; 3:9-20).

4. Abraham was not a Jew! In fact, he was 'justified' before he was circumcised, and thus gives a pattern for today: uncircumcised Gentiles may be justified like him, and so claim him as their 'father' (4:1-25).

5. And this has been Paul's experience: it is simply a fact that Gentile believers have received righteousness by faith in Christ – and this fact must revolutionise our understanding of the ways of God (2:14-16, 26-29; 3:22-24, 29-30; 9:30; 11:17). By the Holy Spirit, they have been transformed (6:17-18; 7:6; 8:9-10).

6. So life in the Spirit, rather than obedience to the Law, is what God now asks of his people. In any case, because of the power of sin, the Law could not deliver what it promised (7:4–8:8).

7. But God has not abandoned Israel! He is still faithful to his covenant promises. But these promises will be fulfilled in the context of the world-wide salvation which he plans (11:1-36).

8. So the Church, made up of Jews and Gentiles together and defined not by loyalty to Moses but by the love of Christ, is the body which can now rightly claim to be the people of God, and must live as such (12:1–15:13)!

An example to be heeded

It appears from chapter 14 that Paul probably also had a particular issue in mind – a conflict in the Roman church between Jewish and Gentile believers over practical issues arising from their life together – the observation of Jewish food laws and festivals. Amazingly, though he has argued strongly that 'Christ is the end of the law' (10:4), Paul gently encourages the Gentile Christians simply to accept their Jewish brothers and sisters, and not to require them to go against their consciences (14:13-23).

Paul's later letters

The New Testament contains a string of seven shorter letters from Paul: Philippians, Ephesians, Colossians, Philemon and the 'Pastoral' letters (1 and 2 Timothy, and Titus). All of these (except possibly Philippians) date from the last few years of Paul's life.

Authorship

Ephesians, Colossians, and the Pastorals are all regarded by some as 'pseudonymous' – that is, written by disciples of Paul and published in his name after his death. This was a not uncommon practice, and in 2 Thessalonians 2:2 Paul expresses the fear that it may have already happened, during his lifetime. The early Church, however, disapproved of it, because the authority of the apostles was unique, and it is highly unlikely that five pseudonymous letters of Paul could have found their way into the New Testament. It seems that Paul's letters were collected at a very early date (Paul himself encourages the process, in Colossians 4:16), when it would have been clear whether they were genuine or not.

Differences

If the later letters are all by Paul, then we are faced with the challenge of explaining the differences between them and his earlier letters. For instance, in Ephesians and Colossians he presents the resurrection as something past (Ephesians 2:5-6; Colossians 3:1), in a way that looks like the view he attacks in 1 Corinthians. The Greek style of the Pastorals is rather different, the great doctrine of justification by faith does not appear, and indeed 'faith' has a different meaning – signifying the faith, the body of truths which Christians believe (e.g. 1 Timothy 3:9; 2 Timothy 3:8). All such differences can be explained either by developments in Paul's thinking or vocabulary, or by the different needs being addressed in these later letters, or by subtleties of thought that unite apparent differences.

Prison letters

Paul was in prison when writing all of the later letters except 1 Timothy and Titus. Which imprisonment is this? Acts mentions two (in Caesarea and in

Stone relief of a Roman soldier.

Rome), and Paul refers to 'frequent' imprisonments (2 Corinthians 11:23). The best suggestion is that all except 2 Timothy were written from the Acts 28 Roman imprisonment, and 2 Timothy from a later imprisonment in Rome, immediately prior to Paul's execution.

The view that Paul was released at the end of Acts 28 rests (a) on the tradition that he was martyred in the persecution by Nero in A.D. 65, and (b) on the references in the Pastorals to various movements by him around the Mediterranean, which cannot be fitted into the Acts narrative.

These marvellous letters are goldmines of teaching and encouragement.

Philippians

This is a thank-you letter, written to acknowledge the church's gift to him (2:25; 4:18). But Paul fills it out into a powerful discourse on facing suffering and death, turning the example of Christ into a pattern for the Christian life (1:18-30; 2:5-11). He writes movingly of the way that pattern has been written into his own experience (3:4-14), and warns against people who dress up worldly ambition as religion (3:17-21).

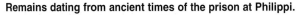

Remains dating from ancient times of the prison at Philippi.

Remains of the massive theatre at Ephesus, site of the riot caused by Paul's visit.

Fact file Paul

59–61	Under house arrest in Rome (*Acts 28:30*) Writes Philippians, Ephesians, Colossians, and Philemon
61	Charges dropped and released?
61–64	Ministers again, possibly in Spain (*Romans 15:24*), Asia Minor (*Philemon 22, 2 Timothy 4:13*), Crete (*Titus 1:5*), Corinth (*2 Timothy 4:20*), Ephesus and Macedonia (*1 Timothy 1:3; 2 Timothy 1:18*) Writes 1 Timothy and Titus
64–65	Re-arrested, tried and executed in Rome (*2 Timothy 4:6,16*) Writes 2 Timothy

Ephesians and Colossians

These letters have much in common, and were clearly written at the same time. Ephesians may have been a circular letter, sent to several congregations in the Ephesus area, for Paul is aware that many of the recipients will not know him now (Ephesians 3:2-4). Ephesians compares with Romans for its power and intensity: Paul focuses on the person of Christ, and displays his cosmic rule as the centre of God's world plan. In Colossians he applies this cosmic picture of Christ to some of the religious conflicts his readers were facing.

Philemon

This letter is a little gem: by a huge coincidence, Paul came into contact, in Rome, with a slave who had run away from his master in the Lycus Valley, 1,000 miles away – and the master turned out to be an old convert of Paul's. Through Paul Onesimus became a Christian, too – and now goes back to his master, Philemon, with this beautiful note entreating forgiveness and acceptance 'no longer as a slave, but better than a slave, as a dear brother' (verse 16). This letter speaks volumes about Paul's attitude to slavery. Clearly he felt that it was incompatible with Christian fellowship that brothers in Christ should also be masters and slaves. But he never attacked slavery as such, preferring to let the gospel make its own appeal.

The Pastoral letters

These letters probably date from a few years later. Timothy and Titus have been co-workers with Paul for about 15 years, and have become leaders of stature in their own right. Paul has left them in charge in Ephesus and Crete respectively, to appoint elders and deacons, to teach and to encourage and lead the churches. In addition, Timothy faced some tricky situations in Ephesus. The Pastorals are thus full of practical advice about church leadership. 2 Timothy contains Paul's moving testimony in the face of imminent death.

An artist's impression of the apostle Paul writing from his prison cell.

Hebrews

The letter to the Hebrews is an enigma. An enormously powerful piece of early Christian theology, clearly the product of a great and original mind – yet we do not know who wrote it, or to whom, or when, or where, or indeed why.

Is it a letter?
The first puzzle concerns its genre. Is it a letter, or a treatise? It has no opening greetings, but it ends like a letter (13:18-25). The style and contents have much in common with the treatises of Philo, the first-century Jewish philosopher, and yet we gather that the author is addressing a particular group of people (e.g. 5:11-12; 10:32-34). The best solution is that the original letter-opening has been lost – which would have given us the author's and recipients' identities.

Who wrote Hebrews?
For many years Hebrews was ascribed to Paul, but this is impossible in the light of Hebrews 2:3-4. Here the author describes himself (or herself) as a second-generation Christian, which Paul refused to do (Galatians 1:12-17). Of the many suggestions, the most compelling is Luther's, that it was written by Apollos, Paul's co-worker in Corinth (1 Corinthians 3:4-7), who came from Alexandria and is described in Acts 18:24 as 'learned' and 'mighty in the Scriptures'. His origin in Alexandria could explain the parallels with Philo, who also came from there, and the author of Hebrews was certainly 'mighty in the Scriptures' – see Acts 18:28.

The readers
Hebrews 13:24 possibly provides a clue about the recipients. 'Those from Italy greet you' suggests that they are in Italy, being greeted by their fellow-countrymen who are with the author outside Italy. If so, Rome would be the best bet. More broadly, they are clearly Jewish Christians who seem to form a distinct community, with their own history (6:10; 10:32-34; 12:4) and leaders (13:17). This would have been possible in Rome, where the church was divided into several house-churches (Romans 16:5, 14, 15).

Identity problems
For such Jewish-Christian groups, identity was a great problem. Where did they belong? Many still felt a strong loyalty to the synagogue, and yet the more they had fellowship with Gentiles, the more difficult their relationship with the synagogue became. If they ate with Gentiles, they would be branded law-breakers – and eventually apostates, if they persisted or deliberately broke off from the synagogue. Either way, they would lose their Jewishness. There seemed to be no cultural and religious middle ground.

The recipients of Hebrews are such a group! The author is clearly very concerned about them. The letter is peppered with warnings – against 'neglecting' their salvation (2:3), 'turning away' (3:12), 'falling short' (4:1), 'dropping off' (6:6), 'shrinking back' (10:39); and with corresponding exhortations to 'pay careful attention' (2:1), 'hold on' (3:6), 'make every effort' (4:11), 'show the same diligence to the end' (6:11), 'draw near to God with confidence' (10:22; 4:16). These verbs illustrate the

Artist's impression of the Jewish high priest in his full regalia.

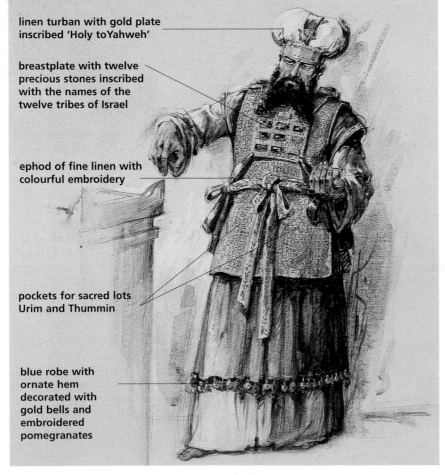

linen turban with gold plate inscribed 'Holy to Yahweh'

breastplate with twelve precious stones inscribed with the names of the twelve tribes of Israel

ephod of fine linen with colourful embroidery

pockets for sacred lots Urim and Thummin

blue robe with ornate hem decorated with gold bells and embroidered pomegranates

The Tabernacle

The author of the book of Hebrews assumes that his readers are well acquainted with the design of the Tabernacle. It was divided into two compartments. The first and larger was the 'Holy Place'. The further and smaller was the 'Most Holy Place', the inner sanctuary. Here stood the Ark, surmounted by its golden lid, the mercy seat, where the Shekinah glory, the visible symbol of God's presence, appeared.

The two 'Places' were separated by a thick curtain called the veil. By this arrangement the Holy One of Israel was teaching his people both his presence among them, and his inaccessibility to them. He was near and yet far; sinners could draw near, but were not permitted to penetrate into his holy presence beyond the veil. Access to God was limited by four conditions, listed in Hebrews 9:7: *only the high priest* might enter the inner sanctuary; but *only once a year* (on the Day of Atonement), *and only taking sacrificial blood* with him, to sprinkle on the mercy seat; and then he would secure remission *only for certain sins* (sins 'committed in ignorance').

For our author, these limitations showed 'that the way into the Most Holy Place had not yet been disclosed' (9:8); once again, the Old Testament reveals its own inadequacy and its need of Jesus. In contrast to the old high priest, Jesus has 'entered the Most Holy Place once for all by his blood, having obtained eternal redemption' (9:12).

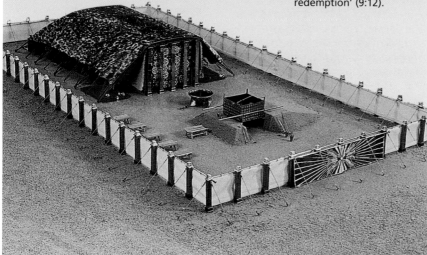

pastoral tone of the whole letter.

What was going on? Two theories have been proposed. Perhaps the recipients were so confused about their identity – Jewish or Christian? – that they were simply not making the progress in their faith that the author desires. He calls them 'sluggish, lazy, slow to learn' in 5:11 and 6:12. Alternatively, he may have heard that they were actually abandoning their Christian commitment in order to stay in fellowship with the synagogue. Hebrews 10:25 reads like a mild encouragement to church attendance: 'Let us not give up meeting together, as is the habit of some . . .' – but we need to read this against the background sketched above, where meeting with Gentiles seriously compromises Jewish identity.

Jesus or Judaism?

Either way, the author's strategy is clear: he presents Jesus as the fulfilment of the Scriptures to the extent that without Jesus the Scriptures are left without coherent meaning. So the readers are faced with a clear choice between the Old Testament, made complete and comprehensible only in Jesus, and Judaism, which has an incomplete Scripture, ineffectual rituals, and no answer to the deepest human needs.

The argument is deep and complex, and highly polemical. In current New Testament scholarship it is popular to suggest that the New Testament does not deny the validity of Judaism – merely adds Christianity alongside it as another 'pathway' to God. But the presence of Hebrews in the New Testament makes this suggestion impossible (though it is hard to square with other New Testament texts, also). The author seeks to claim the Old Testament for Christ, and Christ alone, arguing that, on its own, Israel's covenant with God is 'ageing, near to death, [and] soon to disappear' (8:13). Only in Christ do the Scriptures make sense, because Christ brings the promised 'new covenant' under which sins are truly forgiven (10:11-18). Here Christianity's exclusive claim is expressed at its clearest.

Peter and John

The apostles Peter and John are often linked in the early stories in Acts (3:1; 4:13; 8:14), building on their association in Jesus' inner circle (Mark 5:37; 9:2; 13:3). So it is fitting that the New Testament should include letters from them both, written (probably) when both were in old age, Peter in Rome and John in Ephesus.

1 Peter

The ascription of these letters – two to Peter and three to John – is widely disputed. (We will look at 2 Peter on page 122.)

1 Peter is written in good, lively, idiomatic Greek: is it possible that a Galilean fisherman, whose first language was Aramaic, could have produced it? Though many reply 'No', the better answer is 'Why not?' Recent studies reveal that Galilee was bilingual. Almost certainly Peter would have spoken Greek, as the language of trade. And we must not discount the effect of 25 years of mission

in a Greek-speaking environment – nor the influence of Silas, who helped Peter to write the letter (5:12).

If by Peter, then this first letter was written from Rome (5:13 – 'Babylon' is a code for Rome) at a time when there were Jewish Christians throughout the Roman provinces listed in 1:1. These two factors give the letter a date perhaps in the late 60s. Early church tradition puts Peter in Rome for the last part of his ministry. The letter is addressed, like James, to 'the diaspora', the technical expression for Jews scattered around the world, who are Peter's particular mission responsibility (Galatians 2:7).

Peter's readers

Persecution is clearly looming (1:6-7; 3:13-17; 4:12-19; 5:9-10). Peter knows that his readers feel isolated and vulnerable. They are 'aliens and exiles' (2:11, compare 1:1). Peter skilfully modulates this

The theatre, Hierapolis, seat of Papias.

sense of social alienation into the idea of election: they feel different because they are different (2:9).

Jews in Asia Minor were well integrated into local culture, and many of them participated happily in local festivals, as Peter reminds them (4:3). But now they have stepped back, and incurred suspicion and hostility as a result – especially by refusing to participate in the imperial cult by which people expressed their gratitude and loyalty to the emperor. Slaves and women were particularly vulnerable, for it was culturally unacceptable for them to adopt a religion different from the male head of the household. So Peter gives them special encouragement in the so-called 'Household Code' (2:13–3:7).

Overall, Peter seeks to inspire his readers with a vision of what God has done for them in Christ, and to encourage them to 'do good' in every situation, however difficult (2:12-14, 20; 3:6, 11; 4:19).

John

The letters of John do not identify their author by name, but the ancient manuscripts all include a heading which names 'John'. As in Hebrews, the opening greeting is missing from the first letter, but letters 2 and 3

Theatre, Ephesus.

The remains of the Temple of Artemis (Diana) in Ephesus, with (*inset*) statue of Artemis.

are written by someone calling himself 'the elder' (2 John 1; 3 John 1).

Uncertainty arises at this point, for Papias (bishop of Hierapolis C.A.D. 135) distinguished two 'Johns' among the first-generation Christians known to him: the apostle and 'the elder'. So, even if the author was indeed 'John', we do not know which! But the parallels in theme and style with the fourth Gospel support the traditional view that John the apostle wrote these letters in Ephesus towards the end of his long life. Letters 2 and 3 are addressed to particular churches over which 'the elder' has authority (3 John 9), but letter 1 may be generally addressed to all the churches in the greater Ephesus area, or more widely still.

The two great themes of John's letters are love and truth (see 2 John 1-3). Both are firmly fixed to Jesus Christ, which gives them a particular spin. The great issue in the first letter, for instance, is the departure from the church of a group whom the author calls 'antichrist'. They have denied love because they have broken off from their fellow-believers, and thus must be 'walking in darkness', separated from God who is the light. Fellowship with God is only possible for those who 'walk in the light', which means living in fellowship with one another while 'the blood of Jesus Christ cleanses us from all sin' (1:3, 7; 2:9-10, 18-19).

But this means that a denial of love is also a denial of the truth (that Jesus Christ, by his death for us, binds us into fellowship with himself and with each other). And in the case of this group, their denial of the truth is signalled by their explicit denial 'that Jesus is the Christ' (2:22; 4:2-3). This probably refers to the idea, associated with Cerinthus in the late first century, that 'Jesus' and 'the Christ' were separate beings: the former an ordinary man, the latter a spiritual being who descended upon 'Jesus' at his baptism, but departed again before the crucifixion.

It is better to suffer for doing good – if God so wills – than for doing evil! For Christ also suffered, once for all, for our sins, the righteous for the unrighteous.

1 Peter 3:17-18

Extent of the Church in A.D. 100

By the end of the first century, Christianity was more or less confined to the eastern Roman Empire, except for communities in Rome, Puteoli and around the Bay of Naples. The only church that we know of outside the empire was a possible church at Edessa. Names of cities with Christians are known both from the New Testament, for example, the seven churches of Revelation, and from contemporary correspondence. The early Christian writer Ignatius tells of churches in Magnesia and Tralles, and later writers of a church in Alexandria, the home of Paul's helper Apollos.

Library of Celsus, ancient Ephesus.

Rome

Puteoli

Pompeii

Nicopo

MALTA

MEDITERRANEAN SEA

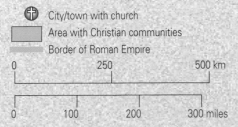

City/town with church

Area with Christian communities

Border of Roman Empire

0   250   500 km

0   100   200   300 miles

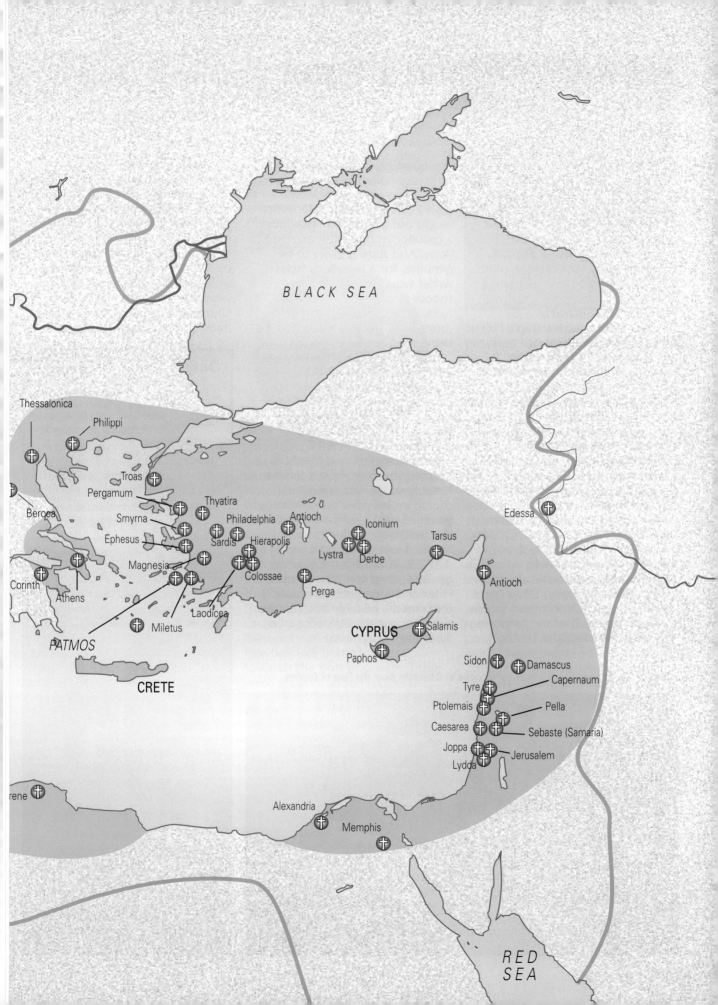

BLACK SEA

Thessalonica

Philippi

Troas

Pergamum

Thyatira

Smyrna

Philadelphia

Antioch

Iconium

Tarsus

Edessa

Beroea

Ephesus

Sardis

Hierapolis

Lystra

Derbe

Magnesia

Colossae

Antioch

Corinth

Athens

Laodicea

Perga

PATMOS

Miletus

CYPRUS

Salamis

CRETE

Paphos

Sidon

Damascus

Tyre

Capernaum

Ptolemais

Pella

Caesarea

Sebaste (Samaria)

Joppa

Jerusalem

Lydda

rene

Alexandria

Memphis

RED
SEA

Clothing

Men's clothes

Most Jewish men wore an inner garment, an outer garment and sandals. Unlike people today, they were not much influenced by fashion and their dress did not change for centuries. Arabs today often wear similar clothes, because they are best suited to the hot climate of their lands in the Middle East.

The tunic

The inner garment, often called a tunic, was like a close-fitting shirt. It was made of wool, linen or cotton. Some tunics just had slits for the arms; others had long sleeves. Sometimes men wore an undergarment called a loincloth beneath the tunic.

The tunic was often held in at the waist by a belt made of leather or cloth. Sometimes the belt had a pouch to keep money in (Mark 6:8). When a man needed to free himself for hard work, he tucked up his tunic into his belt.

In Bible times people had no special nightclothes. At night they simply loosened their belts and lay down in their tunics.

The cloak

Jewish men wore an outer garment called a cloak or robe. This cloak was made of woollen cloth and was wrapped round the body to help keep warm. It had slits for the arms. At night people used their cloaks as bedcovers.

Rich men often had cloaks made of expensive silk or linen, and with wide sleeves and blue fringes (Matthew 23:5).

Jewellery

Jewish men wore various sorts of jewels and decorations. They often wore a ring on the finger, or on a cord around the neck. These rings were sometimes used to press into wax on important letters. Each ring made a special mark, called a seal, to show who the letter came from.

Some people also wore magic charms, believing that they would keep away evil spirits.

Hair-styles

Jewish men cut their hair with scissors and long-bladed razors. Sometimes they made special religious vows, and did not cut their hair for a long time. Men often wore skull-caps, with bands of cloth round the edge.

Below centre:
The costume of a Jewish man.
Below left:
Men often hitched their tunic up when they were working in the fields.
Below right:
Costume of a wealthy Eastern man. Notice his richly-coloured clothing.

Women's clothes

In Bible times, women wore similar clothes to men.

The tunic

Like the men, women wore a tunic of wool, cotton or linen. But women's tunics were usually worn right down to the ankles, and were often blue in colour. Women's tunics also had V-necks, with embroidery along the edges. Like the men, women lifted the hem of their tunics when they were doing heavy work, such as carrying water.

The woman's outer garment was also longer than the man's; it covered the feet, and was fastened with a belt at the waist.

Headgear

Women wore squares of material on their heads, fastened with plaited cords. This helped protect them from the heat of the sun. Especially if they were unmarried, women often wore a veil over their faces out of modesty (Genesis 24:65).

Like the men, women often wore leather sandals. The strap went between the big toe and the second toe, and then round the heel (Luke 3:16).

Jewellery

Jewish women wore many pieces of jewellery, including bracelets on their wrists or above their elbows. They also wore bangles on their ankles, so that they jangled when they walked. The women often also wore earrings.

Jewish women used make-up, painting their eyelashes, and sometimes staining their fingers and toes red with a dye called henna (Isaiah 3:18-21).

Perfume

Women perfumed themselves with scents. They used scents such as frankincense and myrrh from Africa, aloes and nard from India, saffron from Palestine and many others.

Jewish women wore their hair long, and often arranged it in plaits.

Sandals

The poorest people often went barefoot. Others wore simple leather sandals, sometimes with wooden soles. Jesus' disciples wore sandals of this kind (see Mark 6:9). Jewish people took off their shoes when they entered a house. They had their feet washed before going inside.

Left: Costume of a Jewish woman.

Above: Costume of a rich woman. Notice her elaborate headgear and the bright colours of her clothes.

129

Tent life

When Abraham and his family first came to the Promised Land they lived in tents (Genesis 18:1-15). The tents of that time were quite simple. The Bedouin people live in similar tents in the desert today.

Building the tent
To build a tent, they first stuck wooden poles into the sand. Then they stretched a covering of cloth or animal skin, such as goat's hair, over the poles. They fixed down this covering by tying cords to it, and fastening the cords to tent-pegs hammered into the ground.

   The tent covering became waterproof after rain had fallen on it and made it shrink. If the covering got torn, it could be mended by darning it.

Inside the tent
The ground inside the tent was covered with mats and carpets. Curtains divided off different parts of the tent. Cooking pots, food and family belongings were kept inside the tent, beside the tent-poles. The family would dig a little hole in the middle of the tent, and light a fire there to cook food on.

The tent door
The door was simply a flap of cloth that could be raised and lowered. No man was allowed inside the tent, except for the father of the family. Other men had to stay outside at the porch, which had a cloth covering. If a stranger went inside the tent, he could be punished by being put to death (Judges 4:18, 21).

Furniture
Families living in tents had very little furniture. They were continually taking down the tent and moving on. They had to carry the tent poles and coverings with them on the backs of donkeys.

   Tent people had straw mats to sit on, and used animal skins as tables. They kept water, milk and butter in bottles made from goatskins.

Right: The women of Bible times lived in a separate area of the tent, as Bedouin women do today.

Bedouin families still live in traditional style tents in the Judean wilderness.

The house

The poorest people lived in very simple houses with only one room. This room could be as small as 3 metres (10 feet) square.

The house was usually built of mud bricks or of rough stones and rubble. Often insects and snakes lived in the loose walls (Amos 5:19). The walls were built very thick, to keep the house cool in the hot summer days, and warm during the cold winter nights.

Windows and door

There would be one small window, high up in the wall. It had no glass to keep out the wind and rain, but sometimes in winter the window was covered with an animal skin.

The house had a single small door, which was locked at night with a bar that was placed across it (Matthew 5:15).

The lower area

There were usually two levels inside the house. The lower area, near the door, had a floor made of stamped-down earth. Often the family kept their animals, such as the donkey, sheep and guard-dog, in this section at night.

The family sometimes lit a fire in this part of the room, to warm the room and to cook their meals. Most houses had no chimney, so the walls and ceiling became black with soot, and the clouds of smoke set everyone coughing.

The upper area

The second level inside the house was a raised stone platform. On this platform the family would eat their meals, sit talking together and lie down to sleep at night. The family kept their food and pots on shelves or alcoves in the walls.

The roof

The house would have a flat roof made of branches laid across thick beams. After it rained, the roof had

Interior of the house

The house was lit by an oil-lamp. The flat roof was made of branches laid across thick wooden beams. Notice the oil-lamp on the upturned pot.

to be flattened down again with a roller; it was not very watertight. In spring, seeds that had blown on to the roof would start to sprout and make it look green.

The family made great use of the roof, which they reached by stairs up the outside wall of the house (2 Kings 19:26; Matthew 10:27; Acts 10:9). Often they dried grain and fruit on the roof, and stored part of the harvest there.

On hot summer nights, the family would take to the roof to sleep. Often the men would climb up on to the roof to pray, and they also stored their tools there. A law said there had to be a low wall round the edge of the roof

to prevent people falling off (Deuteronomy 22:8).

During the day the family did not spend much time inside the house. They were busy working in the fields, or doing jobs in the courtyard or in the garden.

Furniture

Families usually had very little furniture. Most important was the chest in which they stored food or clothes. Often poor families turned the chest upside down and used it as a dining-table too. Some families had simple wooden stools or chairs to sit on, although many sat on the floor.

Poor people had only animal-skins to sleep on. Richer people had rough mattresses, and sometimes even wooden beds. For pillows, people used goatskins stuffed with wool or feathers.

Every family had an oil-lamp in the house. The cheaper lamps were made of clay; expensive ones were of bronze or other metals. These lamps burned olive oil, pitch or wax and had wicks made of flax. They were left to burn all through the night. The light showed anyone outside that there were people indoors sleeping. It was unheard of not to have a light.

Artist's impression of a peasant's house. Notice the low wall around the roof's edge, built for safety's sake.

Home life

Because they lived in a very hot country, most people got up before day-break so that they could do plenty of work before the sun got too hot. The mother would often get up before anyone else and light the fire, if it had gone out during the night.

After everyone had eaten breakfast, the men and the older boys would go off to the fields to work. The mother and the girls started their daily tasks. The young boys looked after the family's animals, such as the goat or the donkey, just as young Arab boys do today.

Milling
An important job was to grind the grain into flour to bake bread. Women ground the grain in a handmill made of two flat, round stones about 50 centimetres (18 inches) across.

Artist's impression of a market in Bible times.

The bottom stone had a wooden peg in the centre; the top stone, which had a hole in the middle, fitted over this peg.

The woman would put handfuls of grain into the hole in the top stone. Then she slowly turned the handle on the top stone. As the two stones ground against each other, the grain was crushed between them. Fine flour poured on to the cloth that was laid beneath the two millstones. Often two women would do their milling together, to make it less hard work (Matthew 24:41).

Fetching water
Another daily job was fetching water for the family (Genesis 24:11-13). Often the older girls would do this. They would take goatskin bottles to a nearby spring or well and fill them with water. Then they would carefully carry them back, either balanced on their hips or on their shoulders. At the well they might meet other women on the same errand, and stop to chat.

Baking bread
Each day there was also bread to be baked. This, too, was usually done by the women. They mixed the flour that they had milled with a little water. If the bread was to rise, they added a little dough from the previous day's bread, to act as yeast or 'leaven' (Matthew 13:33).

Then the dough was left to warm by the fire, so that the leaven could work its way through the dough. Finally the bread was ready to bake on the hot stones of a hearth.

Bread ovens
Sometimes bread was baked on a big, shallow bowl that was turned upside down over the fire. The dough was rolled out very thin and laid over the top of the dish to bake. Another type of oven looked like an upside-down earthenware cone. A fire was lit at the bottom, and the dough was put inside to bake.

Shopping
Although most families grew a lot of their own food, one or two extra things were usually needed for the evening meal. Some of the girls went to market most days to buy vegetables or meat.

Washing clothes
Sometimes clothes were washed in a fast stream; sometimes dirt was removed by beating dirt out of the wet clothes spread out on flat stones. The women used soap made of olive oil or from a special vegetable.

Rest-time
At midday, when the sun was at its hottest, it was too uncomfortable to work. The family would find a shady place and take a couple of hours' rest. People in hot countries today still rest in the middle of the day.

Women ground the grain in a handmill made of two flat, round stones. Often two women would do their milling together, to make it less hard work.

Jerusalem:
King David's city

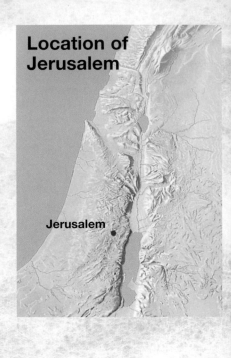

Jerusalem – the city of David, Solomon's showcase, and the most important city in Israel's history – is also a holy place of Islam, and the goal of both medieval Crusaders and modern pilgrims.

The first time Jerusalem is named in the Bible is when Abraham met Melchizedek, a mysterious king from Salem (Jerusalem), who blessed the patriarch (Genesis 14:18-20). Egyptian records – the 'Execration Texts', from as far back as the nineteenth century B.C. – probably refer to Jerusalem, as do fourteenth-century B.C. clay tablets found in Tell el-Amarna, central Egypt, known as the Amarna Letters. When the Israelites entered the Promised Land, they failed to drive the Jebusites from their fortified town of Jebus (Jerusalem). After David became ruler of the united kingdom of Judah and Israel, he needed a new capital city. Jerusalem was ideally positioned, belonging to neither of the two jealous kingdoms. David's commander, Joab, led a successful assault on Jerusalem, which now became known as 'the City of David' (2 Samuel 5:6-10).

An artist's impression of Jerusalem in the time of King David.

Tunnelling into Jerusalem

The Jebusites boasted that Jerusalem – perched on the top of a hill with three steep sides – could never be captured. But David took Jerusalem by surprise when his men climbed a water-shaft which tunnelled beneath the city walls.

A rock-cut sloping shaft was discovered by the English nineteenth century explorer, Col Robert Warren and it leads to a vertical shaft through which a bucket could be lowered to a pool fed by the Gihon spring. The Jebusites enlarged the tunnels to ensure a good water supply during time of siege, and David gained entrance by this means (2 Samuel 5:8, 1 Chronicles 11:6).

King David strengthened Jerusalem's fortifications, and brought the Ark of the Covenant to the city, making it the political and religious centre for God's people. David bought a threshing floor from the Jebusite Araunah and on its site built an altar of sacrifice (2 Samuel 24:13-25). By tradition this is also Mount Moriah, where Abraham so nearly sacrificed his son Isaac (Genesis 22:2). Jerusalem's most important building, the Temple, was to be built on exactly the same site (2 Chronicles 3:1–2).

Jerusalem: Herod the Great

Herod the Great, renowned for his cruelty and ambition.

Herod the Great was infamous for his cruel-heartedness. He murdered his son and expected heir, Antipater, five days before he died himself. History also remembers him for his lavish building programmes.

Herod rebuilt the temple at Samaria, 'out of a desire to make the city more eminent than it had

The fortress of Herodium, built by Herod the Great near Bethlehem.

been before, but principally because he contrived that it might at once be for his own security and a monument of his magnificence' (Josephus). He renamed Samaria Sebaste (meaning Augustus), and built a theatre and forum as a temple dedicated to Augustus.

Herod made Caesarea his capital, and built impressive breakwaters and a vast artificial harbour measuring 500 metres (550 yards) by 270 metres (300 yards), making it into an impressive new port.

Impregnable

King Herod also built an impregnable fortress and summer retreat at Masada, which included two lavish palaces, and his own private bath – with its changing room, cold plunge bath, warm room and hot room – as well as a public bathhouse. At Herodium, near Bethlehem, he built a walled fortress on a hilltop, with four towers to protect it, from which heavy catapults could fire on any besieging force.

But Herod carried out his most ambitious building programme in Jerusalem. He remodelled the *Baris* (fortress) north of the Temple, renaming it the 'Antonia Fortress' in honour of Mark Antony. He built a second

Cleansing the Temple

A great struggle arose during the reign of Antiochus IV Epiphanes (175-163 B.C.), the Seleucid ruler of the Jews. His Jewish subjects were determined to retain their distinctive life and religion; the Seleucid king was equally determined to make Jerusalem a city in the Greek style. The Jews resisted fanatically when pigs (unclean animals for Jews) were offered in sacrifice on Jerusalem's new Greek altars, and the Temple rededicated to the Greek god Zeus. Judas, nicknamed 'the Hammer', led a Jewish guerrilla war, known as the Maccabean Revolt, from the hills surrounding Jerusalem.

Surprisingly, the Seleucids were eventually forced to accept the terms demanded by the Jews. The Temple was reinstated as the focus of Jewish worship and on 14 December 164 B.C., after ritual cleansing, it was rededicated (1 Maccabees 4:36-59). This is celebrated annually by the Jews at the festival of Hanukkah.

Judas' successors now ruled as the Hasmoneans, and successfully governed Jerusalem until the Romans (under Pompey) captured the city in 63 B.C. King Herod the Great was a Hasmonean, but was primarily interested in retaining his throne, as he showed when he ordered the slaughter of all the male children in Bethlehem.

A special Hanukkah candlestick.

The tomb of the family of Herod.

Above: Robinson's arch, part of the structure remaining from Herod's Temple.
Below: A model of Herodian Jerusalem, showing the hippodrome.

fortress, with three massive towers, on the western side of Jerusalem, his Upper Palace linking the two fortresses with a great wall. Herod also built himself a more modest Lower Palace in the centre of Jerusalem.

Far-reaching
Herod also constructed in Jerusalem baths, a theatre, and a hippodrome, or stadium, where he promoted both Greek and Roman games. Two existing pools, just beyond the north-east corner of the Temple area, Herod replaced with the larger Pool of Israel.

Herod's far-reaching building programme for Jerusalem meant that the street plan for the city had to be changed. Jerusalem changed little after his death in 4 B.C., before it was levelled by the Romans in A.D. 70.

141

Jerusalem in A.D. 30

In Jesus' day, Jerusalem was the centre for Jewish faith and worship. It was also the setting for the last week of Jesus' life, and for the most momentous events in God's plan of salvation.

This artist's impression of the city of Jerusalem in Jesus' day shows Herod's Temple, the greatest of Herod's building enterprises, which he started in 19 B.C. and which covered over 15 per cent of the total area of Jerusalem.

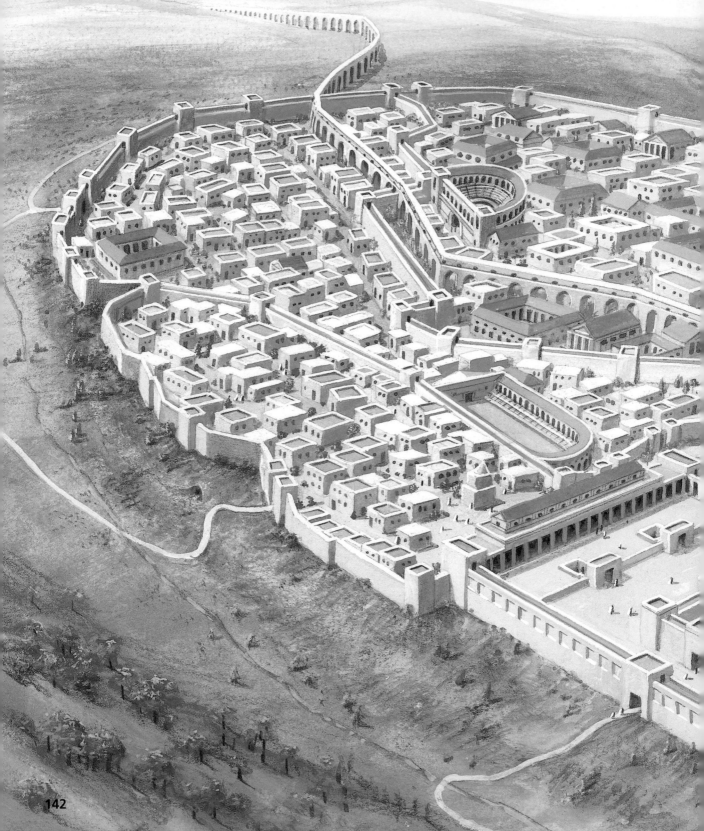

Here, as a baby, Jesus was 'presented' (Luke 2:22), and from its courts Jesus later witnessed the poor widow 'casting her two mites into the treasury' (Luke 21:1-4).

Jesus spoke to his disciples about Jerusalem: 'We are going up to Jerusalem, and everything that is written by the prophets about the Son of Man will be fulfilled. He will be turned over to the Gentiles. They will mock him, insult him, spit on him, flog him and kill him. On the third day he will rise again' (Luke18:31-33).

Jesus revealed his great love for Jerusalem when he said, 'O Jerusalem, Jerusalem, you who kill the prophets and stone those sent to you, how often I have longed to gather your children together, as a hen gathers her chicks under her wings, but you were not willing. Look, your house is left to you desolate' (Matthew 23:37-38).

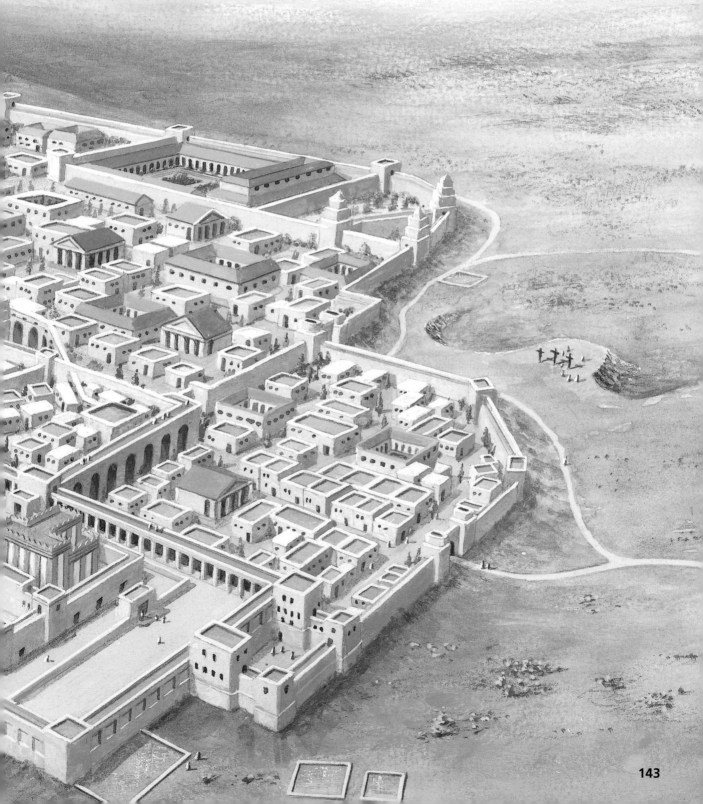

Marriage

In Bible times, young people did not normally decide for themselves who to marry. Their parents usually chose for them.

The bride's price
Once a wife had been chosen for a son, there were financial arrangements to be made. The bride's mother and father had to be paid for losing their daughter. Also, the bride's father gave his daughter a gift of money, called a dowry (Genesis 24:59-61).

Betrothal
Once all the arrangements had been made; the man and woman were bound by vows, or 'betrothed', to be married (Matthew 1:18-20). The time of betrothal lasted a year, while everyone prepared for the wedding itself. The bride's family made her wedding clothes and arranged the wedding feast.

The wedding
At the wedding, the bride and groom made a legal agreement and a blessing was said over them. Then came the wedding feast, when everyone dressed in their wedding clothes. The feast was usually given by the bride's family.

A bride wearing her traditional headdress.

The procession

On the marriage day, there was a procession. The bridegroom, dressed in his best clothes and decorated with jewels, walked with his friends from his home to his bride's home. She would be waiting, having dressed after being bathed by her bridesmaids (Psalm 45:14-15). She wore a veil to cover her face.

The feast
Once the groom arrived, everyone walked back to his house, the guests holding oil-lamps to light the way. When they entered the bridegroom's house, the bride and groom sat down under a decorated canopy and the feast began.

Feasting could last as long as seven days (Judges 14:12), with much drinking, eating, dancing and singing. Jesus once went to a wedding at the village of Cana, near his home town of Nazareth (see John 2).

Artist's impression of a marriage ceremony in Bible times.

Children

Jewish parents believed it was a sign of God's blessing if they had many children (Deuteronomy 28:4). The more children the better, especially if they were boys. If a woman was childless, people made fun of her, or pitied her.

Birth
When a pregnant woman was ready to give birth, the midwife would be called to her house (Exodus 1:15-19). Birth took place at home; there were no hospitals as we know them.

   The newborn baby was first washed, and then rubbed down with salt, water and oil. People thought this was good for the baby's skin. After this, the baby was wrapped up very tightly with strips of bandage. People believed this would help the baby's legs and arms grow straight.

   When a male child was eight days old, there was a special ceremony, called circumcision. The loose skin on his penis was cut off, as a sign that the boy was being given back to God (Genesis 17:10).

Names
At about the same time, the baby was named (Luke 2:21). Names were very important, and each name had its own meaning. For example, David means 'beloved', and Sarah means 'princess'.

Childhood
Up to the age of three children were taught by their mothers. From three to six, boys were taught by their fathers, and their fathers later trained them in their own trade. The mothers taught their daughters how to cook, spin, weave and care for the home. Boys and girls might look after the family's sheep, goats and donkey.

Growing up
When a boy reached the age of thirteen he was regarded as a

Children were taught to ask questions about their nation's past. 'In time to come your children will ask you, "Why did the LORD our God command us to obey all these laws?"' (Deuteronomy 6:20, GNB).

School

Until the time of Jesus, there were no schools. A child's parents taught him or her everything they knew. The children were told about the religious festivals, such as Passover, and what they meant.

   By the time of Jesus, boys of six and over went to school at the 'house of the book'. The teacher was paid by the synagogue, the Jewish meeting-place. The boys would learn by heart passages from Scripture, and be taught to read and write.

Classes
School lasted only about four hours each day. After morning class there

man. There was a special ceremony to mark this stage in his life. When he was twelve, Jesus went to the Temple in Jerusalem with his parents for his last Passover as a child (see Luke 2:41-49). Jewish boys today have a ceremony called the Barmitzvah when they are about thirteen. Afterwards they can go as adults to the synagogue.

Toys and games
Children didn't have many toys to play with. They usually made do

was a long break until afternoon class started, at about three o'clock. But classes went on all the year round – there were no school holidays.

   The teacher sat cross-legged on a little platform in front of the class. Before him was a little rack where he kept scrolls containing parts of the Scripture. The boys sat on the floor in front of their teacher. All the boys were in one class, whatever age they were.

   The boys wrote on wooden tablets covered with a thin layer of wax, using pointed sticks to make marks in the wax (Luke 1:63).

with sticks or bits of string and broken pottery. Balls have also been found. Some children had toys made out of clay, but Jewish children were not allowed to play with dolls or toy animals because the Law forbade the making of 'images'.

   Jesus talks about children playing games in the streets – they sound like dance games (see Matthew 11:16-17.

Health and medicine

The Jews had many rules to make sure they led healthy lives. They were to keep one day in seven as a day of rest. They were not to eat certain unhealthy foods. They were to make sure that their food and their homes were clean.

The Jews believed they should pray to God when they were ill. But sometimes they copied surrounding nations by wearing lucky charms to keep away evil spirits.

Medicines

The Jews gradually began to use simple natural drugs. They knew how to clean wounds and bandage them, using natural ointments for cuts. They used a herb called myrrh mixed with wine as a pain-killer.

Diseases

We know from stories in the Bible that people suffered from many different illnesses and diseases, such as leprosy, blindness, deafness, epilepsy and as cripples (Mark 1:32-34). Many Jews believed that illness came as a result of their sins. If someone was ill, they would ask: 'Was this person a sinner – or his mother or father?' (John 9:2-4).

Doctors

In Jesus' time some doctors were trained by the Greeks to do surgical operations. They took vows promising to put the life of their patient first, and not to give away personal details about their patients.

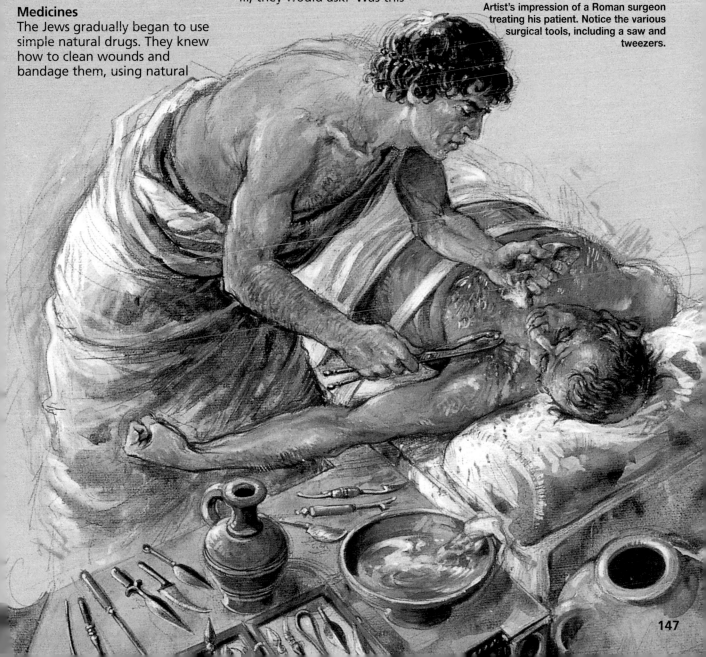

Artist's impression of a Roman surgeon treating his patient. Notice the various surgical tools, including a saw and tweezers.

147

Eating and drinking

Breakfast
Breakfast, the first meal of the day, was not a big meal. The family would usually eat bread and cheese and some dried fruit or olives. The men might take their breakfast with them to the fields.

Evening meal
The main meal of the day was in the evening, when work was finished and the sun was less hot. The women prepared a pot of vegetable stew or lentils (Genesis 25:29, 34), which was simmering over the fire when the men returned from the fields.

Everyone would scoop food out of the pot, using a piece of bread. There were no knives and forks to eat with. They might drink wine with the meal, and on special occasions they might have some meat too. They often finished the meal with fruit.

Feasts
The Jewish people enjoyed having special feasts. They held feasts when people got married, when a baby was born, and when the child was weaned, at burials and at sheep-shearing time. They also ate well if there were guests to entertain. There were religious festivals too – such as Passover, Purim and Harvest (see pages 170-170).

At the festivals, they often added meat to the usual stew. Also, they might have sweet pastries with the fruit. The feasts were very happy times, with plenty of singing and dancing. Wedding feasts lasted for days (see page 144), as they still do in many Arab villages.

Food

Bread
Bread, the basic food, was eaten at every meal. Jesus taught his followers to pray: 'Give us each day our daily bread' (Luke 11:3).

Barley stew with lentils.

Milk
The Jews drank the milk of sheep, and of goats and camels too. They used milk to make cheese and butter (2 Samuel 17:29). They also made a kind of yogurt by shaking milk in a skin bag (Genesis 18:8). The Bedouin people today make yogurt in a similar way.

Vegetables
The Jewish people grew and ate several different vegetables. They had beans, lentils, gherkins and cucumbers for their stews (Ezekiel 4:9). They also had root vegetables, and herbs to flavour their stews.

Fruit and nuts
The Jews ate plenty of fruit. Many different fruit grow well in the warm climate of Israel. When Moses sent spies to explore the Promised Land, they brought back huge bunches of grapes to show how rich the land was.

As well as grapes, the country was rich in pomegranates, figs, dates, olives, almonds and pistachio nuts (Jeremiah 24:2; Genesis 43:11; Deuteronomy 8:8).

Honey
The Jews obtained honey from wild bees (Judges 14:8-9). Honey was important as a sweetener, because they had no sugar. Another sort of honey was made by boiling grape juice down until it was syrupy and sweet. They often spread this syrup on bread to eat.

Meat
Most families did not normally eat meat. They usually only tasted meat at special feasts (1 Kings 4:23). The Jews sometimes ate birds such as pigeons, geese, quails and partridge. The most common meat was the kid, or young goat, but they also ate lamb.

Fish
Fish from the Sea of Galilee and from the River Jordan was a favourite food (Luke 11:11). In the time of Jesus many fishermen sailed on Galilee to bring in fish.

Wine
For most people the main drink was wine. Much of the grape juice was used to make wine. Water was often dirty and full of germs, so it was safer to drink wine.

Olives and grapes

Almost every family had olive trees, often growing in small groves. Olive trees grow well in dry lands like Palestine. They have very deep roots and can find water deep in the earth. It is about 15 years before an olive tree starts to bear fruit; but it can live many years longer than this.

Olive harvest
The olives were ready to pick in September and October. They were gathered in a cloth laid out under the tree. Boys would beat and shake the tree, and the ripe olives would drop into the cloth below. Some of the olives were eaten raw, and others were preserved in salted water. But most of the olives were crushed to make olive oil.

The olive press
The olives were crushed in an olive press. This was made up of a big stone with a hollow on top where the olives were placed for crushing. A stone wheel placed over the olives was turned, pressing the oil out of them. The oil was stored in jars.

Olive oil
Olive oil had many uses. It was used instead of butter on bread, and as cooking fat. It was also used to burn in lamps (Matthew 25:3, 4), and to make soap. Olive oil was also rubbed into the skin to make it shine, and as an ointment for wounds.

Planting grapes
The grape harvest was nearly as important as the grain harvest. Grape vines were best planted on a hillside (Isaiah 5:1). The grapes would catch the sun well there, and the rain would run off the slope. Often the hillside would be stepped into a series of terraces running along the slope. The edge of each terrace was marked with a low wall of stones and rocks.

Before planting new vines, the farmer broke up the soil with his hoe or mattock. Then he planted out the vines, leaving plenty of room between them. While some vines grew along the ground, others needed sticks to climb on.

Pruning
During the winter the farmer cut out dead or broken branches. This left the healthy branches to grow and bear grapes. Jesus talked about pruning grapes (see John 15:1-6).

Grape harvest
When the grapes were ready to pick, in July, August or September, the farmer's family often went to live in a watch-tower among the vines (Isaiah 5:2). At night they could guard the grapes from thieves, and during the day they picked the grapes, collecting them in big baskets.

The grape harvest was a festival time (see page 170). There was much singing and dancing as well as plenty of hard work.

Using the grapes
Some of the grapes were eaten fresh. Some grapes were crushed to make fresh grape-juice. Yet other grapes were spread out to dry in the sun to make raisins.

But most of the grapes were pressed to make wine. These grapes were put into a square tank cut into the rock. People would tread the grapes to press out the juice. As it ran out, the juice was collected in a pot or jar.

Storage
The juice was left for about six months to ferment into wine. Then it was poured into storage jars, carefully leaving behind the waste that had sunk to the bottom (Jeremiah 48:11). Sometimes wine was stored in goatskin bottles instead of jars.

Artist's impression of a farmer pressing olives.

Craft workers

The potter

In Bible times, clay was used to make pots for eating and drinking from, and for storing things. This clay was dug from the ground, and it had to be mixed with water to make it soft enough to shape.

Coil pots

The first potters made bowls and jugs by rolling out long snakes of clay and then coiling them up. Then they smoothed out the bumpy surface and left the pot to dry hard.

Later, potters found they could make smooth round pots by placing the clay on a flat turning wheel. This wheel was often turned by another worker. Then potters learned to turn it by pushing their feet on a second wheel attached below (Ecclesiasticus 38:29).

Decorating the pots

Once the pots had dried, they were often decorated. Sometimes

A potter of Bible times.

red or black was added to make a pattern, or the clay was smoothed to give it a shiny surface.

The potter's mould

If he wanted to make complicated shapes, the potter could not use his wheel. Oil lamps, which had a lip on one side, were made by pressing clay into a wooden mould to shape it. The potter also made some things by hand, such as toys, ornaments and seals.

Firing the clay

Once the clay had dried, the potter put it in a special oven to 'fire' it. The clay pots would come out hard enough to use, but they broke very easily if they were knocked.

The leatherworker

Leather was used to make many different things, such as bottles, belts, soldiers' helmets, shields and slings.

Skinning the animal

First the leatherworker had to prepare his leather. He would skin a goat or ox to get its hide (skin). Then he scraped the skin to remove all the animal's hair. Finally, he soaked the skin and put lime on it, to remove any remaining hair.

Softening the skin

Next the leatherworker softened the leather by soaking it in water with special leaves in it, by rubbing it with dog droppings and by hammering it. His workshop could smell very bad!

Leather goods

Sometimes the tanner, or leatherworker, dyed the leather, before starting to make sandals, belts or other articles to sell.

The carpenter

The carpenter had two jobs – building houses and making furniture. Carpenters had to be tough, strong men.

Building a house

To build a house, the carpenter had to cut down trees. Then he shaped the logs he had cut to use as beams for the roof. He used tools such as a handsaw and an axe to do this work. The axe head was made of stone or bronze and was lashed to a wooden handle.

Making furniture

But the carpenter did many smaller jobs too. He made doors and doorframes, wooden locks, tables, stools and chests for the home. He also made ploughs, yokes and shovels for the farmer.

Working with cloth

The Jewish people made many of their clothes from sheep's wool.

Spinning
Before the wool could be spun, the women had to wash and comb it. Then they spun the wool into lengths on a wooden stick or spindle.

Dyeing
After this the women washed the wool again before dyeing it (Jeremiah 2:22). The dyes they used were made of crushed shells (Acts 16:14), fruit, or even lice eggs, and were mixed with water. The wool was dyed in big pots or basins, then rinsed in water and dried.

An Eastern woman weaves at an outdoor loom.

Weaving
Once the wool had been spun and dyed, it was ready to be woven into cloth. Often the loom was set up outdoors, on a simple wooden frame (Judges 16:13).

First the weaver would fix the long warp threads from end to end. Then she would push the yarn between the warp threads, using a wooden stick to guide it through. Gradually a piece of cloth would be formed, as the weft, or cross-threads, grew.

Important Roman Roads of Asia Minor

AEGEAN SEA

Troas

Pergamum
Sardis
Smyrna
Ephesus — Laodicea
Miletus — Colossae
Antioch
Iconium
Perga — Lystra
Derbe
Attalia — Tarsus
Germanicus
Antioch

MEDITERRANEAN SEA

CRETE

CYPRUS

0   50   100   150   200 mi
0   50   100   150   200   250   300 km

Some rich Romans were carried in chairs by their slaves.

Travel

Because travel was so difficult and dangerous (2 Corinthians 11:26-27), people only left home if they had to, and travelled around in groups. Most people travelled on foot, or on a donkey while those who could afford it went on horseback or by horse-drawn carriage.

Difficult country
Much of Palestine was hilly and there were few good roads. The best roads were built by the Romans. Their roads were straight and level. They enabled the Roman army to march rapidly if trouble arose.

Most people could walk 16 to 20 Roman miles in a day. We know from the Gospels that Jesus and his followers travelled on foot around Galilee. The book of Acts tells how the apostle Paul walked long distances through what we know as Turkey and Greece.

Danger, thief!
The roads were often dangerous, with thieves lying in wait for travellers. Jesus told a story about a traveller who was set upon by thieves (Luke 10:30-35). In his story, the Samaritan who found the wounded traveller took him to a roadside inn. There were many inns like this, where a traveller could find food and a bed for the night.

Chariots and carts
Sometimes farmers or merchants used carts drawn by oxen or by horses to carry grain and other goods. Some rich people could afford to travel in horse-drawn carriages (Acts 8:29).

Pack animals
Poorer people used a donkey or mule to carry their heavy loads, tying sacks on to the animal's back (Genesis 42:25-28). They also used donkeys to turn mill-wheels and water-wheels.

The camel
The camel can store enough water to last several days, making it an ideal creature for travelling in hot deserts. In Bible times the camel was often used by merchants crossing the desert with their goods (Judges 6:5).

Military horseman.

Mule.

Horse-drawn carriage.

Military chariot.

Sea travel

The Jews didn't often travel by sea, because they thought it was very dangerous. Palestine is on the Mediterranean Sea, where it was unsafe to sail in winter because wild storms can arise.

In Jesus' time, the Romans sailed big ships to the ports of Palestine. They used them to carry soldiers, grain and other goods. We know that the apostle Paul sailed to Rome in a grain ship that held 276 people, similar to the ship illustrated below (Acts 27:6). These ships only had one sail on a single mast, and were difficult to handle in stormy weather.

Horse-drawn carriage.

153

Replica of a Roman siege engine and catapult (*background*) near Masada, Israel.

Chariots

Some armies had horse-drawn chariots. The chariots were mainly used to carry archers, so that they could fire their arrows freely at the enemy. Sometimes their arrows had spikes, or barbs, to prevent their being easily pulled out of a wound.

Siege

Often enemy armies surrounded a town and set up a siege. Cities were built with high walls around them to protect them from enemies. An attacking army would try to tunnel beneath the walls, or knock a hole by using a battering-ram. The Romans also used giant catapults that threw great rocks into a city.

The people inside a besieged city would throw stones or boiling oil at the soldiers outside.

The Roman army

The Roman army controlled Palestine in Jesus' time. They were very well organised and equipped; each soldier had armour consisting of a breastplate, helmet and shield (Ephesians 6:13-17). He also had a full set of weapons: a dagger, long sword and javelin. The Romans also trained specialist soldiers such as bowmen, horsemen, surgeons and engineers.

Weapons and war

The Jews were surrounded by enemy nations, but it was not until the time of King Solomon that they could afford to have a regular army. Solomon raised taxes to pay for his army, and built new strongholds to guard the roads.

Weapons

However the Jewish soldiers were often poorly armed. Enemy armies such as the Assyrians had fine coats of mail, and metal shields and helmets, whereas the Jewish soldiers often had only a simple weapon such as a sling. Shields usually consisted of a wooden frame covered with leather. Foot soldiers had a dagger and a throwing spear (1 Samuel 18:10-11), while some soldiers were trained to use slings or bows and arrows.

Egyptian warrior. Philistine warrior. Assyrian spearman. Babylonian spearman. Greek soldier. Israelite archer.

A Roman centurion (*foreground*) and Roman legionary soldier (*background*). The legionary is armed with a long sword, a short sword and a javelin, and has a large shield for protection. The centurion commanded a force of 100 soldiers.

Fishing

In Jesus' time, many fishermen worked on the big lake called the Sea of Galilee, and many fishing villages surrounded the lake. Some of these fishermen used a rod and line, like anglers today.

Cast net

Some fishermen used a cast net (Mark 1:16-17). This was a circular net, about 5 metres (17 feet) across. It had weights tied round the edge, and a rope tied to the middle. When a fisherman could see fish in shallow water by the water's edge, he would wade into the water and drop the net over them. The weights pulled the net down, trapping the fish.

Seine net

If they were fishing from a boat, fishermen would often use a seine net (Luke 5:4). This was a long net, about 3 metres (10 feet) wide, that was let out behind the boat. It had corks fixed to the top to make it float, and stones tied to the bottom to weigh it down.

Fish were caught in the net as the boat sailed along. Sometimes the boat turned in a circle so that the fish were caught in the middle of the net.

Fishing boats

The fishermen used small sailing boats that normally held only about four men. These boats had one big sail, and a long oar to steer with.

When they had finished a day's fishing, the men would lay out their nets to dry, and mend any tears in them.

The shepherd

Sheep were much valued in Bible times. They provided wool, meat and milk. Even the sheep's horns were used – to make trumpets (Leviticus 25:9) or as containers for oil.

Sheep and goats
In Bible times, the shepherd looked after the goats and sheep together in the same flock. Goats gave a lot of milk, and some of it was used to make a kind of yogurt. Goat's hair was used to make a coarse cloth used for covering tents and for rough clothes, while goatskin leather was used to make water bottles.

The shepherd often looked after the sheep and goats belonging to everyone in his village. After the rain had fallen in winter, there was plenty of grass near the village for the flocks to graze on, and when the grain had been cut at harvest, the sheep and goats grazed on the stubble left behind.

New pasture
But when the hot summer sun had dried the grass, the shepherd had to lead the flocks farther away to find pasture (1 Chronicles 4:39-40). He also had to find a brook or well where he could draw water for the sheep and goats to drink.

The shepherd also had to guard his flock from the wild animals that roamed the country (1 Samuel 17:34-36). Lions, bears, jackals and hyena were all looking for animals such as sheep to eat.

Shepherds' tools
The shepherd carried a heavy club spiked with sharp stones to beat off animals (Psalm 23:4). He also had a leather sling.

The shepherd had a staff about 2 metres (6 feet) long. He used this as a walking stick in rough country, and to control his sheep (Ezekiel 20:37-38). Sometimes his rod had a hook, or crook, at one end.

The shepherd also had a leather bag, called a scrip, to carry his food. Some shepherds had a little reed pipe to play while they were watching the sheep and goats.

Shelter
At night the shepherd had to find a safe place to shelter his sheep (Luke 2:8). Often he would take his sheep to a cave, and sleep in the doorway to prevent wild animals from entering (John 10:7). Sometimes, if there was no cave, he had to make a rough stockade out of stones or brushwood.

An Eastern shepherd tends his flock. For such men, little has changed since biblical times.

In the village, there would sometimes be a stone sheepfold, with a little shelter for the guarding shepherd.

The shepherd spent a lot of time alone with his sheep, and learned to know them all by name (John 10:14). He knew which sheep belonged to which family, and could return them to their owners.

An artist's impression of an eastern shepherd leading his flock. Note his stout staff and heavy club.

Sheep-shearing

At the end of summer the sheep would be sheared. When sheep-shearing was finished, the people celebrated with a feast, and plenty of eating and drinking (1 Samuel 25).

Jesus described a shepherd looking for his lost sheep in Luke 15:3-7. There is also a fine description of the shepherd's job in Psalm 23.

Growing grain

Farmers in Bible times grew mainly wheat and barley, and sometimes a grain called millet. Barley could be grown on poorer land, but it was not as popular as wheat.

Sowing seed
The farmer scattered seed from a basket. As he sowed, he ploughed the seed into the soil, to stop the birds flying off with it. Jesus describes a sower at work in Luke 8:5-8.

While the grain was growing, from December to February, the farmer had to weed the land so that the grain was not choked by weeds.

Harvest
Barley was ready to harvest in April or May. The farmer cut it

A farmer harvests the grain with his sickle.

down, using a sharp curved tool called a sickle (Jeremiah 50:16). He cut the barley stalks near the

top, and left the rest of the plant in the ground, so that his sheep could graze there afterwards.

The farmer left some grain standing in the corners of his fields. Poor people were allowed to come and take this grain, or any other grain that the farmer and his workers had missed (Ruth 2).

Threshing
Now the grain had to be separated from the straw stems. The grain was taken to a patch of hard ground (1 Chronicles 21:18-26) where it was beaten with sticks or trampled by oxen to separate it.

Sometimes the farmer used a threshing board. This was a wooden board with stones or iron spikes fixed underneath. Oxen pulled it over the grain, to thresh it.

Ploughing

The farmer started off by ploughing up his land in October or November, when the rain came (Matthew 13:4). The rain helped soften the parched

earth, and made it easier to plough. Often the farmer ploughed and sowed his seed at the same time. The plough was a T-shaped wooden tool with a sharp spike that cut through the soil. It was drawn by two donkeys or two

oxen. If the field was on a hill or near trees, the farmer had to break up the soil by hand. To do this he used a tool like a hoe, called a mattock (Isaiah 7:25).

Artist's impression of a former ploughing with two yoked oxen. Notice the farmer's goad.

Winnowing

After the threshing, the farmer had to separate the grain from the chaff – the bits of straw and the outer husk. He did this by tossing the grain in the air, using a wooden winnowing fork. The chaff was light and was blown away on the wind; but the grain was heavier and fell to the ground.

Finally the farmer shook his grain in a big sieve to get rid of any bits of waste or weeds (Luke 22:31).

Storage

Now the farmer could store his precious grain. He usually put his grain in great earthenware pots or jars (Luke 6:38).

Harvest was a very important time. It provided the grain for another year's bread. So the people celebrated the barley harvest and the wheat harvest each year with special feasts (see page 170).

An artist's impression of labourer winnowing grain.

Religious life

For the Israelites, worshipping God was not merely a matter of going to services three times a year, once a week or even more often. Although services and other religious practices were important, they symbolised that for Israel, being God's people involved the whole of life. For the Jews, there was no difference between 'religious' and 'non-religious' activities. If they treated people unfairly or disobeyed the commandments then religious observance counted for nothing.

Ways of worship

Worshipping God involved living one's life in the way that God had laid down. Family life, working life, social life and political life all had to be carried out in a way that honoured God and reflected his Law. Regulations about

The young boy Samuel aids the high priest Eli in the shrine at Shiloh.

worship practice mingle with laws about farming, fighting, clothing, commerce, loving and learning. All these areas were equally important in the people's relationship with God; all could be seen as part of worship.

But the occasions when people took part in specifically religious activities remained important. We look next at patterns of religious life in Israel.

The Levites

Israel was divided into twelve tribes, of which the tribe of Levi acted as assistants to the priests, looking after the religious aspects of national life. The Levites formed a kind of religious civil service, managing and administering religious activities.

In the early days, when Israel was still travelling in the desert, the Levites were responsible for the care of the Meeting Tent (Tabernacle), and for carrying the tent and Ark of the Covenant from place to place. Later, they were entrusted with cleaning the Temple and looking after the Temple furniture and implements. They also supervised the collection and distribution of gifts for the Temple and the poor.

The Levites did not have an area of the country assigned to them, as did the other tribes. Instead, they were allocated small sections of land throughout the country, so that they could help with local religious activities. The land that the Levites owned was not enough to support the whole tribe, so they also received payment from national funds raised by gifts and taxes upon the whole people.

The priests

The main spiritual leaders of Israel were the priests, who came from one clan of the Levi tribe. The priests were all descendants of Aaron, Moses' brother. Every boy born into a priestly family was prepared from childhood for a priest's work, but worked as a priest only between the age of thirty and fifty.

The priests had to lead worship within the Temple and administer sacrifices. When the people brought sacrifices to offer to God, the priests first had to ensure that they were properly prepared and then offer them. However, only a few priests worked in the Temple at any one time; the rest taught and gave advice. People who had recovered from infectious illnesses or skin diseases such as leprosy had to have their recovery confirmed by priests.

The high priest

One priest was appointed high priest. Once a year, on the Day of Atonement, he alone entered the Most Holy Place in the innermost part of the Temple, where the Covenant Box was kept. The high priest also worked alongside the king and the prophets in leading the nation.

The high priest wore special clothes, including a gold breastplate inlaid with twelve precious stones, to symbolise the unity of the nation gathered to worship God.

> I myself have selected your fellow Levites from among the Israelites as a gift to you, dedicated to the Lord to do the work at the Tent of Meeting.
> Numbers 18:6

Singers and servers

From the time of Solomon, some Levites were trained as singers and as musicians for Temple worship. Artists, woodworkers and needle-workers, who helped design and decorate the Meeting Tent and the Temple, came from other tribes, as did those who served and helped when there were not enough Levites available.

The people

The servers, Levites and priests did not however worship on behalf of the people, or excuse the people from their religious responsibilities. All the people – men, women and children – had an important part to play in Israel's religious life and should be counted among Israel's 'religious personnel'.

Death and burial

In Bible times, many people died before old age. They died through illness, poverty or famine.

When someone died

As soon as someone died, friends and relatives began to wail and lament. This let neighbours know somebody had died. The family would come together to wail.

Sometimes rich families would pay for other people to come and wail for them (Jeremiah 9:17-18). While they were in mourning, people often wore rough goat's-hair clothes, sometimes called sackcloth. Or they tore their clothes, to show how sad they were.

Burial

Because the weather was often very hot, it was important to bury the dead before the body started to rot. Usually the body was washed and wrapped up in linen before being carried on a stretcher to the burying place.

People were often buried in caves, or in specially dug-out tombs in the rock (Judges 8:32). But there were not enough caves for all the bodies. So, when bodies had rotted away, the bones were collected and saved in special bone-boxes (called ossuaries) to make room in the caves for new bodies.

Burial caves

These burial caves were closed up with huge rocks. Sometimes the door was a circular stone that was rolled across the opening in a slot (see Luke 24:1-2).

Poorer people were sometimes buried more simply (Luke 7:14). The stretcher with the body was laid on the ground, covered with earth and surrounded by rocks.

Israel's God

If we see in the Old Testament nothing but Israel's sorry history, a collection of literature or a description of a religion, we have missed the point. At the heart of it is a picture of Israel's glorious God.

We learn about God primarily from the way in which he involves himself in the lives of human beings in real-time situations, not from theological sermons or doctrinal statements.

Nevertheless, gathering together some of what we learn about him helps us understand why belonging to him, being part of his people, was seen as so special and desirable.

Four starting points:
1. *God exists.* This is taken for granted; it is assumed that only a fool would question it (Psalm 14:1).
2. *God allows himself to be known.* He wants people to know him, and reveals himself in many varied ways, through creation, through the Law and the prophets, through visions and by acting in people's lives.
3. *God relates.* The purpose of God's self-revelation is not to give people an intellectual appreciation of who he is, but to allow them to relate to him.
4. *God is majestic and transcendent.* God makes himself known and, despite his greatness, he enters into relationship with human beings. Yet he is also unknowable; greater than any human being can conceive. The prohibition against depicting God in human or other form stems from this belief in God's transcendence (Deuteronomy 4:15-16).

The nature of God
• *He is living.* God is active not static; he reacts to people and to situations. He is Life, and no single picture of him could possibly be adequate. 'By this you shall know

that among you is the living God' (Joshua 3:10).
• *He is personal.* The Old Testament knows nothing of the impersonal 'life-force' of ancient philosophy and modern science fiction. He is a living person; he has a will and gives himself a name. It matters to God what happens (Exodus 3:13-15).
• *He is spirit.* God is personal, but must not be limited by human ideas of personality. He is not a human being. 'For I am God, and not man – the Holy One among you' (Hosea 11:9).
• *He is eternal.* 'Before the mountains were brought forth or ever you had formed the earth and the world, from everlasting to everlasting you are God' (Psalm 90:2).

• *He is one.* God is a unity and God is unique. God is One and there is only one God. 'There is no one beside me; I am the LORD and there is no other' (Isaiah 45:6).
• *He is hidden.* Sometimes God is found at the point where he seems to be missing. 'Truly you are a God who hides himself, O God and Saviour of Israel' (Isaiah 45:15).
• *He is always present*, *always available*. God is not limited to the Temple, or even to the land of Israel, but is equally accessible in Egypt, Babylon or anywhere else.

The character of God
• *God is holy.* Holiness implies purity and apartness. It is a kind of awesome goodness that is simultaneously attractive and terrifying. 'Who is able to stand before this holy God?' (1 Samuel 6:20). God's holiness brings demands for his people. Because he is holy, they must also be holy (Leviticus 19:2).

And the glory of the LORD will be revealed, and all mankind together will see it.

Isaiah 40:5

SOME OLD TESTAMENT NAMES AND TITLES FOR GOD

The LORD is the everlasting God, the Creator of the ends of the earth. . . . He gives strength to the weary and increases the power of the weak.

Isaiah 40:28-29

Ancient of Days
(Aramaic *Attiq yomin*)
Daniel 7:9
The ultimate authority as judge of the world.

Creator *Isaiah 40:28*

Eternal God (Hebrew *El Olam*) *Genesis 21:33*

Father (Greek *Theos ho Pater*) *Malachi 2:10*

God of Mountains
(Hebrew *El Shaddai*)
Genesis 17:1; 49:25
God is all-powerful.

Most High (Hebrew *El Elyon*)
Genesis 14:18-20
God, the maker of heaven and earth.

God of all humanity
Jeremiah 32:27

God of the covenant
(Hebrew *El Berit*)
Judges 9:46
Maker and keeper of his covenants.

God of heaven
Nehemiah 2:4

God of Israel
(Hebrew *El Elohe-Yisra'el*)
Genesis 33:20

Holy One *Job 6:10*

Holy One of Israel
(Hebrew *Qedosh Yisra'el*)
Isaiah 1:4

I AM *Exodus 3:14*

Judge (Hebrew *Shapat*)
Genesis 18:25

King *Jeremiah 10:7*

Living God
Deuteronomy 5:26

LORD (Hebrew *Yahweh*)
Exodus 3:13-16

God of Armies
(Hebrew *Yahweh-seba'ot, Sabaoth*)
1 Samuel 1:11; 17:45
God is all-powerful.

LORD is my Banner
(Hebrew *Yahweh-nissi*)
Exodus 17:15
God gives us victories.

LORD is Peace
(Hebrew *Yahweh-shalom*)
Judges 6:24
God brings us inner harmony.

LORD is There
(Hebrew *Yahweh-shammah*)
Ezekiel 48:35
God will be with his people at the end of history.

Lord, Master (Hebrew *Adonai*) *Psalm 2:4*
God has authority.

LORD Provides
(Hebrew *Yahweh-jireh*)
Genesis 22:14

LORD Our Righteousness
(Hebrew *Yahweh-tsidkenu*) *Jeremiah 23:6*
By God's acts he declares and makes his people righteous.

Most High (Aramaic *Illaya*)
Daniel 7:18
God has final authority.

• *God is all-powerful.* His power is not arbitrary, but purposefully applied, working towards a goal. God is able to fulfil his goals.

• *God is righteous and just.* Righteousness, sometimes seen as an aspect of his holiness, includes – but is more than – doing what is ethically right. For humans, it involves conforming to a norm – to an accepted standard or ideal pattern. So it makes sense to talk about righteous weights and balances, or righteous behaviour, which conforms to the Law. God's righteousness makes him concerned to see that justice is done.

• *God is faithful.* There is no adequate equivalent in English for the Hebrew word *chesed*, which is sometimes translated as loving-kindness or steadfast love, but also includes faithfulness, loyalty and total dependability. It is one of the commonest words used to describe God's attitude towards Israel.

• *God is love.* God's love for Israel is what makes the covenant more than a formal agreement. Many words are used for God's love, meaning desiring, taking pleasure in, attaching oneself to, knowing, caring about – and there is a strong link with *chesed*. Love involves both the will and strong emotion. God's love for Israel is spontaneous; it is not a result of Israel's deserving it. God chose to love them.

• *God is jealous.* God's jealousy is linked to his holiness and power – but also to his love. He is sovereign, and cannot share the love and worship of his people with other gods. The Hebrew word for this includes no sense of petulance or envy, so perhaps the term 'jealous' is misleading; 'zealous' might be a better translation.

• *God is angry.* God's jealousy may express itself in anger, which is linked with his holiness. It is different from human anger, and is never malicious or capricious. God is angry about evil. Unlike his love, his anger is momentary. 'His anger lasts only a moment, but his favour lasts a lifetime' (Psalm 30:5).

• *God is merciful and gracious.* This too is linked with *chesed* and with love. God's sovereignty means that he is free to give human beings more than they deserve, and he delights to do this. Mercy and forgiveness are pictured as freely available to those who, in repentance and faith, turn back to God. God cares about human beings and longs for their restoration. His mercy is never grudging.

The Jewish festivals

Passover (Pesach) and **Unleavened Bread**
Commemorated Israel's deliverance from Egypt
Exodus 12:11-30; Leviticus 23:4-8; Numbers 28:16-25; Matthew 26:17
Each family celebrated the deliverance of the Hebrews from slavery in Egypt, and symbolically re-enacted the first Passover as they ate their own special meal. The celebration continued for seven days as they commemorated the Exodus and wilderness wanderings by eating unleavened bread, recalling the haste with which they left Egypt, when they did not have time to let the bread rise.

Firstfruits
Leviticus 23:9-14; Numbers 28:26-31
A barley harvest feast at the end of the seven-day Passover festival

Second Passover
Numbers 9:9-13; 2 Chronicles 30:2-3
For those unable to keep the first Passover

Pentecost
(Shavuot, Weeks, Firstfruits, Harvest)
A celebration of harvest
Leviticus 23:9-22; Deuteronomy 16:9-12; Acts 2:1
At Pentecost, seven weeks after Passover, the Jews celebrated the gathering in of the wheat harvest. The priests offered symbolically two loaves made from new flour. This feast also celebrated the giving of the Law to Moses at Mount Sinai.

Trumpets
(Rosh Hashanah, New Year, Judgement and Memorial)
A time of reckoning with God
Leviticus 23:23-25; Numbers 29:1-6
This two-day celebration marked by the blowing of trumpets to greet the civil new year, was also the beginning of the most solemn month in the year. The Israelites prepared themselves for Yom Kippur, which comes ten days later, by praising God, whose standard they had failed to meet, and recounting his greatness, love and mercy.

Day of Atonement
(Yom Kippur)
The most holy day in the Jewish year
Leviticus 16; 23:26-32; Numbers 29:7-11
On Yom Kippur Israel confessed the nation's sins, and asked forgiveness and cleansing. A scapegoat was sent into the desert, carrying symbolically the people's sin. The high priest entered the Most Holy Place of the Temple on this day alone. Recognising this day as the holiest of feast days, Jews neither ate nor drank for 24 hours.

Tabernacles
(Succoth, Booths, Ingathering)
Commemorated Israel's wanderings in the wilderness
Leviticus 23:33-44; Numbers 29:12-40; John 7:2
A joyful harvest festival celebrating the gathering of the grapes. During the seven-day celebration the people thanked God for protecting them in the wilderness and for the harvest. For seven days they lived in shelters made of branches, to remind them of their time living in tents in the wilderness.

The Hebrew calendar

Month	Name (name before Exile)	Modern equivalent
1	**Nisan** (Abib)	March/April
2	**Iyyar** (Ziv)	April/May
3	**Sivan**	May/June
4	**Tammuz**	June/July
5	**Abu** (Ab)	July/August
6	**Elul**	August/September
7	**Tishri** (Ethanim)	September/October
8	**Heshvan** (Bul) = Marcheshvan	October/November
9	**Chislev**	November/December
10	**Tebeth**	December/January
11	**Shebat**	January/February
12	**Adar**	February/March

The Jewish year is strictly lunar, with lunar months averaging 29.5 days, giving 354 days in a year. A thirteenth month, Veader, was added about every three years to align the calendar with the solar year.

A Jewish family celebrate Passover in modern Israel.

the expulsion of the Syrians by Judas Maccabeus in 164 BC, and the cleansing and rededication of the Jerusalem Temple, which the Syrians had desecrated. Lighting a new candle each day for eight days, the Jews commemorated the miracle of the Temple's holy candelabrum: for the rededication they had only one day's worth of consecrated oil but it burnt for eight full days, the time required to consecrate more oil.

Purim (Lots)
Celebrated the failure of Haman's plot to destroy the Jews
Esther 9:21, 27-28
A time of feasting and joy when the people celebrated the deliverance of the Jews from death through the bravery of Queen Esther of Persia.

Simhath Torah
(Rejoicing in the Law)
Marked the end of the annual reading of the entire cycle of the Law
A joyful celebration giving thanks for the Pentateuch – the first five books of the Hebrew Bible.

Dedication
(Hanukkah, Lights, Maccabees)
Commemorated the rededication of the Temple in 164 BC
1 Maccabees 4:41-49;
John 10:22
On Hanukkah the Jews celebrated

Weather	Harvests/agriculture	Festivals/Holy days
Rain ('latter rain')	Flax harvest	•14th Passover •15th–21st Unleavened Bread •16th Firstfruits
Dry	Barley harvest	•14th Second Passover
Warm and dry	Wheat harvest	•6th Pentecost (= Harvest, Firstfruits, Shavuot, Weeks)
Hot and dry		
Very hot and dry		
Very hot and dry	Date harvest Grape harvest Summer fig harvest	
Rain begins	Olive harvest Grape harvest	• 1st Trumpets (= Rosh Hashanah) •10th Day of Atonement (= Yom Kippur) •15th–21st Tabernacles (= Ingathering, Succoth, Booths) •22nd Simhath Torah (= Solemn Assembly)
Rainy ('former rain') Ploughing	Olive harvest	
Cool and rainy	Winter fig harvest Sowing	•25th–2nd Tebeth Dedication (= Hanukkah, Lights)
Cold, hail and snow	Sowing	
Warmer and rainy	Almond blossoms Sowing	
Thunder and hail	Citrus fruit harvest Sowing	•14th–15th Purim (= Lots)

171

The Tabernacle – God's tent

About 50 chapters of the Bible are concerned with the Tabernacle, indicating its importance in the development of the religious life of Israel.

Why the Tabernacle?
The Tabernacle was a portable sanctuary – a holy place for worshipping God – created in the desert in response to the demand for mobility. It symbolised God's presence with his people, and was a place where his will was communicated.

When the people of Israel were journeying from Egypt through the wilderness towards the Promised Land they were living in tents, so the Tabernacle was also a tent. It was designed so that it could easily be dismantled when the Israelites moved their camp and reassembled at the next halting place.

The Tabernacle and the Temple

The Israelites anticipated that once peace and security had been secured, a permanent national shrine would be set up (Deuteronomy 12:10-11). However, this was not realised until the time of King Solomon, when the first Temple was erected (2 Samuel 7:10-13; 1 Kings 5:1-5). The Tabernacle was thus a forerunner of the Temple. The Tabernacle and Temple are closely linked both historically, and by their similarity in construction and underlying theology.

How we know about the Tabernacle

The fullest and most reliable source of information about the Tabernacle is in the book of Exodus. Exodus 25–28 prescribes the construction and furniture of the Tabernacle, while Exodus 35–40 describes how it was made. We are also helped by the specifications for Solomon's Temple (1 Kings 6; 2 Chronicles 3–4), and the Temple seen in a vision by the prophet Ezekiel (Ezekiel 40–43), both of which followed the basic plan of the Tabernacle.

An artist's impression of the Tabernacle in the wilderness near Mount Sinai. Notice the camp of Israel is set up around the central Tabernacle.

The outer courtyard
and its furniture

The courtyard
(Exodus 27:9-18; 38:9-20)
The courtyard was a rectangle, 100 cubits (about 150 feet/46 metres) long on its north and south sides and 50 cubits (about 75 feet/23 metres) wide on its east and west sides.

See page 117 for a description of the Tabernacle.

The framework of the fence

Enclosing this space was a fence, with a framework consisting of 60 acacia wood pillars, 5 cubits (about 7.5 feet/2.3 metres) high (Exodus 27:18). The pillars were probably round, and about 5 inches (12 centimetres) in diameter, with 20 on each side and 10 at each end. The base of each pillar stood in a brass socket, and each pillar was held upright by cords (Exodus 35:18) fastened to brass tent pegs (Exodus 27:19) driven into the ground, both inside and outside the court.

Curtain rods ('bands') rested on hooks near the top of the pillars, serving as the top rail of the fence, and keeping the pillars the right distance apart. These rods were made of shittim wood, covered with silver; the hooks and protecting caps on the pillars were also made of silver (38:17, 19). There were also hooks at the bottom of the pillars, to which the bottom edge of the curtains was fastened.

The curtains

Curtains of fine-twined linen (probably like modern duck) and probably white or natural in colour were sewn together end to end, to form a continuous screen all around the Tabernacle area. Each curtain was 22.5 feet (about 6.9 metres) long, and the curtains were 7.5 feet (about 2.3 metres) high so that no one could look over the fence.

The entrance
(Exodus 27:16-18; 38:18)

A central entrance about 30 feet (about 9 metres) wide and 5 cubits (about 7.5 feet/2.3 metres) high was located in the eastern end of the Tabernacle court. The entrance was screened by an embroidered curtain woven from blue, purple and scarlet material, and 'finely twisted linen' (Exodus 38:18) – that is, the warp consisted of bleached linen threads and the woof of strips of wool dyed alternately blue, purple and scarlet. The entrance curtain was probably set back from the fence, allowing entry at both ends. This was the only entrance into the Tabernacle courtyard.

The altar of burnt offering
(Exodus 27:1-8; 38:1-7)

Anyone entering the Tabernacle court immediately confronted the bronze altar of burnt offering, where sacrifices were offered to God. According to the Mosaic Law, this was the only place where sacrifices could be made. The altar stood at the east end of the court, probably about halfway between the entrance and the Tabernacle itself (Exodus 40:29), reminding the people that they could not approach God except by the place of sacrifice.

The altar was a hollow box of acacia wood, 5 cubits (about 7.5 feet/2.3 metres) square by 3 cubits (about 4.5 feet/1.4 metres) high – small compared with the gigantic altar in Solomon's Temple (2 Chronicles 4:1). It was lined with sheets of bronze inside and out to protect it from the heat, and was light enough to be carried on bronze-covered poles that passed through bronze rings fixed at each corner.

An artist's impression of sacrifice at the altar of burnt offering.

The history of the Tabernacle

The wilderness years

It was at Mount Sinai, today identified with Jebel Musa, at the base of which stands St Catherine's Monastery, that Moses received the Law. When the Jews turned from God and started to worship the golden calf in the wilderness, Moses angrily shattered the tablets of stone inscribed with the Ten Commandments. After the people repented, Moses climbed Mount Sinai again to intercede with God.

Constructing the Tabernacle
God renewed his covenant with Israel, gave them a second copy of the Law, and invited them to offer materials with which to construct the Tabernacle. The people responded generously, and gave much more than was needed (Exodus 36:5-6); the work went ahead under the direction of Bezalel and Oholiab (Exodus 35:30; 36:2).

The Tabernacle was completed on the first day of the first Jewish month (Abib, March-April) in the second year after the Exodus from Egypt. The cycle of sacrifices and worship that God had laid down for the new sanctuary now began (Exodus 40:2).

The Tabernacle in the camp
Unlike the provisional tabernacle (Exodus 33:7-14), this permanent Tabernacle stood in the very centre of the Jewish encampment. It must have appeared very impressive, with Mount Sinai as its backdrop. Moses and Aaron set up their tents on the east side of the Tabernacle, and the other three families of priests on the other three sides – the family of Kohath to the south; the family of Gershon on the west; and the family of Merari on the north – acting as the 'bodyguard' of Israel's ruler, God. This prevented any unauthorised intrusion into

the sacred area. This pattern is still followed by tent-dwellers in the Middle East. In a Bedouin camp the chieftain's tent occupies a central position with the families grouped around it in their allotted positions.

Outside the inner square, in a wider square, the tribes of Judah, Zebulun and Issachar camped on the eastern side, under the standard of Judah; Ephraim, Manasseh and Benjamin to the west, under the standard of

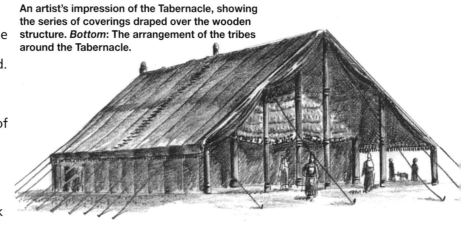

An artist's impression of the Tabernacle, showing the series of coverings draped over the wooden structure. *Bottom*: The arrangement of the tribes around the Tabernacle.

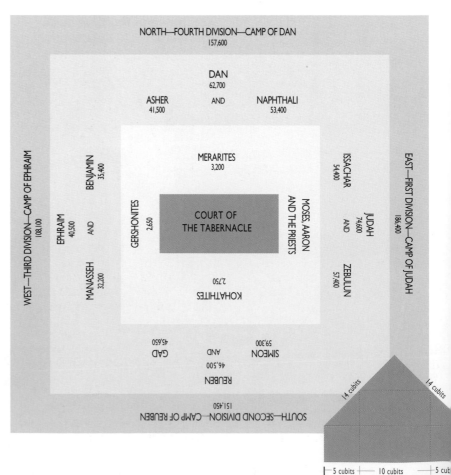

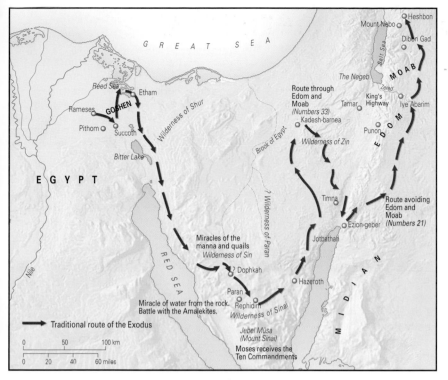

A nineteenth century engraving of Mount Sinai, or Mount Horeb.

named in the itinerary in Numbers 33 are today unknown. Two sites can be definitely identified: Hazeroth and Kadesh. Hazeroth has usually been identified with Ein Hudra, an oasis west of the Red Sea. Kadesh-barnea is today usually identified with the valley of Ein el-Qudeirat, a lush oasis based around the biggest spring in the area. It is situated in northern Sinai, at the crossroads of two major routes across the desert, a site surveyed by the British archaeologist Leonard Woolley and T.E. Lawrence – 'Lawrence of Arabia' – just before World War I.

Rebellion in the camp
The Israelites arrived at Kadesh nearly a year after leaving Sinai, and it was from here that Moses sent out twelve spies to reconnoitre the Promised Land (Numbers 13). When all the spies except Joshua and Caleb returned with discouraging reports, the Israelites panicked. Their fear turned to fury, and there was a mass uprising. Moses' and Aaron's lives were saved only by the direct intervention of God at the Tabernacle (Numbers 14:1-10). Because of their failure to trust God, the Israelites were condemned to remain in the wilderness until all the adults who had left Egypt had died (Numbers 14:20-25).

A fresh start
It was 38 years before the Israelites, with the Tabernacle in their midst, again set out for the Promised Land. After leaving Kadesh-barnea, circling round Edom, and defeating the Amorites and Og, king of Bashan, they encamped on the Plains of Moab (Numbers 33:48-49), at the oasis formed by springs in the foothills of Moab. From here, Moses climbed Mount Pisgah (also known as Nebo; Deuteronomy 34:1) to look at the Promised Land which he was not to be permitted to enter (Deuteronomy 3:27).

Ephraim; the less conspicuous tribes, Dan, Asher and Naphtali to the north, under the standard of Dan; and Reuben, Simeon and Gad on the south side, under the standard of Reuben.

Breaking camp
The Israelites remained at the foot of Mount Sinai for a year, until the Tabernacle and its furnishings were completed. Then they set out again, heading for the Promised Land (Numbers

10:11). When the Israelite army organised the people for the march, the Tabernacle, carried on the shoulders of Levites, remained at the centre, with the tribes from the east and south sides of the camp marching in front of it, those from the north and west to the rear (Numbers 2).

En route
Although the Bible records the route taken by the Israelites in the wilderness, most of the places

Into the Promised Land

Crossing the River Jordan

When Moses died, Joshua took over the leadership of the people. After sending two spies across the Jordan and into the ancient city of Jericho, he prepared the Israelites to enter the promised land of Canaan. The Ark of the Covenant was taken to the head of the Israelite marching column and the people were ordered to follow the Ark, carried as usual by the Levites, across the River Jordan (Joshua 3:3-4), which dried up for their crossing.

Gilgal, the site of the Israelites' first camp on the west side of the Jordan, became their first permanent settlement, and during the early stages of the Israelite conquest of Canaan, the Tabernacle was located here (Joshua 4:19; 5:10; 9:6; 10:6, 43).

Taking Jericho

The Ark figured prominently in the destruction of Jericho, being carried around the walls of the city every day for seven days, before the 'great shout' on the seventh day, when the city walls fell.

After the Israelites failed to take the city of Ai, through the sin of one man, Achan, Joshua and the elders of the nation fell in front of the Ark and asked God's help.

The central sanctuary

When the Israelites had captured the central highlands of Palestine, the Tabernacle was transferred there. Although the exact location is not clear, it was probably sited in turn at Shiloh, near Bethel, in the mountains of Ephraim (modern Seilun; Joshua 18:1, 10; 22:9, 12); Shechem, a city lying between Mount Gebel and Mount Gerizim, where the desert covenant was renewed (Joshua 8:30-35; 24); at Mizpah (Judges 20:1); and at Bethel (Judges 20:18, 26).

Finally the Ark was moved back to Shiloh, perhaps because of the town's central position, and because it belonged to the powerful tribe of Ephraim.

The Tabernacle remained in Shiloh for the entire period of the judges; but the Ark of the Covenant was taken from it in the time of Eli (1 Samuel 4:4) and never returned. By the time of the prophet Samuel, the sanctuary at Shiloh, now called the 'house of the Lord', appears as a more permanent structure with doors (1 Samuel 1:7; 3:3, 15; see also the Mishnah). Probably this building replaced the earlier Tabernacle, which, with the passing of years and the wear and tear of moving, had deteriorated. It is certainly unlikely that the Moses' Tabernacle survived beyond the period of the judges.

The capture of the Ark

During the time of Samuel, the warlike 'Sea-Peoples' or Philistines, who lived along the Mediterranean coast, threatened the existence of the Israelites. In about 1050 BC, after a major defeat at Aphek, the leaders of Israel took the Ark into battle with them to try to compel God to fight for his people (1 Samuel 4:1-11). But the Philistines were again victorious. They captured the Ark and destroyed the sanctuary at Shiloh (as archaeologists have shown).

After the battle, the Philistines first took the Ark to Ashdod, where its presence caused the Philistine deity Dagon to collapse, and plague to break out. It was therefore moved on to Gath and then to Ekron, but the plague went with it. At last, seven months after its capture, the terrified people of plague-ridden Ekron returned the Ark to Beth-shemesh in Israel (1 Samuel 6:12).

From Beth-shemesh, the Ark was sent to Kiriath-jearim, above the modern village of Abu Ghosh, only 8 miles from Jerusalem, where it was kept for 20 years (1 Samuel 7:1-2). Here Eleazar looked after it in his own house.

King David's Tabernacle

When David became king over all Israel, he made Jerusalem his capital city. Here, on Mount Zion, next to his palace, he set up a new tabernacle for the Ark.

In his first attempt to bring the Ark to its new home, David did not observe the scriptural instruction for it to be carried on priests' shoulders, but transported it in a cart. When the oxen stumbled, Uzziah held the Ark to steady it, and was killed for his lack of reverence (1 Samuel 6:1-7).

Frightened by this disaster, David now stored the Ark for a further 20 years in the house of the foreigner Obed-Edom (2 Samuel 6:10).

The Ark was finally carried into Jerusalem on the shoulders of Levites (1 Chronicles 15–16), with David dancing before it.

Other tabernacles

There are references to a tabernacle at Nob in the reign of King Saul

---

The Ark of the Covenant

The ark was the portable holy chest built to hold the most sacred relics from Israel's history. It was made according to instructions given to Moses by God, and is sometimes also known as "the ark of the Testimony" and "the ark of God". It measured 1.1 x 0.7 x 0.7 metres, and was made of acacia wood overlaid with gold. Two cherubim stood on top.

The ark served as a container for the two tablets of the law that Moses brought down Mount Sinai, a sample jar of manna and Aaron's rod that budded. The ark's cover, also known as the "mercy-seat", was the place where the high priest came once a year on the Day of Atonement to spill blood to atone for the people's sins. The Israelites believed that God's presence was manifest between the two cherubim on the lid of the ark. This made the ark the holiest item in the worship of ancient Israel.

The Philistine deity Dagon.

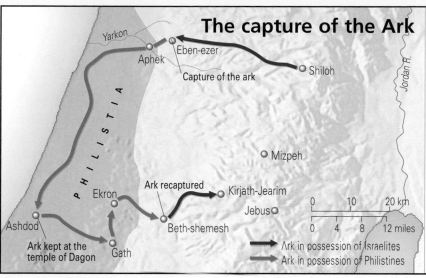

The capture of the Ark

Yarkon

Aphek
Eben-ezer
Shiloh
Capture of the ark

Jordan R.

P H I L I S T I A

Mizpeh

Ark recaptured
Ekron
Kirjath-Jearim
Jebus

Ashdod
Beth-shemesh

Ark kept at the temple of Dagon
Gath

0   10   20 km
0 4 8 12 miles

→ Ark in possession of Israelites
→ Ark in possession of Philistines

Artist's impression of the Ark of the Covenant.

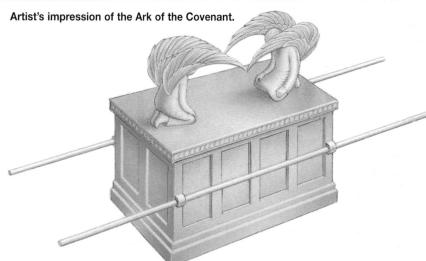

Upon its return to Israel, the Ark was kept at Kiriath-jearim for 20 years.

(1 Samuel 21:1-6) and at Gibeon (1 Chronicles 16:39; 20:29). In David's day the bread of the Presence was kept at Nob (21:1-6), implying that at least some of the Tabernacle's sacred furniture was also situated there.

We know that at the close of David's reign the high place at Gibeon possessed relics from the original Tabernacle, including the altar of burnt offering, which was still in use (1 Chronicles 16:39; 21:29; see also 1 Kings 14; 2 Chronicles 1:3-6).

Solomon's Temple

An artist's impression of Solomon's Temple, with the great laver, or bronze ritual washing basin. The capitals of the pillars on either side of the Temple doorway were each decorated with 200 pomegranates.

King David was not permitted to build a Temple, though he collected money and materials for its construction. His son, Solomon, built the first Temple in Jerusalem. It was twice the size of the portable Tabernacle which it replaced and on which it was modelled.

Solomon used the forced labour of foreigners living in the country– 80,000 quarrymen and 70,000 porters – to cut and transport the huge stones for building the Temple; 30,000 Israelites collected cedar and juniper wood from Lebanon; and there were 3.850 supervisors. The Temple was panelled with cedar, on which skilled Phoenician craftsmen carved cherubim, flowers and palm trees, before the whole interior was overlaid in gold.

Outside the Temple stood a three-tiered bronze altar and a great bronze basin (the laver) for ritual washing. It was supported by twelve bronze oxen, three at each point of the compass.

The double doors of cypress wood, which opened into the Holy Place, were flanked by two pillars, on the right Jachin, and on the left Boaz.

Solomon's Temple, a fulfilment of King David's dream, was a monument to the glory of God (see 1 Kings 6–7; 2 Chronicles 3–4).

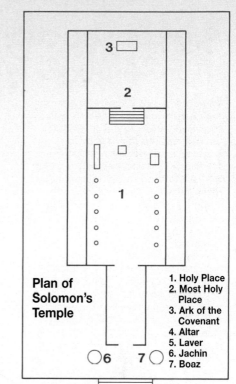

Plan of Solomon's Temple

1. Holy Place
2. Most Holy Place
3. Ark of the Covenant
4. Altar
5. Laver
6. Jachin
7. Boaz

A reconstruction of Solomon's Temple

David purchased the site for a temple for 50 silver shekels from Araunah the Jebusite. This site is identified with Mount Moriah – today the Temple Mount, Jerusalem – where Abraham had years before been told to sacrifice his son Isaac. The building of the Temple began in the fourth year of Solomon's reign, about 959 B.C., and took seven years to complete. It was a national project of immense size. To preserve the holiness of the Temple site, and minimise noise, most of the masonry and carpentry was completed elsewhere, before the components were assembled on the actual site. Detailed accounts of the Temple's construction in the Bible enable us to make a quite accurate reconstruction of Solomon's Temple.

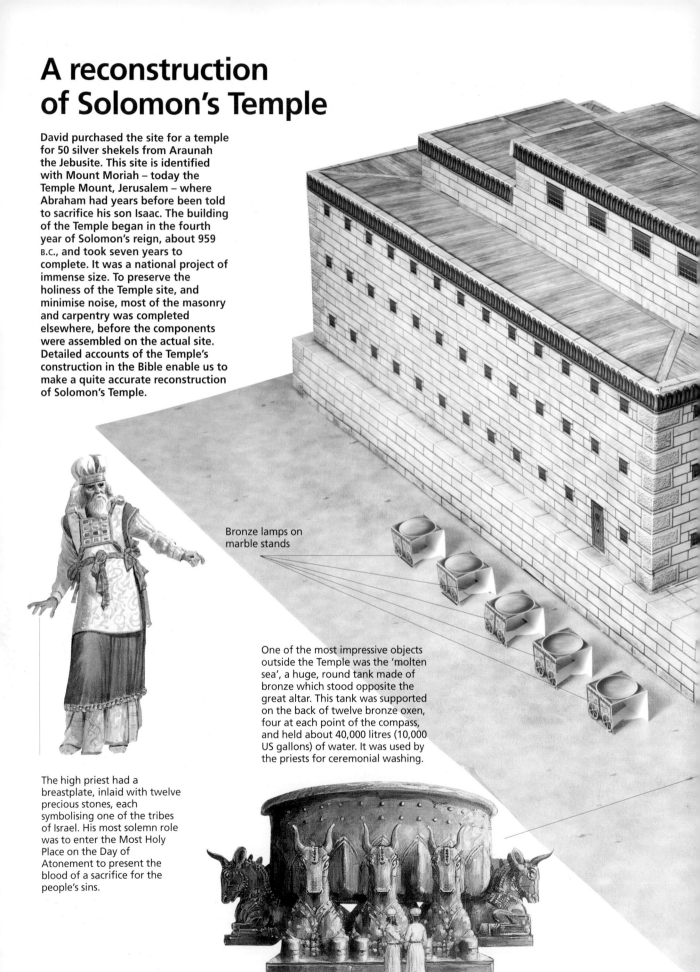

Bronze lamps on marble stands

One of the most impressive objects outside the Temple was the 'molten sea', a huge, round tank made of bronze which stood opposite the great altar. This tank was supported on the back of twelve bronze oxen, four at each point of the compass, and held about 40,000 litres (10,000 US gallons) of water. It was used by the priests for ceremonial washing.

The high priest had a breastplate, inlaid with twelve precious stones, each symbolising one of the tribes of Israel. His most solemn role was to enter the Most Holy Place on the Day of Atonement to present the blood of a sacrifice for the people's sins.

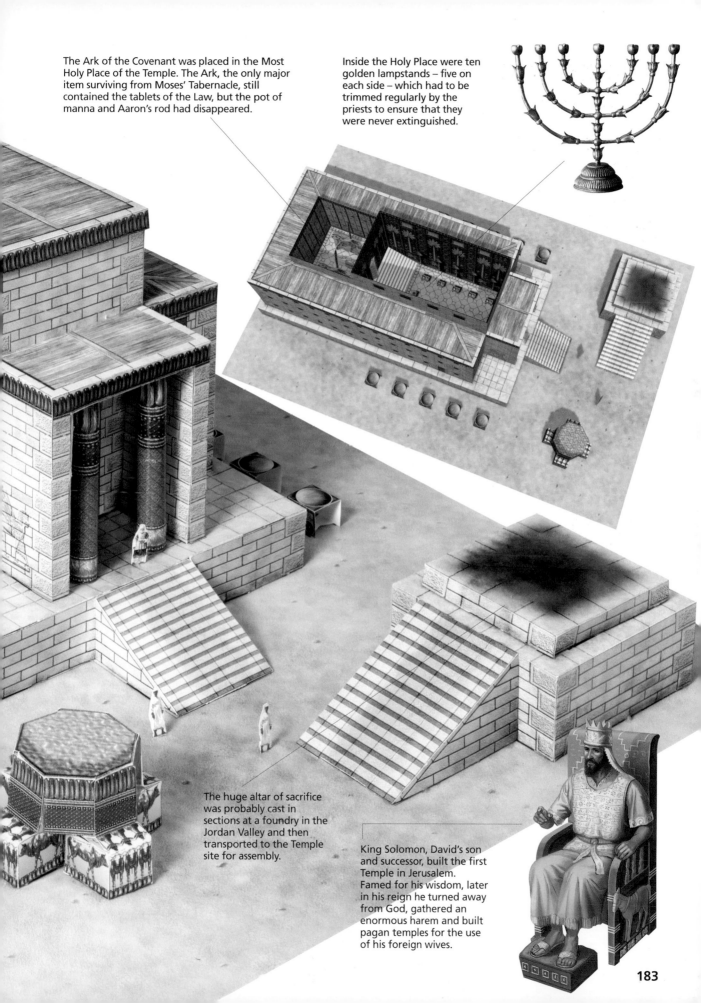

The Ark of the Covenant was placed in the Most Holy Place of the Temple. The Ark, the only major item surviving from Moses' Tabernacle, still contained the tablets of the Law, but the pot of manna and Aaron's rod had disappeared.

Inside the Holy Place were ten golden lampstands – five on each side – which had to be trimmed regularly by the priests to ensure that they were never extinguished.

The huge altar of sacrifice was probably cast in sections at a foundry in the Jordan Valley and then transported to the Temple site for assembly.

King Solomon, David's son and successor, built the first Temple in Jerusalem. Famed for his wisdom, later in his reign he turned away from God, gathered an enormous harem and built pagan temples for the use of his foreign wives.

183

The synagogue

In Jesus' time, there was at least one synagogue in nearly every town and village (Luke 4:14-30). The Jews started having services in synagogues during the Exile, when they had no access to the Temple. The synagogues developed their own form of service, parallel to that of the Temple.

There were synagogue services every Sabbath, and on the Jewish festival days. The synagogue was also open for prayer three times a day.

In the main room of the synagogue stood a seven-branched lampstand, or *Menorah,* and a lamp of eternity. During worship there would be prayers, Scripture readings and praise.

The sacred rolls of the Law (the *Torah*) were kept in a special cupboard.

Sometimes in larger buildings there would be a courtyard with small rooms leading off it built on to the main structure.

Women and children
Women and children were allowed only into the gallery of the synagogue.

Above: The fourth-century Capernaum synagogue has been carefully excavated and partially reconstructed.

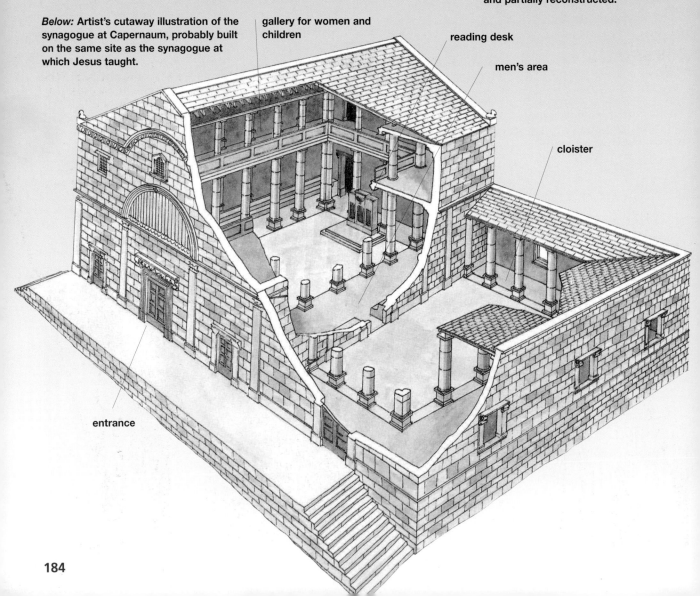

Below: Artist's cutaway illustration of the synagogue at Capernaum, probably built on the same site as the synagogue at which Jesus taught.

gallery for women and children

reading desk

men's area

cloister

entrance

Jewish sects and parties

In New Testament times there were a number of political, religious and social groups.

RELIGIOUS

Pharisees
First called the *Hasidim* ('pious ones'), this religious group supported the Maccabeans in the revolt against Antiochus. They studied both the Jewish Law (written Law), and the traditions that had been added to the Law (the spoken Law). They believed that their strict observance of these traditions made them the only righteous Jews. Later they became known as Pharisees ('separate ones'), and held religious power in Jerusalem during Jesus' ministry (Matthew 5:20; Luke 11:42), when some of them were Jesus' most bitter opponents.

Sadducees
A small Jewish sect made up mainly of priests and members of the Sanhedrin council (Acts 4:1; 5:17). Their dislike of all change and a desire to keep everything as it was led to frequent quarrels with the Pharisees. Their name means 'righteous ones' in Hebrew. Their Bible was limited to the Pentateuch and they rejected doctrines not found there. They held that no oral law or tradition was equal to Scripture. In contrast to the Pharisees, they did not believe in a resurrection, angels or spirits (Mark 12:18; Acts 23:8). The Sadducees kept on good terms with the Romans when they came to power.

Essenes
A Jewish sect whose members lived a form of monastic life. Living in isolated communities such as Qumran, their name means 'saintly' ones. They sought purity and communion with God through self-denial, temperance and contemplation.

POLITICAL

Herodians
A sect of Jews who agreed to subject themselves to Roman rule. They believed that Herod and his descendants were the last hope for Israel to maintain their own national government. They helped plot the death of Jesus (Mark 12:13; Matthew 22:16).

Zealots
A strongly nationalistic Jewish sect. They combined the religious practices of the Pharisees with hatred for any non-Jewish government. They believed it was God's will for Jews to take military action against Rome. (Matthew 10:4).

Galileans
A sect that believed that foreign control of Israel was against Scripture, and therefore refused to acknowledge foreign rulers. Similar politically to the Zealots, the Galileans were eventually absorbed into that sect (Acts 5:37).

SOCIAL

Scribes
Jewish men who copied, taught and explained the Law. Many scribes were Pharisees, and, like them, believed in the authority of oral traditions (Luke 20:46). As teachers of the Law, they were important in Jewish society, and also served as judges or lawyers.

Nazirites
Jews who took a vow of separation for a limited time or for life. Easily recognised because they vowed never to cut their hair, Nazirites separated themselves by their lifestyle to be close to God (Numbers 6:2, 4-6; Judges 13:5; 1 Samuel 1:11; Acts 18:18; 21:23-24).

Proselytes
A non-Jew who had been converted to Judaism. By being circumcised, a convert was thought to have joined the family of Abraham and was expected to follow the Law.

Publicans
Jews who collected taxes for the Roman government. Their willingness to work in the government was seen as disloyal to Israel (Luke 19:1-9).

Some of the Levites (Temple assistants) served as Temple guards.

Pharisee.

Sadducee.

High Priest.

Herod's Temple

Opposite: The Court of Priests (*background*) and the Court of Women (*foreground*), from Alec Garrard's model.

From Solomon to Herod

Solomon's splendid Temple had a chequered history of neglect, plunder (King Shishak of Egypt captured some of its treasures during the reign of Solomon's son, Rehoboam), misuse (King Manasseh reintroduced pagan practices and 'built altars to all the starry hosts' – 2 Kings 21:4–5) and looting and destruction under the Assyrian King Nebuchadnezzar in 587 B.C. The Ark of the Covenant disappeared at the time of the Exile, and was never recovered or replaced.

Under the leadership of King Zerubbabel and the high priest Joshua, the Israelites rebuilt Solomon's Temple, but on a far inferior scale. When the foundation stone of this Temple was laid, many of 'the older priests wept aloud' in disappointment (Ezra 3:7-13).

The prophets of the Old Testament encouraged the returned Jewish exiles to complete the restoration of the Temple and worship God faithfully there. The prophet Haggai asked pointedly, 'Is it a time for you yourselves to be living in your panelled houses, while this house [the Temple] remains a ruin' (Haggai 1:4)?

The Second Temple was probably improved and more elaborately adorned during the third and second centuries B.C., but we know little about this period in its history. On 15 December 167 B.C. Antiochus IV, the Seleucid king, set up a pagan altar in the Temple, thereby ritually polluting it for the Jews. When the Jewish heroes the Maccabees defeated the Seleucids, they had to cleanse the Temple and rededicate it (1 Maccabees 4:36-59). In 63 B.C. the Roman general Pompey captured Jerusalem.

A political move

King Herod now rebuilt the Temple. While his Temple was unquestionably the largest and most magnificent of the three Temples, it was not built by him for the glory of God, but to curry favour with the Jews, whom he had to keep in order if he wanted to remain a puppet king within the Roman Empire.

The Court of the Women was also known as the Court of Prayer; beyond it women were not allowed to penetrate the innermost courts of the Temple. Worshippers came to the Court of Prayer to meet the priests at the hour of prayer, bringing with them their various sacrifices. Within the Court of Prayer stood four enormous lampstands, lit on special occasions, such as the Festival of Lights.

The Court of the Priests was the innermost court of the Temple, and also the holiest; at its name implies, only priests could enter it. At its centre stood the Temple sanctuary itself, with other buildings and porticoes surrounding it.

Herod the Great

Herodium

Herod loved grandiose building projects. The Herodium ranks as one of the largest fortresses ever built for the protection of one man, and as the greatest engineering feat yet discovered in the inter-testamental period. Built on top of a huge cone-shaped mount 11 kilometres (7 miles) south of Jerusalem, with four towers (three semi-circular, and one rounded), it was protected by an outer double wall with a 3 metres (10 foot) passageway between the walls.

When Jerusalem was destroyed in A.D. 70, the Herodium was one of three major sites of Jewish resistance outside Jerusalem. The second century Jewish Bar Kokhba Revolt also used the Herodium as its headquarters.

Masada

Masada, Herod's other palace fortress, was located overlooking the western shore of the Dead Sea, and served as his summer resort. This virtually impregnable bolt-hole was lavishly furnished, as the excavated bathhouse and storerooms have revealed.

Fanatical Jewish zealots made their last stand against Rome in A.D. 73 at Masada. Rather than be captured by the Romans, they entered into a suicide pact, first killing their wives and children and then themselves.

The remains of Herod's northern palace in profile at Masada.

The Temple and its courts

This overall view of the Temple constructed by Mr Alec Garrard gives a fine impression of the structure and extensive surrounding courts.

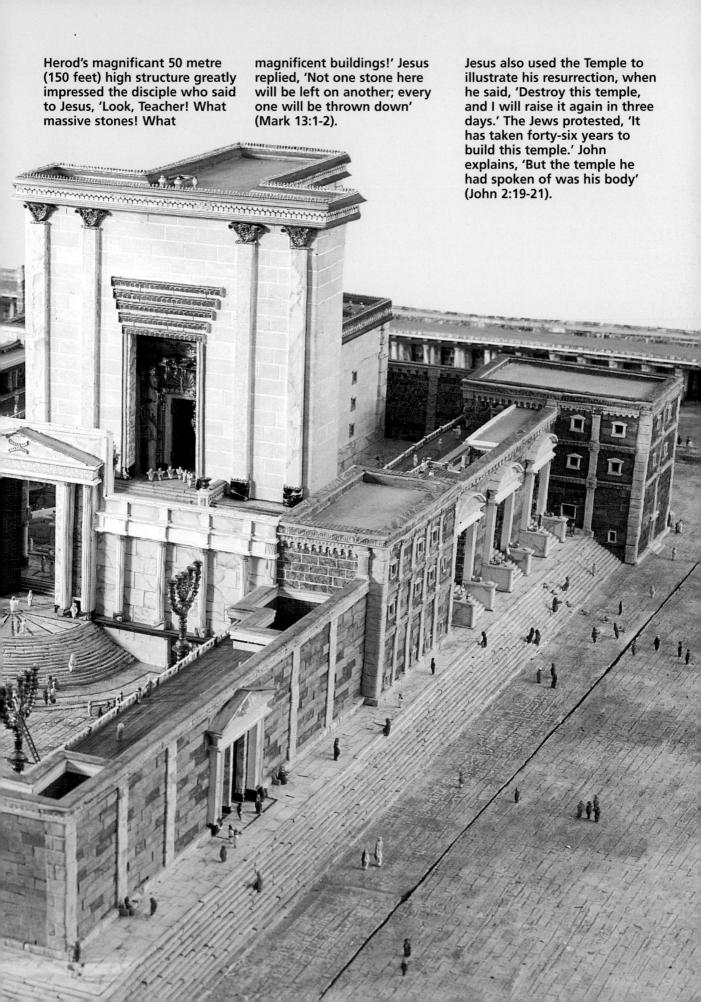

Herod's magnificent 50 metre (150 feet) high structure greatly impressed the disciple who said to Jesus, 'Look, Teacher! What massive stones! What magnificent buildings!' Jesus replied, 'Not one stone here will be left on another; every one will be thrown down' (Mark 13:1-2).

Jesus also used the Temple to illustrate his resurrection, when he said, 'Destroy this temple, and I will raise it again in three days.' The Jews protested, 'It has taken forty-six years to build this temple.' John explains, 'But the temple he had spoken of was his body' (John 2:19-21).

The Temple destroyed

In A.D. 66 the Jews rebelled against their Roman masters. Herod's Temple became the focal point of resistance, from where the Jews held out against the might of Rome. By August of A.D. 70 all of Jerusalem except the Temple was in Roman hands.

As the Temple was one of the wonders of the ancient world, the Romans hesitated before destroying it. But the stubborn zealots refused to surrender, even though they stood no chance against the overwhelming numbers, war-machines, armaments and discipline of the world's best army.

The Romans, under Titus, responded by torching the Temple, setting fire to all its woodwork, and even throwing a lighted torch into the sanctuary itself. Before the building was reduced to a heap of rubble the Romans grabbed some of its priceless furnishings, thinking what excellent trophies they would make for their victory parade back in Rome.

In literal fulfilment of Jesus' prophecy that 'not one stone here will be left on another; every one will be thrown down' (Matthew 24:2), all that remained of Herod's Temple by the time the Roman army had finished was the platform on which it was built.

The massacre

The Romans were always ruthlessly efficient in warfare. In crushing the resistance of the Jewish zealots, the Romans massacred all the inhabitants who had failed to flee to the surrounding mountains. From the time that Titus had laid siege to

The Emperor Vespasian A.D. 69-79.

the city to the time the last stone of the Temple was pulled down it is estimated that more than one million Jews were slaughtered.

The Titus Arch, Rome, built to commemorate Titus' victory over the Jews.

Titus, the successful Roman commander, who crushed the Jews and destroyed their Temple in A.D. 70.

A hoard of silver shekels, dating from A.D. 66–70, with the oil lamp within which they were discovered by archaeologists. They were probably hidden by a frightened Jewish family during the Roman assault on Jerusalem in A.D. 70.

The Temple plundered

Rome was no friend to the early Christians. Under Nero, the emperor who preceded Vespasian, the Christians had been persecuted and blamed for its great fire, and the apostle Paul martyred.

Rome was proud of her military victories. The Titus Arch (*opposite*) was built in Rome and showed soldiers carrying off the priceless treasures they had plundered from the Jerusalem Temple in A.D. 70.

The relief below shows the Romans triumphantly carrying the seven-branched golden lampstand and the table of the showbread. This is the only contemporary depiction of furniture from the Temple extant today.

Varieties of religion in Bible times

False gods of Bible times

Name	Country	Description	Scripture
Artemis (Diana)	Asia	many-breasted fertility goddess	*Acts 19:28*
Asherah symbol – a pole	Canaan	goddess of the sea wife of Baal	*Judges 3:7* *1 Kings 18:19* *2 Kings 21:3* *2 Chronicles 15:16; 24:18*
Ashtoreth (Astarte Queen of Heaven)	Canaan Sidon	mother-goddess fertility goddess	*Judges 2:13; 10:6* *1 Samuel 12:10* *1 Kings 11:5, 33* *Jeremiah 7:18; 44:17-25*
Baal	Canaan	young storm god chief god of Canaan until the Exile; the name Baal is often linked with place names, such as Gad, Peor, etc.	*Judges 2:13;* *1 Kings 16:31-32;18:18-29*
Baal-Zebub	Philistia	god of Ekron	*2 Kings 1:2*
Castor, Pollux	Greece	twin sons of Zeus	*Acts 28:11*
Chemosh	Moab ?Ammon	national god of war	*Numbers 21:29* *Judges 11:24* *1 Kings 11:7, 33* *Jeremiah 48:7*
Dagon	Philistia	national god of rain/agriculture	*Judges 16:23* *1 Samuel 5:2-7*
Hermes (Mercury)	Greece	messenger god, god of cunning, theft	*Acts 14:12*
Marduk (Bel)	Babylon	young storm/war god chief god	*Isaiah 46:1* *Jeremiah 50:2; 51:44*
Molech (Malcam) (Milcom) (Moloch) (?Rephan)	Ammon Israel	national god worshipped with child sacrifice	*Zephaniah 1:5* *Jeremiah 49:1, 3* *Kings 11:5, 7, 33* *Acts 7:43* *Acts 7:43*
Nebo (Nabu)	Babylon	son of Marduk god of wisdom, literature, arts	*Isaiah 46:1*
Nergal	Babylon	god of hunting/the underworld	*2 Kings 17:30*
Rimmon (Hadad)	Damascus	god of thunder, lightning, rain	*2 Kings 5:18*
Tammuz	Babylon	fertility god	*Ezekiel 8:14*
Zeus	Greece	chief of Greek gods	*Acts 14:12*

( ) = alternative name

Men and Women of the Bible

The first families

The families of Adam and Eve, Noah and Abraham and Sarah

Adam and Eve.

Adam *'mankind'*
Adam was the first person created by God. When he ate the forbidden fruit from the tree of the knowledge of good and evil, he brought sin into the world, and with Eve, his wife, had to leave the Garden of Eden.
Genesis 2–3; Luke 3:38; Romans 5:14-19; 1 Corinthians 15:22, 45

Eve *'life'*
Eve, created out of Adam's side, was the first woman and became the mother of all human beings. Tempted by the serpent, she disobeyed God and gave Adam the forbidden fruit to eat.
Genesis 2:18–3:20

Cain *'acquire'*
Cain, Adam and Eve's eldest son, was an arable farmer. God rejected Cain's offering of produce, but accepted his brother's animal sacrifice. This so infuriated Cain that he murdered his brother.
Genesis 4:1-25; Hebrews 11:4

Abel *'shepherd'*
Abel, Adam and Eve's second son, sacrificed the firstborn of his flock, which was accepted by God. Abel was murdered by his jealous brother, Cain.
Genesis 4:1-25; Hebrews 11:4

Noah *'rest'*
Noah, a 'preacher of righteousness', was the only blameless man in a corrupt world. On God's instructions he built a three-tiered ark, 150 metres/450 feet long, in which he and his family were kept safe during the great flood. After the flood, God made a covenant with Noah, and gave the rainbow as a sign that he would never again destroy the world.
Genesis 5–9; Luke 3:36; 1 Peter 3:20; 2 Peter 2:5

Ham *'hot'*
Ham was Noah's youngest son. After the flood, Noah cursed Canaan, one of Ham's four sons, because of Ham's indecent behaviour when Noah was drunk.
Genesis 5:32; 9:18–10:6

Shem *'name' or 'renown'*
Shem, Noah's eldest son, was an ancestor of Jesus Christ.
Genesis 5:32; 9:18-23; 10:21-29; 11:10-26; Luke 3:36

Japheth *'may God enlarge'*
Japheth was Noah's second son.
Genesis 5:32; 9:18-23; 10:2-5

Methuselah *'man of the javelin'*
Methuselah is renowned for being the oldest man to have lived – he was 969 when he died.
Genesis 5:21-27; Luke 3:37

Enoch *'teacher'*
Enoch is one of only two people (the other is Elijah) whom the Bible records as being 'translated' to heaven without dying.
Genesis 5:18-24

Job *'persecuted'*
Job, a godly man who lived in Uz, endured terrible and undeserved sufferings. He lost his family, fabulous wealth, status and health. Job's three friends, Eliphaz, Bildad and Zophar, tried unsuccessfully to counsel him, as did a younger man, Elihu. Nothing helped Job until he humbled himself in God's presence. After Job had prayed for his friends, God restored his health and his fortune.
Job 1–42

Noah and his family leave the ark after the great flood.

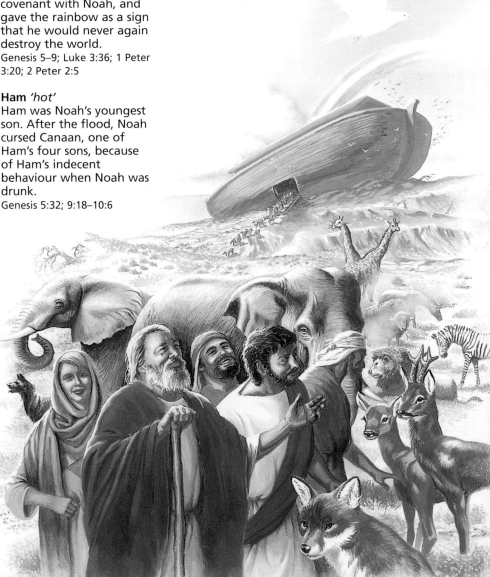

Abraham (Abram) *'father of multitudes'*
Abram was the founder of the Jewish nation. His life was characterised by outstanding faith and by prayer. He lived about 2000 B.C., growing up in the prosperous town of Ur in Mesopotamia. At God's call he set off into the unknown with his wife, Sarah, his father, Terah, and nephew, Lot. After spending some years in Haran, where his father died, he travelled to Canaan. There he lived in the highlands, probably as a wealthy nomad. He believed God's promise that a great nation would descend from him, and he believed that his wife, Sarah, would have a son, though she was past child-bearing years. Later he was willing to obey God's command to sacrifice his son Isaac, believing that God would raise Isaac from the dead. Abraham 'believed God and it was credited to him as righteousness'.
Genesis 11:1–25.11; Matthew 1:1-2; Acts 7:2-3; Hebrews 11:8-19

Sarah *'princess'*
Sarah was Abraham's wife. In fulfilment of God's promise she became the mother of Isaac, in her old age.
Genesis 17:1–18:15; 20:1–21:7; Hebrews 11:11; 1 Peter 3:6

Terah *'turning'*
Terah, born in Ur, travelled with his son Abraham to Haran, where he died.
Genesis 11:24-32; Luke 3:34

Lot *'covering'*
Lot, Terah's grandson and Abraham's nephew, chose to live in the evil town of Sodom. He escaped just before Sodom was destroyed, but his wife was turned into a 'pillar of salt' because she looked back as she fled.
Genesis 11:31–14:16; 19

Isaac *'laughing'*
Isaac was the long-awaited son whom God had promised to Abraham and Sarah. Isaac and his wife, Rebekah, had twin sons, Esau and Jacob. In Isaac's old age, he was tricked into blessing Jacob with the blessing he had reserved for Esau.
Genesis 21:1–27:40; Matthew 1:2

Jacob *'supplanter'*
Jacob was the son of Isaac and Rebekah, and the younger twin brother of Esau. By devious means, he supplanted his brother and so inherited God's blessing to Abraham. Jacob escaped to Mesopotamia, where he married his uncle Laban's two daughters, Rachel and Leah. As he was returning to Canaan he had an all-night wrestling match with an angel of God and was told, 'Your name will be Israel' *('he struggles with God')*. His twelve sons were the founders of the twelve tribes of Israel.
Genesis 25:21–35:29; 37:1; 42:1–50:14

Rachel *'ewe'*
Jacob worked for Laban for 14 years to win his daughter Rachel in marriage. Joseph and Benjamin were her sons.
Genesis 29–30; 35:18-20

Rebekah *'flattering'*
Rebekah was the granddaughter of Abraham's brother, Nahor, who had remained in Mesopotamia, and she was Laban's sister. She married Isaac. It was Rebekah's idea to trick Isaac into giving Jacob the blessing.
Genesis 24–28

Esau *'hairy'*
The son of Isaac and Rebekah, and elder twin of Jacob, Esau became a skilful hunter. He was the founder of the nation of Edom.
Genesis 25:1–28:9; 32–33; 36; Hebrews 12:16-17

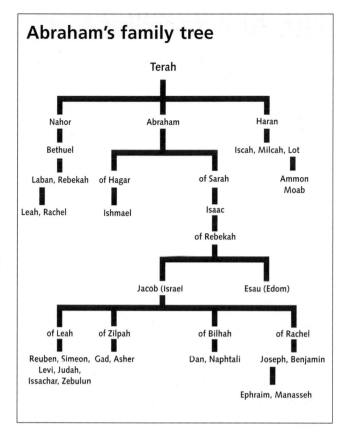

Abraham's family tree

Hagar *'flight'*
Hagar was Sarah's Egyptian servant, who, at Sarah's suggestion, became Abraham's secondary wife. Sadly, when Ishmael was born to Hagar and Abraham, Hagar despised the childless Sarah, and Sarah was jealous of Hagar. After the birth of Isaac, Hagar and Ishmael were sent away.
Genesis 16; 21:8-21; Galatians 4:21-31

Ishmael *'God heard'*
Ishmael, son of Hagar, Sarah's servant, and Abraham, teased his young half-brother Isaac. Sarah forced Abraham to expel Ishmael and Hagar into the desert, where an angel led them to water. Ishmael had twelve sons, each of whom became a tribal chief.
Genesis 16–17; 25:12-18; 1 Chronicles 1

Melchizedek *'king of righteousness'*
Melchizedek is one of the Bible's most mysterious people, 'without father or mother, without beginning of days or end of life . . .'. He was king of Salem (Jerusalem), priest of the most high God, and he blessed Abraham. Melchizedek was a 'type', or prophetic symbol, of Jesus Christ, who was both king and priest.
Genesis 14:18-20; Psalm 110:4; Hebrews 5:6; 7

Into Egypt – and out

God cares for the Israelites, making Joseph prime minister and Moses their rescuer.

Joseph with two of his brothers.

Joshua.

Joseph *'increaser'*

Joseph, Rachel and Jacob's first son, was given an ornamented coat ('coat of many colours') by his doting father. Joseph's brothers sold him as a slave to passing traders, who in turn sold him to Potiphar in Egypt. Wrongfully thrown into prison, he was set free after he had correctly interpreted Pharaoh's mysterious dreams. Pharaoh appointed him prime minister of Egypt, responsible for collecting and storing food in preparation for the seven years of famine which he had predicted. Famine forced Joseph's family to come to Egypt, where Joseph cared for them all.
Genesis 30:22-24; 37–50

Pharaoh *'great house'*

Some eleven pharaohs are mentioned in the Bible. The pharaoh of Joseph's time was probably not Egyptian but a foreign 'Hyksos' ruler, a Semite like the Hebrews. The 'new' pharaoh in the time of Moses was Rameses II, who re-established an Egyptian dynasty. He treated the Hebrews with great cruelty, forcing them

to be slaves
Genesis 40–41 Exodus 1–15

Benjamin *'son of the right hand'*

Benjamin was Jacob's youngest son and Joseph's brother. His mother Rachel died as he was born. When Benjamin went to Egypt, Joseph kept him there, accusing him of stealing a silver cup. As a result of this trick, Jacob was persuaded to go to Egypt, where he was reunited with Joseph.
Genesis 35:18, 24; 42:4, 36; 43–45

Ephraim *'fruit'*

Ephraim was Joseph's second son and brother of Manasseh. Even though he was the younger of Joseph's sons, his grandfather Jacob gave him the blessing reserved for the firstborn son. Ephraim was an ancestor of one of the twelve tribes of Israel.
Genesis 41:52; 46:20; 48; 50:23

Zipporah *'bird'*

Zipporah was one of seven daughters of Jethro, a priest in Midian, who gave Moses a home when he fled from Egypt. Zipporah became Moses' wife and they had two sons, Gershom and Eliezer.
Exodus 2:16-22; 4:24-26; 18:2-4

Miriam *'loved by God'*

Miriam was Moses' sister. As a child she helped her mother hide her baby brother and kept watch until he was rescued. As an adult, she was a prophetess. For a time she opposed Moses' leadership, and was temporarily punished with leprosy.
Exodus 2:4, 7–8; 15:20-21; Numbers 12; 20:1

Aaron *'enlightened'*

Aaron was Moses' elder brother. Because Moses had protested to God that he was not a good speaker, Aaron became Moses' spokesman to Pharaoh. In the desert Aaron gave in to the Israelites' demand for gods and helped them to make a golden calf. He

became Israel's first high priest and was in charge of God's tent of worship, the Tabernacle.
Exodus 4:14, 30; 5–12; 28–29; 32

Joshua *'God is salvation'*

Joshua had courage and faith. He was both a spiritual and military leader. As Moses' right-hand man in the wilderness, he went to spy out the land of Canaan and, with Caleb, encouraged the people to attack. Though this advice was ignored, he eventually led the people to victory in Canaan, having taken over the leadership on Moses' death. At the end of his life, Joshua challenged the Israelites to follow God faithfully, and said, 'As for me and my household, we will serve the Lord.'
Exodus 17:9-13; 24:13; Numbers 13–14; Joshua

Shrine built over the traditional site in Hebron of the Cave of Machpelah, burial place of the Patriarchs.

Judah *'praise'*

Judah, the fourth son of Jacob and Leah, gained the birthright Reuben forfeited. After his brothers had planned to kill Joseph, Judah persuaded them to sell him to traders instead.
Genesis 29:35; 37:26-28; 38; 43:3-10

Levi *'joined'*

Levi was the third son of Jacob and Leah. With his brother Simeon, he avenged his sister Dinah's rape in a dreadful slaughter of the people of Shechem. Levi was the ancestor of the Levites, the Israelite tribe who served God and his priests in the Tabernacle and later in the Temple.
Genesis 29:34; 34:25-31; 49:5-7

Manasseh *'one who causes forgetfulness'*

Joseph's elder son, Manasseh, was adopted, with his brother Ephraim, by his grandfather Jacob, and so became an ancestor of one of the twelve tribes of Israel. Jacob, however, gave the blessing for the firstborn son to Ephraim and not to Manasseh.
Genesis 41:51; 48

Potiphar *'belonging to the sun-god'*

Potiphar was a captain of the guard, a high-ranking Egyptian official. He bought Joseph from the Ishmaelite traders, and when he saw that 'the Lord was with Joseph' he put him in charge of all his household. Potiphar later threw Joseph into prison, after his wife falsely accused Joseph of attempted rape.
Genesis 37:36; 39

Reuben *'see, a son'*

Reuben, the first of Jacob and Leah's six sons, tried to rescue Joseph after his brothers had planned to kill him.
Genesis 29:32; 35:22-23; 37:21-29; 42:37-38

Moses and Aaron plead with Pharaoh to let their people go.

Moses *'drawer out'*

When Moses was a baby he was saved from death by Pharaoh's daughter, who found him hidden in a reed basket among the bulrushes. She brought him up as her son, a prince of Egypt. But when he was a young man he 'refused to be known as the son of Pharaoh's daughter. He chose to be ill-treated along with the people of God'. After killing an Egyptian taskmaster, he fled to Midian, where he became a shepherd and married Zipporah.

The Exodus

When he went to look at a burning bush in the desert, Moses received God's call to return to Egypt and rescue the people, with his brother Aaron as his spokesman. Moses confronted Pharaoh, but only after the land had been devastated by plagues and all the firstborn Egyptian sons had died did Pharaoh give permission for them to leave – an event remembered every year in the Jewish Passover festival.

In the desert

After leading the people to safety on dry land through the Sea of Reeds, Moses brought them to Mount Sinai, where God gave him the Ten Commandments. He also gave detailed rules for daily living and instructions for the building of the Tabernacle. Moses led the often rebellious people through the desert for 40 years, supervising their conversion from a rabble of discontented slaves to a fighting force. His fiery temper cost him the privilege of entering the Promised Land.

Moses was the first and greatest of the prophets. He gave the Law, and revealed God as *'Yahweh'* ('I am'). He was a man to whom 'God spoke face to face as a man speaks with his friend'.
Exodus 2 – Deuteronomy; Luke 9:28-36; Hebrews 11:23-29

Simeon *'hearing'*

Simeon was Jacob and Leah's second son. With his brother Levi, he avenged his sister Dinah's rape by slaughtering the people of Shechem.
Genesis 29:33; 34:25-30; 49:5-7

Caleb *'dog'*

Caleb was one of the twelve men Moses sent to spy out the Promised Land.

He and Joshua submitted a minority report that, with God's help, they could conquer the land, a courageous stand which almost cost Caleb his life. Out of all those who left Egypt, only Joshua and Caleb eventually entered Canaan.
Numbers 13–14; 26:65

Achan *'troubler'*

Achan stole some of the rich treasures of the conquered city of Jericho, and hid them in his tent. This led to Israel's defeat in the battle against Ai. When Achan's crime was discovered, he was stoned to death and Ai was then captured.
Joshua 7:1–8:29

Judges

Judges were rulers of Israelite tribes when the Israelites were settling down in the Promised Land. A judge was a military leader, who rescued his tribe, or a group of neighbouring tribes, from the enemy, and became a peacetime governor.

Samson *'distinguished'*
Samson, famed for his superhuman strength, ruled Israel for 20 years. Often single-handed, Samson tried to free the Israelites from the 40-year-long domination of the Philistines. As a Nazirite, dedicated to God, Samson never cut his hair. His downfall, which proved to be fatal, was his attraction to women. He revealed to Delilah that the secret of his strength lay in his long hair. While he was asleep, she had his hair cut off.

Philistines, hiding in her room, seized him and blinded him, making him their prisoner. As his hair grew, Samson's strength returned. One day when he was in the Philistine temple, he pushed down its two central pillars. The building collapsed, killing Samson and all the leading Philistine rulers and warriors.
Judges 13–16; Hebrews 11:32

Jael *'mountain goat'*
Jael is remembered for the gruesome way in which she killed the commander of the Canaanite army, Sisera. As he slept in her tent, Jael drove a tent peg through his temples.
Judges 4:17-21; 5:24-27

Sisera *'meditation'*
Sisera commanded Canaan's army for King Jabin. He deployed 900 iron chariots to oppress the Israelites. After one battle he took refuge in

Samson and Delilah.

the tent of Jael, who, after welcoming him with traditional oriental hospitality, drove a tent peg through his head, as he slept.
Judges 4–5

Barak *'lightning'*
After 20 years' oppression at the hands of the Canaanites, Barak, commander of the Israelite army, gained an important victory over Jabin, king of Canaan, thus freeing the Israelites.
Judges 4–5

Deborah *'honey bee'*
Deborah was one of the most successful judges of Israel (and the only woman judge). She made Barak her commander and he defeated the Philistines, ushering in a period of 40 years of freedom from foreign domination.
Judges 4–5

Delilah *'dainty'*
Using her beauty and charm, Delilah badgered Samson into revealing the secret of his strength – the fact that his hair had never been cut. Delilah, who was herself a Philistine, then betrayed Samson into the hands of her people. For this treachery she received a large reward.
Judges 16

Gideon overcomes the Midianites by his midnight surprise attack.

Gideon *'great warrior'*
Though Gideon's family, with at least ten servants, must have been a leading family, Gideon himself had little self-confidence. When called upon by an angel to rescue his tribe from Midianites – fierce nomads from the desert – he protested his insignificance and inability. Told to pull down his father's Baal idol, he did so at night. Instructed to summon an army, it took two 'signs' of a wet, and then a dry, fleece to encourage him, and

a dream whose retelling he overheard, to strengthen his resolve. However, at God's command he reduced his army to a mere 300, and, with a brilliant midnight ploy, his small force terrified and overcame the vast numbers of the enemy. After this victory Gideon became a judge over his tribe. Sadly, he let go of his hard-won dependence on God, allowing his family and tribe to worship a golden ephod.
Judges 6–8

Jephtha *'he opens'*

Before Jephtha, Israel's eighth judge, went into battle against the Ammonites he rashly vowed that, if he won, he would sacrifice the first person who came out of his house to meet him. His only daughter met him, dancing and singing, and Jephtha did as he had vowed.
Judges 11–12

Naomi *'pleasantness'* or *'my joy'*

Naomi was Ruth's mother-in-law. With her husband, Elimelech, she moved from Bethlehem to Moab, where her husband and their two sons, Mahlon and Kilion, died. Naomi would have been destitute if Mahlon's wife, Ruth, had not returned with her to Bethlehem. As a result of Ruth's second marriage, Naomi became the great-great-grandmother of King David.
Ruth

Ruth *'companion'*

Ruth married one of Naomi's sons, Mahlon. Ruth's husband, father-in-law and brother-in-law all died. But Ruth left her home country of Moab to return to Naomi's home in Bethlehem, saying, 'Where you go I will go, and where you stay I will stay. Your people will be my people and your God my God. Where you die I will die and there I will be buried.' In Bethlehem Ruth married a relative of Naomi's, Boaz. Ruth's son, Obed, was the father of Jesse, whose son was King David.
Ruth; Matthew 1:5

Boaz *'quickness'* or *'strength'*

Boaz, a wealthy landowner, lived in the time of the judges. When the foreigner Ruth gleaned for grain in his fields, he protected her from the rough workmen and gave her extra grain. Boaz is

Nebi Samwil, by tradition the burial place of Samuel.

Samuel *'asked of God'*

Samuel, the son of Elkanah and Hannah, was the last great warrior-judge of Israel, and one of the first prophets. His call to be a prophet came when he was still a child serving God in the tabernacle in Shiloh. He did not recognize the voice that spoke his name in the night, and the first three times thought that the old priest Eli was calling him. Samuel's rule marked the transition between the period of judges and kings. In his old age, much against his better judgement, Samuel yielded to the Israelites' desire to be like the other nations and have their own king. Samuel anointed Saul as Israel's first king. But, to Samuel's intense disappointment, Saul betrayed his early promise. Samuel broke off all contact with Saul and anointed David as Saul's successor.
1 Samuel 1–4; 7–16

called a 'kinsman redeemer' as he was a relative (kinsman) of Naomi (Ruth's mother-in-law). When Boaz married Ruth he bought back (redeemed) the property Naomi and her husband had lost when they left Bethlehem. Boaz became the great-grandfather of King David.
Ruth; Matthew 1:5; Luke 3:32

Abimelech *'my father is king'*

Abimelech, Gideon's son, ruled Israel as judge for three years, but killed 70 of his half-brothers to achieve this. He came to a violent end himself, being crushed to death by a millstone.
Judges 8–9

Hannah *'grace'*

Hannah, married to Elkanah, had no children, but Elkanah had children, and Hannah suffered the taunts and jeers of her husband's second wife. During her annual visit to the shrine of Shiloh, Hannah prayed for a son, and vowed that she would dedicate any son of hers to God's service. When God gave her the gift of a son, Samuel, she waited until he was weaned and then gave him to Eli to serve in the sanctuary at Shiloh. Each year Hannah brought Samuel a coat. As a result of Eli's prayers, Hannah had five more children.
1 Samuel 1–2

Eli *'God is exalted'*

Eli was both a priest and a judge over Israel. As priest in the sanctuary at Shiloh, he trained the boy Samuel. But his failure to discipline his two sons, Hophni and Phinehas, brought God's judgement on Israel. The sons were killed by the Philistines, God's covenant-box, the Ark, was captured and Eli, on hearing the news, fell from his chair, broke his neck and died.
1 Samuel 1–4

The first kings

Israel's most illustrious king was David, whom God called 'a man after my own heart'.

King Saul.

Saul *'asked'*
Saul, a Benjamite, the son of Kish, was anointed by Samuel to be Israel's first king. As a young man Saul was outstandingly good-looking. A courageous and charismatic military leader, he was also a genuinely humble and trusting man of God. Sadly, he grew proud and disobedient, so that God rejected him. In his times of madness, David calmed him down by playing the harp, but Saul became jealous of David's popularity and drove him from the court, and from the country. In a battle against the Philistines at Mount Gilboa, Saul was wounded and killed himself.
1 Samuel 8–31; 2 Samuel 1

Jesse *'God exists'*
Jesse, who lived in Bethlehem, was the grandson of Ruth and Boaz, and the father of King David.
Ruth 4:16-22;
1 Samuel 16–17

Jonathan *'God is given'*
Jonathan was King Saul's eldest son. Even though he knew that David, and not he, would be the next king, he was David's best and closest friend. A brave warrior, Jonathan was killed in battle by the Philistines.
1 Samuel 13–14, 18–20, 23, 31; 2 Samuel 1

Goliath *'an exile'* or *'soothsayer'*
Goliath was the Philistine champion and over 3 metres (9 feet) tall. He was heavily armoured, the iron point of his spear alone weighing 7 kilograms. (15 pounds). A stone from David's sling silenced his jeers; he fell unconscious to the ground and David cut off his head.
1 Samuel 17; 22:10

David *'beloved'*
Despite some spectacular failures, including adultery with Bathsheba and the murder of Bathsheba's husband, Uriah, David was Israel's greatest king. He was the youngest son of Jesse and had numerous talents. He played the harp, composed music, wrote poetry (including some of the most beautiful psalms), killed the giant Goliath, defeated Israel's enemies, established Jerusalem as the capital city and ushered in a golden age for Israel. His passionate love for God made him 'a man after God's own heart', and the people saw him as the model for the future Messiah.
1 and 2 Samuel;
1 Chronicles 11–29

David meets the Philistine champion, Goliath.

Absalom *'father of peace'*
Absalom was the deeply loved and ill-disciplined son of David. In his quest to take over the throne, Absalom stole the hearts of the Israelites from his father, King David. A fierce civil war followed. As Absalom was fleeing for his life, his mule went under an oak tree and his long hair was caught in the branches. Against David's orders, Joab then killed him.
2 Samuel 3:3; 13–19

Michal *'who is like God?'*
Michal was Saul's younger daughter and David's first wife. She saved David's life when Saul tried to kill him.
1 Samuel 18–19; 25:44;
2 Samuel 3:13; 6

Bathsheba *'the seventh daughter'*
One evening as David was walking on the palace roof, he saw Bathsheba bathing. David committed adultery with her, had her husband Uriah killed and then married Bathsheba. David was severely rebuked by the prophet Nathan for his sin. Bathsheba and David's first son died, but their next son, Solomon, succeeded David as king.
2 Samuel 11–12; 1 Kings 1–2

Nabal *'foolish'*
Nabal, a wealthy man from Carmel, refused hospitality to David and his men, whereupon his wife, Abigail, sent food. Ten days later, 'the Lord struck Nabal and he died'.
1 Samuel 25

Joab *'God is father'*
Joab was King David's commander-in-chief and his nephew. He was notorious for his ruthlessness, and he killed David's son Absalom when he rebelled against David. Solomon had Joab killed for killing Abner and Amasa, two other army commanders.
2 Samuel 2–3; 14; 18–20; 1 Kings 2:28-35

Solomon *'peace'*
Solomon, son of Bathsheba and King David, whom he succeeded as king of Israel, built and dedicated to God the magnificent Temple in Jerusalem. Unlike his father, Solomon was not a man of war, but excelled at diplomacy. Inheriting a peaceful kingdom, he strengthened it by means of lucrative trading partnerships and marriage alliances. His kingdom became a byword for wealth and luxury. Solomon was internationally renowned for his wisdom. But his many foreign wives led him to lose his first love for God. High taxes, introduced to finance his building projects, left his country impoverished and the people angry.
2 Samuel 12:24; 1 Kings 1–11; 1 Chronicles 22; 28; 29; 2 Chronicles 1–9

Uriah *'God is my light'*
Uriah the Hittite was a totally loyal officer in David's army. David, who had committed adultery with Uriah's wife, Bathsheba, arranged for Uriah to fight in the most dangerous position, where he was killed.
2 Samuel 11–12

Abigail *'source of joy'*
Abigail saved her husband, Nabal, from David's fury with gifts of food for him and his men, including 200 cakes of pressed figs. David, who greatly appreciated her 'good judgement', married Abigail when her husband died.
1 Samuel 25; 27:3; 30:5; 2 Samuel 2:2

Adonijah *'God is my lord'*
Adonijah, David's fourth son, tried, unsuccessfully, to gain the throne of Israel from his weak and very elderly father. Although David forgave Adonijah, Solomon had Adonijah executed for threatening the throne again.
2 Samuel 3:4; 1 Kings 1:1–2:25

Hiram *'my brother is exalted'*
As king of Tyre, Hiram was an ally of both David and Solomon. He supplied cedars from Lebanon and pine logs for the building of the Temple.
2 Samuel 5:11; 1 Kings 5, 9:11-14

Ish-Bosheth *'man of shame'*
When King Saul was killed, the commander of Saul's army, Abner, crowned Saul's son Ish-Bosheth king of the eleven northern tribes of Israel. After Ish-Bosheth's death, David became king of both Judah and Israel.
2 Samuel 2–4

Amnon *'faithful'*
Amnon was King David's first son, who raped his half-sister Tamar. Though David was furious, he failed to punish Amnon. Absalom, Tamar's brother, could never forgive Amnon and killed him two years later, against David's wishes.
2 Samuel 3:2; 13:1-39

Abner *'my father of light'*
Abner, the commander of Saul's army and King Saul's

The Queen of Sheba visits King Solomon.

cousin, crowned Ish-Bosheth as king on Saul's death. Abner became disenchanted with Ish-Bosheth and joined David's army, only to be killed by David's commander, Joab, in revenge for Abner's slaughter of Joab's brother.
1 Samuel 14:50; 17:55-58; 26:7-16; 2 Samuel 2:12-3:39

Ahithophel *'brother of foolishness'*
When David's son, Absalom, revolted against his father, Ahithophel deserted David's service and joined Absalom. The advice Ahithophel gave was 'like that of one who inquired of God'. When Absalom refused Ahithophel's advice, preferring the advice of Hushai, who was in fact a 'mole' planted by David, Ahithophel committed suicide.
2 Samuel 15–17

Abiathar *'father of abundance'*
King Saul had Abiathar's father and the other 84

priests of Nob slaughtered, because they had assisted David. Abiathar, the sole survivor, became joint high priest with Zadok under King David. When David was old and ineffective, Abiathar was one of those who supported David's son Adonijah in his usurpation of sovereignty, but for this he was banished by Solomon.
1 Samuel 22–23; 2 Samuel 8:17; 1 Kings 1:7, 19; 2:26-27; 1 Chronicles 15:11-15; 18:16

Zadok *'righteous'*
Zadok was joint high priest with Abiathar in King David's reign. While Abiathar supported Adonijah's claim to the throne, Zadok remained faithful to David and crowned Solomon as the next king of Israel. Solomon kept Zadok as high priest.
2 Samuel 8:17; 15:24-36; 17:15; 19:11; 1 Kings 1:8; 2:35

Judah's prophets and kings

After Solomon's death, the united kingdom of Israel split into two, with ten tribes forming the northern kingdom of Israel and two tribes forming the southern kingdom of Judah.

Rehoboam in a war chariot.

Rehoboam *'freer of the people'*
Rehoboam, King Solomon's son and successor, inherited a kingdom that, though outwardly peaceful and prosperous, was seething with discontent. When he refused to lessen the burden of taxes, threatening instead to increase taxation, the Israelites rebelled. Only the tribes of Benjamin and Judah stayed loyal to Rehoboam and the house of David.
1 Kings 12; 14:21-31;
2 Chronicles 10-12

Abijah *'the Lord is my father'*
Abijah, Judah's second king, was the son of King Rehoboam. He ruled for three years. Though not a godly king, when an emergency came and his army was threatened, he cried to God for help. His troops rallied and he won a great victory.
1 Kings 14:1–15:8;
1 Chronicles 12

Asa *'healer'*
Asa, Judah's third king, attempted to remove pagan worship from Judah.
1 Kings 15:9-24;
2 Chronicles 14–16

Jehoshaphat *'God is judge'*
Jehoshaphat, Asa's son, was Judah' s fourth king . Though he allied himself with wicked King Ahab, he was himself a godly king, destroying idols and upholding God's laws.
1 Kings 22; 2 Kings 3;
2 Chronicles 17:1–21:3

Jehoram *'God is high'*
Jehoram, the son and successor of Jehoshaphat, married Athaliah, daughter of Queen Jezebel and King Ahab, who led him away from his father's right ways. He murdered his six brothers and allowed the people to worship idols. As Elijah predicted, he died of an incurable disease.
2 Kings 8:16-24;
2 Chronicles 21:4-20

Ahaziah *'God sustains'*
Son of Jehoram, Ahaziah was the sixth king of Judah. Influenced by his mother, Athaliah, he 'did evil in God's sight'. He ruled for less than a year, being murdered by a military commander, Jehu, while visiting his uncle Joram, king of Israel.
2 Kings 8:25-29; 9:14-29;
2 Chronicles 22:1-9

Athaliah *'God is strong'*
Judah's only queen, when Athaliah's son King Ahaziah died, she murdered her grandchildren in order to gain the throne, and behaved like her evil mother, Jezebel. Unbeknown to her, one grandchild, Joash, survived and was kept hidden till he was seven years old. He was then proclaimed king and soldiers murdered Athaliah.
2 Kings 11; 2 Chronicles 22:10–23:21

Joash *'God has given'*
Joash, son of King Ahaziah, became king of Judah when he was seven years old. Under the influence of Jehoiada, the priest, Joash restored the Temple and removed Baal worship. When Jehoiada died, Joash lost his commitment to God, and allowed idol worship to creep back. He ruled for 40 years before his courtiers murdered him.
2 Kings 11–12;
2 Chronicles 24

Amaziah *'God has strength'*
Amaziah, the son of Joash, began well but gradually turned away from God's ways, reintroducing idols. He was assassinated at Lachish after ruling for 29 years.
2 Kings 14:1–22;
2 Chronicles 25

Azariah *'God has helped'*
Azariah, also called Uzziah, was Amaziah's son. He became king when he was 16. Though he served God, Azariah failed to remove the idolatrous 'high places'. For usurping the role of a priest and attempting to offer incense in the Temple, he was afflicted with leprosy, and had to live in isolation.
2 Kings 15:1-6
2 Chronicles 26

Isaiah *'salvation of God'*
Isaiah prophesied in Jerusalem during the reigns of Uzziah, Jotham, Ahaz and Hezekiah, kings of Judah, a period of about 40 years. Isaiah was married to a prophetess and his two sons were given symbolic names; Shear-Jashub, meaning *'a remnant will return'*, and Maher-Shalal-Hash-Baz, meaning *'quick to the plunder'*. Isaiah's call to be a prophet came in an awe-inspiring vision of the holiness of God, recorded in Isaiah 6. His book speaks strongly of the power of God, combining outrage against sin and prophecies of catastrophic judgement with tender and beautiful visions of future peace and blessing. It is Isaiah who first portrays the Messiah as a suffering servant, killed for the sins of his people. He was a courtly adviser of kings, strongly warning against foreign political alliances and preaching the necessity of total trust in God.
Isaiah (especially 1:1; 6; 7:3; 8:1; 53; 61)

Jotham *'God is perfect'*
Jotham followed in the godly ways of his father, King Uzziah. He was crowned king in Uzziah's lifetime, when leprosy forced Uzziah to live in isolation.
2 Kings 15; 32–38;
2 Chronicles 27

Ahaz *'he holds'*
Ahaz, the son of Jotham, encouraged Baal worship, and even made human sacrifices of his own sons. When the armies of Aram and Israel marched against him he panicked. Ignoring Isaiah's advice, he went to Tiglath-Pileser III of Assyria for help, but ended up being subject to him.
2 Kings 16; 2 Chronicles 28;
Isaiah 7

Hezekiah *'God is strength'*
Unlike his father, Ahaz, Hezekiah held fast to God, and introduced wide-ranging and thorough religious reforms. His dependence on God led him to rebel against Assyria. In preparation for an Assyrian attack, he built a famous aqueduct (533 metres/1,745 feet long) through solid limestone, so that the city of Jerusalem would always have a secret water supply when under siege. When the Assyrians called on him to surrender, he turned to God for help, and God routed the army.
2 Kings 18–20;
2 Chronicles 29–32;
Isaiah 36–39

Manasseh *'causing forgetfulness'*
Manasseh was as evil as his father, Hezekiah, had been good. He burned his own son as a child sacrifice, took advice from mediums and fortune-tellers, and practised magic. He 'filled Jerusalem from one end to the other with the blood of innocent people'. He was captured by the Assyrians and exiled to Babylon, but he returned to Judah a reformed man, trusting God.
2 Kings 21:1-18;
2 Chronicles 33:1-20

King Hezekiah.

Amon *'workman'*
Amon, the son of Manasseh, succeeded his father to the throne, and followed the same evil practices. After two years, he was murdered by his court officials.
2 Kings 21:18-23;
2 Chronicles 33:20-25

Josiah *'God supports'*
Josiah, the boy-king of Judah, was crowned when he was eight, when his father, Amon, was killed. Under Josiah, idolatry was purged and the Temple in Jerusalem was repaired. In the Temple, a copy of the lost scroll of the Law was found and Josiah obeyed the instructions found there.
2 Kings 21:26-23:30;
2 Chronicles 33:20-25:27

Jehoiakim *'God establishes'*
King Jehoiakim reversed the godly reforms introduced by his father, Josiah, and reinstated Baal worship. He opposed the prophet Habakkuk and had Jeremiah's scrolls burned.
2 Kings 23:36–24:7;
2 Chronicles 36; Jeremiah 36

Jehoiachin *'God will establish'*
The Babylonians appointed King Jehoiachin in the place of his father, Jehoiakim. Fourteen weeks later he was exiled to Babylon by King Nebuchadnezzar.
2 Kings 24:8-16;
2 Chronicles 36:9-10;
Jeremiah 52:31-34

Zedekiah *'Jehovah is my righteousness'*
Zedekiah was the last king of Judah, taking over from his nephew Jehoiachin. Although he was King Nebuchadnezzar's puppet king, Zedekiah rebelled. This brought about Jerusalem's destruction.
2 Kings 24:17-25; 2 Chronicles 36:10-23; Jeremiah 21; 32; 34; 37–39

Habakkuk *'God is strength'*
Habakkuk wrote his prophetic book during the reigns of Jehoiakim and Josiah. He warned that the Babylonians would capture Judah, and this would be God's punishment for their violence, idolatry and corruption. Habakkuk emphasised the importance of personal faith, writing that the 'just shall live by faith'. Habakkuk

Nahum *'comforter'*
Nahum's short prophecy encouraged the people of Judah as they faced defeat by the Babylonians. Nahum predicted the overthrow of Nineveh, the capital of the Assyrians, who had long oppressed the Israelites. This took place in 612 B.C.
Nahum

Jeremiah *'God is high'*
Jeremiah, whose prophecies are recorded in the books of Jeremiah and Lamentations, lived in the grim days of the last five kings of Judah: Josiah, Jehoahaz, Jehoiakim, Jehoiachin and Zedekiah. Jeremiah was hated and called a traitor because he urged the people not to resist the Babylonian armies, declaring that the impending destruction of Jerusalem was God's judgement against idolatry. His book vividly communicates the horror and misery he felt as he contemplated the destruction of his beloved homeland. Jeremiah was probably taken off to Egypt after Jerusalem fell into the hands of King Nebuchadnezzar in 587 B.C. His prophecy that the Jews would return to Jerusalem 70 years after its fall also came true.
Jeremiah; Lamentations

Micah *'who is like God?'*
Micah prophesied against the southern kingdom of Judah (during the reigns of Jotham, Ahaz and Hezekiah), and also against the northern kingdom of

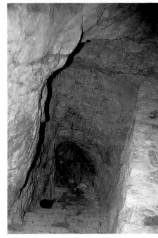

Hezekiah's tunnel, Jerusalem.

Israel (during the reigns of Pekah and Hoshea). While Micah spoke out against evil practices and God's impending judgement (saying that Samaria would become 'a heap of rubble'), he was also a prophet of hope, and predicted that a great ruler over Israel would come from Bethlehem.
Micah

Zephaniah *'God has treasured'*
The prophet Zephaniah was the great-great-great-grandson of King Hezekiah. His message of judgement on Judah was delivered during Josiah's reign. He predicted that a small number (a 'remnant') would return to Jerusalem.
Zephaniah

Obadiah *'servant of God'*
Obadiah prophesied against the people of Edom, Judah's persistent enemy.
Obadiah

Huldah *'weasel'*
Huldah, a prophetess, was consulted by Hilkiah the priest, on behalf of King Josiah, after the book of the Law had been discovered in the Temple.
2 Kings 22:14-20;
2 Chronicles 34:22-28

Israel's prophets and kings

In the 210 years from Jeroboam I to Hoshea, the northern kingdom of Israel had nine dynasties and nineteen kings. Kings' sons did not succeed their fathers, as in the southern kingdom (which had a single dynasty), but were often ambitious and bloodthirsty officials or military leaders.

Jeroboam I *'the people multiplied'*
Jeroboam was a talented young officer in Solomon's court, in charge of the entire labour force of the country, when the prophet Ahijah met him and prophesied that he would be king over the ten northern tribes. When Solomon consequently tried to kill him, he fled to Egypt until Solomon's death. Jeroboam became Israel's first king, after Israel had split into the two kingdoms of Judah (in the south) and Israel (in the north). In order to stop the people in Israel travelling to Jerusalem to worship God, he set up rival religious sanctuaries in Bethel and Dan, where the same religious festivals were held, but on different days, and sacrifices were offered by priests not descended from the family of Aaron. This counterfeit system of worship was supported by all the subsequent kings of Israel.
1 Kings 11:26–14:20

Omri *'God apportions'* or *'people'*
Omri, a commander-in-chief in King Elah's army, came to Israel's throne as its sixth king by defeating commander Zimri, who had killed King Elah. Omri 'sinned more than all those before him'. He established the strategic hill town of Samaria as Israel's new capital.
1 Kings 16:15-28

Ahab *'father is brother'*
Ahab, son and successor of Omri, was one of Israel's most successful (yet evil) kings. He married evil Jezebel, daughter of Ethbaal, king of the Sidonians, and so began to worship Baal. He set up an altar for Baal in the temple of Baal that he built. Ahab's death, during his third war against Syria, was seen as God's punishment on one of Israel's most wicked kings.
1 Kings 16:29-18; 20:1–22:40

Ahaziah *'God sustains'*
Ahaziah followed in the evil footsteps of his father, Ahab, and consulted the god of Ekron, Baal-Zebub, rather than the Lord. When he fell from his balcony, he never recovered, as Elijah the prophet had pronounced.
1 Kings 22:51-53; 2 Kings 1

Jehoram (Joram) *'God is exalted'*
Jehoram did evil in the eyes of the Lord, but not to the extent that his father (Ahab) and mother (Jezebel) had done, because he did at least make an attempt to end Baal worship. He was murdered by Jehu.
2 Kings 3; 9:14-29

Jehu *'he is Yahweh'*
Jehu was an army commander when he was anointed by a prophet to be the next king of Israel. He killed Jehoram, Jezebel, all members of the royal family and all the priests of Baal. Though he claimed that he would worship God, he maintained the false worship introduced by Jehoram.
2 Kings 9-10

Black obelisk, showing Jehu giving tribute to Shalmaneser.

Jehoahaz *'God has grasped'*
Israel's eleventh king, Jehoahaz, was a failure. He led the Israelites away from worshipping God, and was defeated by two kings of Syria, Hazael and Ben-Hadad.
2 Kings 13:1-9

Jehoash *'God has given'*
Jehoash (sometimes known as Joash) consulted the dying prophet Elisha and was told that he would defeat Syria three times. Although he did this, he still worshipped idols.
2 Kings 13:10–14:16

Jeroboam II *'the people multiplied'*
Jeroboam II's military achievements in recovering Damascus and Hamath for Israel were notable, but he continued Baal worship.
2 Kings 14:23-29

Elisha *'God is Saviour'*
Elisha was Elijah's disciple, assistant and successor as God's faithful prophet in Israel. He worked as a prophet for 55 years during the reigns of Joram, Jehu, Jehoahaz and Joash. Fourteen miracles were performed through Elisha, most notably the healing of commander Naaman's leprosy.
1 Kings 19:16, 19-21; 2 Kings 2-9; 13:14-20

Gehazi *'valley of vision'*
Gehazi, Elijah's dishonest servant, secretly accepted gifts of silver and clothes from Naaman, which Elijah had declined. Gehazi was punished and became 'as white as snow' with Naaman's leprosy.
2 Kings 4:25–5:27; 8:1-6

Naaman *'pleasantness'*
Naaman, the Syrian army commander, was a valiant warrior, but also suffered from leprosy. A captured Hebrew girl told him about the prophet Elisha. Naaman visited him and was told to dip himself seven times in the River Jordan. Naaman at first proudly refused, but when he complied, he was immediately cured.
2 Kings 5

Amos *'burden-bearer'*
Amos was a shepherd and cultivator of sycamore-fig trees in Judah when God sent him to Israel to prophesy against the moral corruption, dishonesty, mistreatment of the poor, and the luxurious living that was rampant in the northern kingdom of Israel.
Amos

Naboth *'a sprout'*
Naboth refused to sell his vineyard to King Ahab, and for this Queen Jezebel had him killed.
1 Kings 21; 2 Kings 9:30-37

Hoshea *'deliverer'*
Hoshea, the last king of Israel, acquired the throne by killing his predecessor,

Elijah's sacrifice on Mount Carmel is consumed by fire from heaven.

Elijah *'the Lord is my God'*
Elijah, the most prominent prophet of his day in Israel, opposed King Ahab and his foreign queen, Jezebel, in their attempts to make Baal worship the official religion of Israel. God sent a severe drought, during which Elijah was fed with food brought by ravens. He also multiplied food for a widow, and brought her son back to life. Elijah challenged Ahab and the 450 prophets of Baal to a contest on Mount Carmel. While Baal's prophets could do nothing, fire came on Elijah's sacrifice, in answer to his prayer. The prophets of Baal were then all killed and God again sent rain. After this 'mountain-top' experience Elijah suffered deep depression. He travelled to Mount Horeb in the wilderness and there God spoke to him as a 'still small voice'. Elijah did not die in the normal way, but was 'translated' and caught up in a chariot of fire. With Moses. Elijah appeared at Jesus' transfiguration.
1 Kings 17–19; 21; 2 Kings 1:1–2:18; Luke 9:28-36

King Pekah. It was during his reign that final disaster struck the northern kingdom. After a three-year siege in the ninth year of Hoshea's reign the king of Assyria (Shalmaneser) captured Samaria (the capital of Israel) and deported the Israelites to Assyria. In this way the prophetic warnings came true, and Israel was punished for its sin of worshipping other gods and refusing to obey God's law of justice and love.
2 Kings 15:30; 17-18

Joel *'the Lord is God'*
Joel warned the southern kingdom of Judah that God's judgement ('the day of the Lord') would fall on Judah like a devastating plague of locusts, if they did not return to following God.
Joel

Hosea *'God has saved'*
Hosea denounced the people of Israel for their idolatry, likening them in their unfaithfulness to God to his adulterous wife, Gomer. In his deeply moving prophecies Hosea shows that, just as he loved his wife and brought her back, so God loves his wayward people and brings them back to himself.
Hosea

Jonah *'dove'*
Jonah was the first Hebrew prophet sent to a pagan country. God told him to warn the ungodly people of Nineveh to turn away from their sins. Jonah, trying to run away from this thankless task, found himself swallowed by a great fish. When he eventually preached to the people of Nineveh, and they repented and turned to God, Jonah was furious. Jonah, and through Jonah the Jewish people, had to learn that God cares for people of all nations - and for their animals too. The book of Jonah takes its name from the prophet.
Jonah

Exile and return

After a 70-year exile in Babylon, the Jews of Jerusalem returned to rebuild their ruined city.

Sennacherib *'Sin [the moon-god] has multiplied the brothers'*
Sennacherib, king of Assyria, defeated the Babylonians and then besieged King Hezekiah of Judah. In fulfilment of Isaiah's prediction that God would save Jerusalem, 185,000 Assyrian soldiers mysteriously died in the night, killed by 'the angel of the Lord'. Sennacherib returned to Nineveh, where two of his sons killed him.
2 Kings 18:17–19:37; 2 Chronicles 32; Isaiah 36-37

Nebuchadnezzar *'may the god Nebo defend the boundary'*
Nebuchadnezzar, the powerful king of Babylon, defeated the Israelites of Judah, captured Jerusalem, and exiled the majority of the people to Babylon. Nebuchadnezzar built many beautiful buildings and temples in Babylon, including the fabulous hanging gardens of Babylon, which were later counted among the seven wonders of the ancient world. For seven years Nebuchadnezzar was insane – God's punishment on him for his overweening pride. His sanity was restored when he gave praise to God.
2 Kings 24-25; 2 Chronicles 36:6-20; Daniel 1–4

Ezekiel *'God strengthens'*
The son of Buzi the priest, Ezekiel lived in Jerusalem until he was deported in 597 B.C. and taken to Babylon, along with the king and most of the ruling families of the city. Until 587 B.C., when Jerusalem was destroyed, Ezekiel lived by the River Kebar, from where he urged the people left in Jerusalem to repent. Later, after the destruction of Jerusalem, Ezekiel preached a message of hope, and prophesied a future return to Jerusalem. In this way he comforted the captured Jews, who had lost their homes, their land and their Temple, and who felt as if they had been abandoned by God. He showed that faith in God could continue even in a foreign land and without the Temple. He often acted out his prophecies in dramatic, and sometimes bizarre, ways.
Ezekiel

Abednego *'servant of Nego'*
Abednego was one of Daniel's three close friends among the Jewish exiles in Babylon. With Shadrach and Meshach, Abednego refused to bow down and worship the statue of Nebuchadnezzar. For this rebellion he was thrown into a blazing furnace, but miraculously survived unscathed.
Daniel 1–3

Belshazzar *'Bel protect the king'*
As co-regent and successor to King Nebuchadnezzar, Belshazzar was Babylon's last king. During a banquet Belshazzar called Daniel to interpret strange writing that had appeared on the wall. Daniel's interpretation was that Belshazzar had been weighed in God's balances of judgement and been found deficient. As a result he was about to lose his throne to the Medes and Persians. 'That very night,' we are told, 'Belshazzar was slain', bringing to an end the vast power of Babylon.
Daniel 5

Cyrus *'sun, splendour'*
Cyrus, founder of the Persian Empire, captured Babylon in 539 B.C. He was noted for his enlightened and humane rule. In keeping with this, he allowed the exiled Jews to return to Jerusalem and rebuild the Temple, at the expense of his royal treasury.
Ezra 1–6

Daniel *'God is my judge'*
Daniel, who came from an aristocratic Jerusalem family, was exiled to Babylon when he was in his teens. Sent to court to train to be an administrator, he rose to high rank in the Babylonian, and then the Persian, kingdoms. Daniel was a man of outstanding faith and prayer. He was noted for his courage and his wisdom, including the ability to interpret dreams. Because of his refusal to deny his faith he was thrown into a lions' den, where he was miraculously preserved. He was a visionary, and the second half of the book named after him records the revelation God gave him of future world events.
Daniel

Darius *'he that informs himself'*
Darius the Mede, who succeeded Belshazzar as king of Babylon, was tricked by his officials into having Daniel thrown into the lions' den. When he saw Daniel's miraculous deliverance, he said, 'In every part of my kingdom people must fear and reverence the God of Daniel.'
Daniel 5–6

Daniel in the lions' den.

Part of the 'broad wall' of Jerusalem mentioned in Nehemiah 3:8.

Nehemiah 'the Lord comforts'

Nehemiah grew up in Babylon during the time of the Jewish Exile. He rose to the influential position of cupbearer to King Artaxerxes of Persia. When Jews were allowed back to Jerusalem, Nehemiah's family stayed behind. He was deeply upset when he heard that the returned exiles had not succeeded in rebuilding Jerusalem's walls. After praying and fasting for four months, Nehemiah asked if he could return to Jerusalem and organise the people to rebuild the ruined walls of the city. Nehemiah's building programme was opposed by Sanballat, Tobiah, the Arabs, the Ammonites and the men of Ashdod, but as a result of hard work and prayerful vigilance the wall was rebuilt.
Nehemiah

Ezra 'the Lord helps'

Ezra, a priest and scribe, led the third group of Israelites from exile in Babylon back to Jerusalem. He had written permission to enforce God's Law as the law of the land. The Temple had been rebuilt, but he found the people had grown lax and were neglecting God's laws. Thirteen years after Ezra's arrival, Nehemiah came to Jerusalem as governor, and the people experienced a spiritual revival.
Ezra

Zerubbabel 'seed of Babylon'

Zerubbabel was the leader, and later governor, of the first group of Israelites to return to Jerusalem from exile in Babylon. With the encouragement of the prophets Haggai and Zechariah, and against violent opposition, he rebuilt and dedicated the Temple.
Ezra 1–5; Haggai

Queen Esther.

Esther 'myrtle'

Esther, a beautiful young Jewess, grew up in Susa, the capital of Persia. She was an orphan, cared for by her cousin Mordecai. King Xerxes chose her to be his consort after Queen Vashti fell from favour. At first Esther did not reveal that she was a Jewess, but when Haman planned to massacre all Jews in his empire, Esther, after prayer and fasting, devised a courageous plan to save her nation.
Esther

Xerxes (or Ahasuerus)

Xerxes was the king of Persia who married the Jewess Esther after dismissing his first wife, Vashti.
Esther

Haggai 'born on a feast day'

Haggai rebuked the returned exiles for living in expensively panelled houses while the Temple was still in ruins. Zerubbabel, Judah's governor, and Jehozadak, the high priest, followed Haggai's instructions and rebuilt the Temple.
Haggai

Haman

Haman became prime minister to Xerxes, king of Persia, and in his hatred for Mordecai used his wealth and position to mastermind the massacre of all the Jewish people in Persia. His evil plan would have succeeded but for Esther. Haman was hanged on the 75-foot (25-metre) high gallows he had built for the execution of Mordecai the Jew.
Esther 3–9

Malachi 'my messenger'

Malachi rebuked the Jews for replacing enthusiasm for God with the ritual of services in the new Temple.
Malachi

Mordecai 'dedicated to Mars'

Mordecai was a Jewish exile who lived in the Persian capital of Susa. His cousin, Esther, became King Xerxes' wife. By exposing a plot to kill Xerxes, Mordecai saved the king's life. He later incurred Haman's fury for his fearless refusal to bow down to him. In his anger, Haman resolved to slaughter all Jews and have Mordecai hanged on a gallows. It was Mordecai who made sure that Esther got news of the plot and acted to save her people. Mordecai was then made prime minister.
Esther

Sanballat 'the god Sin has given life'

Sanballat, governor of Samaria, with Tobiah and Geshem, opposed Nehemiah's governorship, and did all he could to prevent the rebuilding of Jerusalem's walls.
Nehemiah 2:19-20; 6:1-14; 13:28-29

Tobiah 'the Lord is good'

Tobiah the Ammonite, with Sanballat and Geshem the Arab, fought against Nehemiah's rebuilding of Jerusalem. Tobiah taunted the Jews, saying that if a fox trod on their walls they would collapse.
Nehemiah 2:19-20; 4:3-9; 6:28-29; 13:1-9

Zechariah 'the Lord remembers'

Zechariah's prophecies roused the Jews who had returned to Jerusalem out of their apathy, spiritual sloth and evil ways. He was a priest as well as a prophet, a descendant of one of Judah's ancient high priestly families. He had been born in exile in Babylonia, but returned with the first group of Jews and prophesied alongside Haggai.
Zechariah

Jesus of Nazareth

All the prophecies about God's promised Messiah were fulfilled in the birth, life, death, resurrection and ascension of Jesus.

John the Baptist.

Mary *'loved by God'*
Mary, a young Jewish virgin who was engaged to a carpenter called Joseph, was chosen by God to conceive and bear his Son, Jesus Christ, by the power of the Holy Spirit. The angel Gabriel announced this to Mary in Nazareth, and she responded with humility and trust. Her *Magnificat,* or song of praise to God, which she sang when she went to visit her cousin, Elizabeth, shows her love and devotion for God. Mary's deeply thoughtful nature is shown after Jesus' birth in Bethlehem, and the visit of the shepherds with their astounding story of angels in the sky. Mary, we are told, married Joseph and had several other children. Jesus' first sign, when he changed water into wine,

Mary.

was performed at the instigation of Mary , who was with him during at least part of his three-year public ministry. Mary stood at the foot of the cross as Jesus died, and Jesus told the apostle John to look after her. We find her again in the upper room on the day of Pentecost.
Matthew 1; Mark 6:3; Luke 1–2; John 2:1-11; 19:25-27; Acts 1

Joseph *'may (God) add'*
Joseph was 'engaged' to Mary when they discovered that Mary was pregnant through the action of the Holy Spirit. Joseph married Mary and became foster father to Jesus. Being warned in a dream, Joseph took Mary and Jesus from Bethlehem to Egypt to escape Herod's massacre of baby boys in Bethlehem. After Herod's death, Joseph returned to his home town of Nazareth, where he was a carpenter. After Jesus' visit to the Jerusalem Temple, aged twelve, Joseph is never heard of again, and it is assumed that he must have died when Jesus was still young.
Matthew 1–2; Luke 1:27–2:52

Elizabeth *'God is my oath'*
Elizabeth, wife of the priest Zechariah, was visited by her cousin Mary, the mother of Jesus, when they were both pregnant. Elizabeth greeted Mary with the words, 'Blessed are you among women, and blessed is the child you shall bear.' Elizabeth's son was John the Baptist.
Luke 1

John the Baptist *'the Lord is gracious'*
John the Baptist, son of Elizabeth and Zechariah, lived in the Judean wilderness. John wore clothes made from camels' hair, with a leather belt around his waist, as the prophet Elijah had done centuries earlier. He fearlessly preached a message of repentance, paving the way for his cousin, Jesus Christ, whom he baptised in the River Jordan. Speaking about himself and Jesus, John said, 'Jesus must become greater; I must become less.' John was imprisoned, and later beheaded, because he spoke out against Herod Antipas' marriage to his brother Philip's wife, Herodias.
Matthew 3; 11:1-19; 14:1-12; Mark 1:1-8; Luke 1; John 1:1-34

Salome *'clothing'*
Salome was Herodias' daughter and Herod's step-daughter. At a great feast held on Herod's birthday, she danced a passionate dance, for which Herod promised her any gift she desired. At her mother's request, she asked for John the Baptist's head on a plate.
Matthew 14:6-11; Mark 6:21-28

Anna *'grace'*
Anna, a very elderly, widowed prophetess, spent her life worshipping God in the Jerusalem Temple. She recognised the baby Jesus as the Messiah when he was consecrated in the Temple.
Luke 2:36-38

Herodias *'heroic'*
While Herodias' husband, Herod Philip, was still alive, she married his brother-in-law, Herod Antipas. Herodias detested John the Baptist because he spoke out against this marriage. She had him thrown in prison, and was responsible for his execution.
Matthew 14:1-12; Mark 6:14-29

Simeon *'he hears'*
A devout Jew who lived in Jerusalem, Simeon had been told by the Holy Spirit that, before he died, he would see the Lord's Christ. When Mary and Joseph brought the baby Jesus to the Temple, Simeon took him in his arms and praised God. His beautiful song of peace and joy is called the *Nunc Dimittis* and is sung regularly in many churches.
Luke 2:25-35

Tiberius *'son of the Tiber'*
Tiberius, also known as Claudius Caesar Augustus, was Roman emperor from A.D. 14 to A.D. 37. He ruled during most of Jesus' lifetime.
Luke 3:1

Herod the Great *'heroic'*
Herod, the evil king of Judah from 34 to about 4 B.C., was visited by the 'wise men', and subsequently ordered all male babies in Bethlehem under two years of age to be slaughtered. He was called 'the Great' because the country was very prosperous during his long reign and he built many beautiful buildings, including the magnificent new Temple in Jerusalem. But he was loathed for his vicious cruelty, and kept himself in power by fawning on the Romans and by killing all possible rivals.
Matthew 2; Luke 1:5

Augustus *'august'*
Augustus, the nephew and successor of Julius Caesar, took the title Octavian and became the first Roman emperor, ruling from 31 B.C. to A.D. 14. Augustus ordered the census which brought Joseph and Mary from Nazareth to Bethlehem for Jesus' birth.
Luke 2:1

Zechariah *'the Lord remembers'*
Old Zechariah, a godly priest and husband of Elizabeth, was told by an angel that they would have a son who must be called John, and who would bring many people back to God. Since Elizabeth was well advanced in years and had always been childless, Zechariah greeted this news with incredulity. For this he was struck dumb, and remained unable to speak until the baby was born and named John.
Luke 1

Jesus teaching his disciples in the hills around Galilee.

Jesus *'the Lord is salvation'*
Jesus Christ is portrayed in the New Testament as the Saviour of the world, and the name 'Jesus' itself means 'Saviour'. As John wrote at the end of his Gospel, 'These miraculous signs are written that you may believe that Jesus is the Christ, the Son of God, and that by believing you may have life in his name.'

Childhood
Jesus' mother, Mary, laid the baby Jesus in a manger at his birth in Bethlehem, where shepherds visited him. Jesus was presented in the Temple, and then Mary and Joseph, Jesus' foster father, fled to Egypt with Jesus after the 'wise men' had visited them. They later returned to Nazareth, where Joseph worked as a carpenter. Apart from Jesus' visit to the Temple when he was twelve, where he listened to the teachers and asked them questions, nothing else is known about his childhood.

Three years of ministry
When Jesus was about 35 years old, John the Baptist baptized him in the River Jordan, before Jesus went into the desert to be tempted by Satan. After this, Jesus started his public ministry , choosing twelve apostles to be with him. Jesus performed many miracles, such as changing water into wine at Cana, and many healings, such as Jairus' daughter being brought back to life. He also preached often, as in the Sermon on the Mount, and told numerous memorable parables, such as the Good Samaritan and the Prodigal Son.

Last week
The four Gospel writers concentrate on the last seven days of Jesus' life. On the Sunday before his death, Jesus entered Jerusalem on a donkey, to the cheers of the crowds. The following Thursday, Jesus ate the Last Supper with his disciples, before going to the Garden of Gethsemane to pray, where Judas betrayed him. Jesus was arrested, given unfair trials, unjustly condemned to death, crucified like a common criminal and buried. But on the Sunday his tomb was found to be empty, as he had been raised from the dead. Forty days later Jesus ascended into heaven, after many resurrection appearances, promising that he would one day return.
Matthew; Mark; Luke; John

The Twelve

Jesus chose twelve men to be with him during his three years' work of preaching and teaching. He called them 'apostles' , meaning 'those who are sent'.

Andrew *'manly'*
Andrew introduced his brother, Peter, to Jesus when they were disciples of John the Baptist. Andrew and Peter were fishermen on Lake Galilee. Andrew brought to Jesus a boy who had two small fish and five barley loaves, which Jesus miraculously used to feed 5,000 people.
Matthew 4:18-20; Mark 1:16-18; John 1:35-42; 6:8-9

Bartholomew *'son of Talmai'*
Nothing is known about Bartholomew. The only time his name appears is in the list of all Jesus' apostles.
Matthew 10:3

James (form of Jacob 'supplanter') James was a fisherman, working with his brother, John, and father, Zebedee, in the family business. He was mending nets when Jesus first called him, and he followed Jesus at once. Jesus gave John and James the nickname 'sons of thunder', because they had stormy natures. They suggested, for example, that Jesus should ask God to rain down fire on an unbelieving village. James became one of Jesus' three closest apostles, whom Jesus chose to have with him at special moments, such as the transfiguration. James was beheaded for his Christian faith by Herod Agrippa I about ten years after the death of Jesus.
Matthew 4:21-22; 10:2; 17:1-13; 26:37; Mark 5:37; 10:35-45; Luke 9:51-56; Acts 12:2

James (form of Jacob) *'supplanter'*
There were two apostles called James. The James who was not John's brother was the son of Alphaeus, and nothing else is known about him.
Matthew 10:3; Acts 1:13

John *'the Lord is gracious'*
John, a fisherman and son of Zebedee, was one of Jesus' inner circle of three very close apostles; along with his brother, James, he was given the nickname 'sons of thunder'. John, who leaned on Jesus at the Last Supper, was Jesus' closest friend, and as Jesus was dying, he asked John to look after Mary, his mother. John wrote one Gospel, the book of Revelation (during his exile on the island of Patmos), and three short letters. In his Gospel, John never mentions himself by name, but uses the words 'the disciple Jesus loved' instead. John became a leader in the early Church.
Matthew 4:21-22; 10:2; 20:20-23; John 13:23-25; 19:25-27; Acts 1:13; 3-4; Galatians 2:9; 1, 2 and 3 John; Revelation 1:1

Judas *'praise'*
The Judas who did not betray Jesus is called 'Judas, not Iscariot', and is probably the same person as Thaddaeus.
Luke 6:16; Acts 1:13

Judas Iscariot
Judas Iscariot was the treasurer for the twelve apostles. For 30 silver pieces he betrayed Jesus with a kiss in the Garden of Gethsemane. When Judas saw that Jesus had been condemned to death, he was overtaken by remorse, and returned the silver to the elders, saying, 'I have sinned for I have betrayed innocent blood.' Judas then hanged himself. Judas is always the last name in the list of the apostles.
Matthew 26:1–27:10; Acts 1:15-26

Matthew *'gift of the Lord'*
Matthew, also known as Levi, was called from being a tax-collector to follow Jesus. He abandoned everything and held a feast in his house for Jesus and many tax-collectors and 'sinners'. He is the traditional author of the first Gospel.
Matthew 9:9-10

Nathanael *'God has given'*
Nathanael is most probably the same person as Bartholomew. Philip told Nathanael about Jesus. When Nathanael met Jesus, Jesus said of him, 'Here is a true Israelite, in whom there is nothing false.'
John 1:43-51

Thomas *'twin'*
Thomas, whose name is Didymus in Greek, showed

Jesus eats the Last Supper with the Twelve.

his courage when he was prepared to die for Jesus, before Jesus went to raise Lazarus. At the Last Supper, Thomas asked Jesus, 'How can we know the way?' and Jesus replied, 'I am the way, the truth and the life.' Thomas is remembered as 'doubting' Thomas because he said that he would never believe in Jesus' resurrection unless he saw Jesus for himself and touched his wounds. When the risen Lord Jesus did appear to him, Thomas immediately worshipped him and called him his Lord and God.
Matthew 10:3; John 11:16; 14:5-6; 20:24-28

Simon *'hearing'*

Simon, not to be confused with Simon Peter, is known as Simon the Zealot, because he was probably a member of a Jewish revolutionary group dedicated to driving the Romans from Israel.
Matthew 10:4

Peter betrays Jesus on the night of his arrest.

Peter *'rock'*

Peter, the outspoken and often brash leader of the twelve, always heads the lists of the apostles. With his brother, Andrew, Peter left his fishing at Christ's command and became one of Jesus' three closest disciples. At Caesarea Philippi, Peter told Jesus that he was 'the Christ, the Son of the living God'. Peter boasted that he would die for Jesus, but denied him three times. After Jesus' resurrection, Jesus told Peter to be a shepherd and 'feed his sheep'. Peter led the first Christians, preaching fearlessly on the day of Pentecost, when 3,000 people accepted his message and were baptised. With John, Peter healed a cripple outside the Temple gate called Beautiful. As the number of Christians swelled to over 5,000, Peter and John were thrown into prison for teaching the people that the resurrection of the dead comes through Jesus. Peter wrote two short letters, and much of Mark's Gospel is usually seen as a summary of his teaching. Jesus predicted that Peter would be martyred, and it is thought that he was executed by Nero in Rome.
Matthew 4:18-20; 10:2; 14:25-31; 16:13-23; 17:1-13; 26:31-35, 69-75; 1 and 2 Peter

Philip *'lover of horses'*

Philip, who, like Andrew and Peter, was from Bethsaida, brought Nathanael (Bartholomew) to meet Jesus. When 5,000 hungry people needed food, Jesus tested Philip's faith. At the Last Supper, Philip asked Jesus to show them the Father, and Jesus replied, 'I am in the Father and the Father is in me.'
John 1:43–51; 6:5-7; 12:20-22; 14:8-9

Jesus' friends and foes

In addition to his twelve apostles, Jesus had many devoted followers and friends, although some of the religious leaders opposed him.

Zacchaeus *'pure'*
Zacchaeus, a wealthy, dishonest tax-collector, climbed a tree to have a good view of Jesus as he passed through Jericho. Jesus told Zacchaeus to come down and then went to his house, where Zacchaeus called Jesus 'Lord' and announced that he would give away half of his money to the poor and pay back four times over the money he had gained by cheating.
Luke 19

Mary Magdalene (form of Miriam) *'strong'*
Mary was named Magdalene after the town she came from, Magdala. Jesus drove seven demons from her and she became his follower, standing close to his cross when he died. Mary Magdalene was the first person Jesus appeared to after his resurrection.
Matthew 27:55; 28:1-10; Mark 15:40; 16:1-8; Luke 8:2; John 19:25; 20:1-18

Nicodemus *'conqueror of the people'*
Nicodemus, a leading Pharisee, visited Jesus at night and was told that he needed to be born again. As a member of the Jewish ruling council, Nicodemus stood up for Jesus, saying that they ought to give him a hearing before they condemned him. Nicodemus helped Joseph of Arimathea to place Jesus in the tomb, and brought myrrh and aloes to embalm him.
John 3:1-21; 7:45-52; 19:39

Simon *'he hears'*
On his way into Jerusalem from the country, Simon of Cyrene was pressed into carrying Jesus' cross as Jesus went to the place of execution.
Matthew 27:32; Mark 15:21; Luke 23:26

Bartimaeus *'son of Timaeus'*
As Jesus went through Jericho, a blind roadside beggar shouted out to him. Jesus stopped, called Bartimaeus to him and healed him of his blindness. Bartimaeus then followed Jesus along the road.
Mark 10:46-52

Joseph of Arimathea *'may (God) add'*
Joseph of Arimathea, a wealthy Jewish member of the Sanhedrin council, was a secret follower of Jesus. As soon as Jesus had died on the cross, Joseph asked Pilate for permission to take Jesus' body for burial. Accompanied by Nicodemus, who brought the spices, Joseph took Jesus' body to a new tomb in which nobody had ever been laid, and wrapped the body with the spices in strips of linen. This was in accordance with Jewish burial customs.
Matthew 27:57-61; Mark 15:42-44; Luke 23:50-55; John 19:38-42

Jairus *'he will enlighten'*;
Jairus, a ruler of the synagogue at Capernaum, asked Jesus to heal his sick twelve-year-old daughter. As Jesus was on the way to the house, news came that the daughter had died. Nevertheless, Jesus went with Jairus to his home, took the dead girl by the hand and healed her.
Mark 5:21-43

Barabbas *'father's son'*
Barabbas had been condemned to death for murder. At the time of the feast of the Passover it was the custom for the governor to release one prisoner of the crowd's choice. Pilate wanted to release Jesus, but the crowd asked for Barabbas' release and for Jesus to be executed. Pilate gave in to their wishes.
Matthew 27:11-26; Mark 15:1-15; Luke 23:18; John 18:40

Jesus talks to Nicodemus.

Annas *'grace'*

After Jesus was betrayed by Judas in the Garden of Gethsemane, he was arrested, bound and taken to Annas for questioning. Annas, who had been high priest from A.D. 6 to 13, then sent Jesus to his son-in-law, Caiaphas, who was the high priest that year. After Jesus' ascension, Peter and John were also questioned before Annas, because of their Christian preaching.
John 18:12-14, 19-23; Acts 4:6

Caiaphas *'depression'*

Caiaphas, son-in-law of Annas, held a dominant position among the Sadducees and the Jewish priesthood for many years, and was high priest in Jerusalem from A.D. 18 to 36. He masterminded Jesus' arrest, advising the Jewish authorities that one man, Jesus, should die for all the people. Caiaphas presided over the illegal trial of Jesus by the Sanhedrin, pronouncing Jesus guilty of blasphemy. Caiaphas, who had no power to enforce the death sentence, then sent Jesus to Pilate for sentencing. Caiaphas is referred to simply as the 'high priest' in Acts, and was responsible for persecuting the first Christians.
Matthew 26:3-5, 57-68; Mark 14:53-55; Luke 3:2; John 11:49-51; 18:12-14, 19-24; Acts 5:27

Pilate *'javelin carrier'*

As commander-in-chief of the Roman soldiers, Pontius Pilate was all-powerful as Roman governor of Judea (A.D. 26–36), and was the only person who could pass the death sentence. Caiaphas sent Jesus to Pilate, who recognised that Christ was innocent, and even tried to release Jesus as the one prisoner given free pardon each year. Pilate's wife told Pilate that he should have nothing to do with Jesus, for she had been troubled by a dream about him and believed

Mary, Martha and Lazarus at their Bethany home.

Lazarus *'God has helped'*

Lazarus, brother of Mary and Martha, was loved by Jesus. Lazarus died, and four days later Jesus came to his home town of Bethany, wept with his two grieving sisters and then brought Lazarus back to life, explaining that he was the resurrection and the life. The Pharisees tried to kill Lazarus as well as Jesus because many people put their faith in Jesus on account of this miracle.
John 11:1–12:11

Mary (form of Miriam) *'strong'*

Mary, the sister of Martha and Lazarus, loved to sit at Jesus' feet and listen to his teaching. A short time before Jesus' death, Mary anointed his feet with expensive perfume, wiping his feet dry with her hair.
Mark 14:3-9; Luke 10:38-42; John 11:1–12:8

Martha *'lady'*

With her sister, Mary, and brother, Lazarus, Martha often entertained Jesus in her home in Bethany, some two miles from Jerusalem. Martha once complained to Jesus that Mary just sat and listened to Jesus while she was left to do all the work. Jesus, however, replied that Mary had chosen what was better.
Luke 10:38-42; John 11:1–12:8

him to be innocent. But when the crowds shouted to Pilate that if he let Jesus go he would be opposing Caesar, he handed Jesus over to be crucified. Pilate had a notice prepared and fastened to the cross. It read, 'JESUS OF NAZARETH, THE KING OF THE JEWS'.

Matthew 27:11-26; Mark 15:1-15; Luke 22:66–23:25; John 18:28–19:22

The first Christians

The Acts of the Apostles describes people who became followers of Christ in the first exciting days of the early Church.

Stephen defends himself before the Sanhedrin.

Stephen *'crown'*
Stephen was the leading deacon of seven that the Jerusalem church appointed to care for the poor widows. Some Jews objected to Stephen's preaching and the miracles he performed, and so he was brought before the Jewish council of the Sanhedrin. They listened to Stephen's long defence until he accused them of killing 'the Righteous One', which so angered them that they dragged him out of the city and stoned him to death. Stephen, the first Christian martyr, prayed for the forgiveness of those who stoned him. His death was witnessed by Saul (Paul).
Acts 6:1–8:2

Ananias *'protected by the Lord'*
Ananias, in league with his wife, Sapphira, sold a piece of property and gave part of the proceeds to the apostles, while pretending that the money he gave was the total sale price.

Peter accused Ananias of lying to the Holy Spirit and to God, as well as to the apostles, at which Ananias fell down and died.
Acts 5:1-11

Sapphira *'beautiful'*
Sapphira, together with her husband, Ananias, tried to deceive the apostles by giving only part of the money they received for selling some land. When questioned about this by Peter, Sapphira lied and at once died.
Acts 5:1-11

Cleopas *'renowned father'*
Cleopas was one of two disciples who had a conversation with the risen Christ on their way from Jerusalem to Emmaus. Jesus warmed their hearts, as he explained to them from the Old Testament that the Messiah had to suffer before he could be glorified. It was not until Jesus 'broke bread' with them that they recognised him, as he vanished from their sight. Cleopas and his friend returned to Jerusalem to share their experience with the eleven apostles.
Luke 24:13-49

Cornelius *'of a horn'*
Cornelius, a Roman centurion, was respected by the Jews at Caesarea, where he was well known as a generous and devout man of prayer. An angel spoke to him in a vision, telling him to fetch Peter from Joppa. As a result of Peter's visit and preaching, Cornelius and his household believed in Christ, received the Holy Spirit and were baptised. They are the first Gentiles on record to become followers of Jesus.
Acts 10

Matthias *'gift of God'*
After Judas Iscariot's suicide, the remaining eleven apostles drew lots to choose between Barsabbas and Matthias, to see who would replace him. Both men had travelled with Jesus during his three-year public ministry. Matthias was chosen.
Acts 1:15-26

Rhoda *'rose'*
Rhoda worked as a servant in the house of Mary, the mother of John Mark. When Peter was miraculously delivered from prison and knocked on the door of Mary's house, Rhoda ran and announced to the praying Christians that Peter was outside. In her excitement she forgot to open the door.
Acts 12:1-19

Peter meets the centurion Cornelius.

James brother of Jesus (form of Jacob) *'supplanter'*
James was one of Jesus' brothers. During Jesus' lifetime, his brothers did not believe in him, but after Jesus' resurrection James became the leader of the church in Jerusalem. James probably wrote the letter of James.
Matthew 13:55; Mark 6:3; Acts 12:2; 15:13-21; 21:17-26; Galatians 1:19; 2:9

Agabus *'locust'*
Agabus, a prophet from Jerusalem, prophesied at Antioch about an impending famine which would spread across the Roman Empire. He also accurately predicted that Paul would 'be bound' if he went to Jerusalem. But other details of this prophecy were not accurately fulfilled.
Acts 11:27-30; 21:10-11

Simon (Magus) *'one heard'*
Simon Magus of Samaria astonished people with his magic. After hearing Philip preach about Jesus Christ, Simon himself believed and was baptised. However, when Simon saw that the Spirit had been given to believers after the apostles laid their hands on the people, he tried to buy this power from Peter and John. Peter rebuked Simon severely for this, and told him to repent of his sin. Simon asked them to pray for him.
Acts 8:9-25

Jude from *'praise'*
Jude, one of Jesus' brothers, sometimes called Judas, believed in Jesus only after his resurrection. He was probably the writer of the letter of Jude, but never says he was Jesus' brother, preferring humbly to call himself 'brother of James'.
Matthew 13:55; John 7:5; Acts 1

Philip *'lover of horses'*
Philip, along with Stephen the martyr, was one of seven deacons appointed by the Jerusalem church. Philip became a leading evangelist among the Samaritans and Gentiles. He told a travelling Ethiopian official the good news about Jesus, which resulted in the man's immediate baptism.
Acts 6:5; 8:4-13, 26-40; 21:8

Ethiopian eunuch
The unnamed Ethiopian eunuch, Queen Candace's chief officer, who was in charge of all her treasure, was returning from worshipping in Jerusalem. In his chariot he was reading chapter 53 of the Old Testament book of Isaiah. He could not make sense of it until Philip joined him and explained that Isaiah's prophecies applied to Christ, whereupon the Ethiopian put his trust in Jesus. When they saw some water, Philip baptised him.
Acts 8:26-39

Philip explains the book of Isaiah to the Ethiopian.

Crippled beggar at Beautiful Gate
Each day 'a man crippled from birth was carried to the Temple gate called Beautiful, where he was put to beg from those going into the Temple courts'. Peter and John did not give him money, but healed him. He went into the Temple courts 'walking, jumping and praising God'.
Acts 3:1-10

Aeneas *'praise'*
Aeneas, a cripple who lived in Lydda, had been unable to get out of bed for eight years. Peter visited him and said, 'Jesus Christ heals you.' Immediately Aeneas was able to walk again.
Acts 9:32-35

Dorcas *'gazelle'*
Dorcas was a Christian widow who lived in Joppa. She was 'always doing good and helping the poor'. When she fell ill and died, her friends sent for Peter. As soon as he arrived, the widows crowded around him, crying and showing him the clothes Dorcas had made for them. After praying, Peter brought Dorcas back to life.
Acts 9:36-43

Sergius Paulus
Paul and Barnabas visited the island of Cyprus, where Sergius Paulus, 'an intelligent man', was the Roman proconsul. After the sorcerer Elymas had been struck blind by Paul, Sergius Paulus believed, 'for he was amazed at the teaching about the Lord'.
Acts 13:4-12

Philippian jailer
When Paul and Silas were thrown into prison in the town of Philippi, little did they think that they would witness one of the most dramatic conversions in the early Church. 'About midnight . . . there was such a violent earthquake that the foundations of the prison were shaken.' Their unnamed jailer woke up and drew his sword to kill himself, because he thought the prisoners had escaped. Paul assured him, 'We are all here!' At this the jailer asked Paul and Silas, 'What must I do to be saved?' Paul and Silas told him about Jesus. Then the jailer and his whole family 'believed in the Lord Jesus Christ' and were baptised.
Acts 16:22-40

Paul and his circle

Silas *'wood-dweller'*
A leader of the church in Jerusalem, Silas travelled with Paul on his second missionary journey, and was jailed with Paul at Philippi. When Paul travelled on to Athens, Silas stayed in Berea, rejoining Paul at Corinth. Silas is probably the 'Silvanus', mentioned in several of Paul's letters, who helped Peter write his first letters.
Acts 15–18; 2 Corinthians 1; 1 Thessalonians 1; 1 Peter 5

Titus *'honoured'*
Titus was a Gentile Christian, and friend and helper of Paul. We know he once visited Jerusalem with Paul, and he probably often travelled with him. Titus worked in Corinth, breaking down the bad feeling between the Christians and Paul. He also delivered Paul's second letter to the Corinthians, and helped collect money in Corinth for poor Christians in Judea. Paul wrote his letter to Titus while Titus was working in Crete.
1 Corinthians 16; 2 Corinthians 7–8; Galatians 2; Titus

Tychicus *'fortunate'*
Tychicus, a friend of Paul, probably came from Ephesus, and it seems was chosen by the churches of Asia Minor to take the money they collected to poor Christians in Judea. Tychicus was with Paul in prison in Rome, and delivered Paul's letters to the churches at Colossae and Ephesus.
Ephesians 6; 1 Corinthians 4; 2 Timothy 4; Titus 3

John Mark *Mark: 'polite'*
Mark, writer of the second Gospel, lived in Jerusalem, where the first Christians met in his mother's house.

Mark, cousin of Barnabas, accompanied Paul and Barnabas on their first missionary journey, but he left them half-way, and Paul refused to take him on his second trip. But later Mark joined Paul in Rome, and was described by Paul as 'my son Mark'. By tradition, Mark's Gospel is based on Peter's preaching.
Mark 14; Acts 12–15; 2 Timothy 4; Philemon

Barnabas *'son of encouragement'*
Barnabas, a native of Cyprus and member of the Jerusalem church, sold land to give money to poor Christians in Judea. When Paul came to Jerusalem after his conversion, Barnabas befriended him, although others were suspicious of him. The Jerusalem church sent Barnabas to Antioch to build up the church, and he asked Paul to join him. Barnabas accompanied Paul on his first missionary journey from Antioch, but on the second trip they disagreed over taking John Mark with them. They separated, Barnabas taking Mark with him to Cyprus, but Paul always spoke well of Barnabas.
Acts 4, 9, 11, 12, 15; Galatians 2

Erastus *'desired'*
An assistant of Paul, Erastus joined Timothy to work in Macedonia while Paul remained in Asia Minor.
Acts 19; 2 Timothy 4

Timothy *'honouring God'*
Born to a Jewish Christian mother and Greek father in Lystra, Timothy became a friend and aide of Paul. He assisted on Paul's second missionary journey, staying in Thessalonica to help the persecuted believers there. Paul also

John Mark and Barnabas in Asia Minor.

The theatre at Perga, visited by Paul during his first missionary journey.

sent Timothy from Ephesus to teach the church at Corinth. Although he lacked confidence and needed Paul's support, he became leader of the church at Ephesus; Paul's two letters to him are full of advice to leaders in the church.
Acts 16, 17; 1 & 2 Timothy

Paul

Paul *'small'*
The great apostle and pioneering missionary, whose letters form a large part of the New Testament, Paul was both a Jew and a Roman citizen. Born in Tarsus, he was given the name Saul, and educated by the rabbi Gamaliel in Jerusalem. Saul, who belonged to the Pharisee sect, was strongly opposed to the Christians, and he watched the stoning of Stephen.

On his way to Damascus to arrest Christians, Saul saw a dazzling light and heard Jesus ask: 'Why do you persecute me?' Blinded by the light, he was led into Damascus, where Ananias restored his sight. After Saul had been baptised, he started preaching the gospel; but when Jews in Damascus plotted to kill him, he fled to Jerusalem, where the Christians were at first frightened of him. But Barnabas befriended him and introduced him to the apostles. After another plot to kill him, Saul returned to Tarsus.

First mission
Some years later Barnabas fetched Saul to help the church at Antioch in Syria. This church later sent them to Asia Minor to spread the gospel. Following their visit to Cyprus, Saul became known as Paul (the Greek form of his Hebrew name). He returned to Antioch and told the church what they had achieved. Paul also helped Jewish Christians in Jerusalem accept that Jesus is the Saviour of all, not solely of the Jews. On his second missionary journey Paul was accompanied by Silas, first visiting Christian converts in Galatia. They were joined in Lystra by a young man named Timothy, and sailed to Greece from Troas, where they were joined by Luke. They started a new church in Philippi, but Paul and Silas were beaten and jailed. After their release, they travelled on through Greece, Paul preaching in Athens and settling in Corinth for eighteen months. Paul then returned to Jerusalem, taking gifts for poor Christians from believers in Greece and Asia Minor.

Trial
Paul stayed a time in Syria before departing again for Ephesus, where he worked and preached for nearly three years, before revisiting Corinth, and returning, via Greece and Asia Minor, to Jerusalem. On arriving back in Jerusalem, Paul was arrested once more and sent to Caesarea for trial. After two years on remand in gaol, Paul appealed for trial before Caesar and was sent to Rome. His ship was wrecked off the coast of Malta, but no lives were lost. Paul eventually reached Rome safely, where he was kept under house arrest for two years, writing many of his letters from confinement. He was probably released following his trial, but rearrested and executed by the Emperor Nero around A.D. 67.
Acts 7, 9–28; Paul's letters

Luke, the physician.

Gaius *'lord'*
A Macedonian Christian who joined Paul on his third missionary journey, Gaius was dragged into the amphitheatre during the silversmiths' riot at Ephesus.
Acts 19

Luke *'light-giving'*
A Greek-speaking doctor who wrote the third Gospel, Luke was also a friend of Paul. He accompanied the apostle on some of his journeys, and recorded his experiences in the book of Acts. Luke sailed to Rome with Paul, staying with him while he was a prisoner in the imperial capital.
Colossians 4; 2 Timothy 4; Luke-Acts

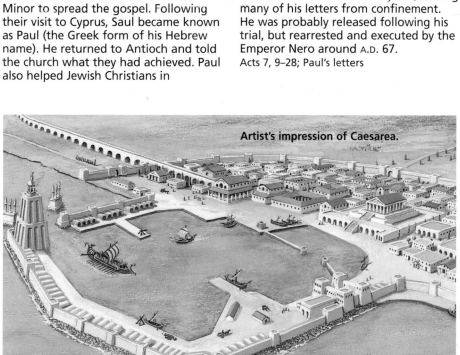

Artist's impression of Caesarea.

217

Paul's converts and opponents

As a travelling missionary, Paul made many close friends who were eager to help him in the cause of Christ – as well as not a few opponents.

Aquila *'eagle'*
A godly Jewish Christian, husband of Priscilla, and friend and faithful supporter of Paul, Aquila was born in Pontus and expelled from Rome by Claudius. Aquila met Paul in Corinth, where they were both tentmakers, and Paul worked and stayed with him. Aquila and Priscilla travelled with Paul to Ephesus. Later, after Claudius' edict had been revoked, they returned to Rome. In Ephesus and Rome the church met in their homes.
Acts 18; Romans 16:3;
1 Corinthians 16:19

Priscilla *'ancient one'*
Six out of the seven times Priscilla and Aquila are mentioned in the New Testament, Priscilla's name comes before Aquila's, and from this it has been concluded that Priscilla was exceptional in some way. They invited Apollos to speak in their home when they lived in Ephesus. Paul greatly valued Priscilla and Aquila, calling them his 'fellow-workers in Christ', who risked their lives for him and to whom all the Gentile churches were indebted.
Acts 18; Romans 16:3;
1 Corinthians 16:19;
2 Timothy 4:19

Apollos *'a destroyer'*
Apollos, a Jewish Christian from Alexandria, is described by Luke as 'a learned man, with a thorough knowledge of the Scriptures. He had been instructed in the way of the Lord, and he spoke with great fervour and taught about Jesus accurately'. Priscilla and Aquila were able to teach him more about God. Apollos greatly encouraged the Christians of southern Greece, and refuted the Jews in public debate, 'proving from the Scriptures that Jesus was the Christ'.
Acts 18:24–19:1;
1 Corinthians 16:12

Crescens *'increasing'*
Crescens was a companion of Paul's during his imprisonment in Rome.
2 Timothy 4:10

Crispus *'curled'*
As a result of Paul's preaching in the synagogue in Corinth, where Crispus was the synagogue ruler, Crispus and his entire household believed in the Lord. Because of this, many people in Corinth believed and were baptised. Gaius, Crispus and his household were the only people Paul baptised in Corinth.
Acts 18:7-11;
1 Corinthians 1:14

Demetrius *'belonging to Demeter'*
Demetrius was a silversmith in Ephesus who made silver shrines of the local goddess, Artemis. Such a trade was profitable in that city. Because Paul's preaching of the gospel threatened this trade, Demetrius organised a riot, with people chanting 'Great is Artemis of the Ephesians!' Paul made a hasty exit for Macedonia.
Acts 19:23–20:1

Demas *'popular'*
Demas was one of Paul's friends and helpers, but deserted Paul during his imprisonment in Rome because he was 'in love with this world'.
Colossians 4:14;
2 Timothy 4:10; Philemon 24

Dionysius *'Bacchus'*
Dionysius was a member of the Areopagus council in Athens. After Paul spoke to this council about the resurrection of Jesus, Dionysius was one of the people who became a follower of Paul and believed.
Acts 17:34

Elymas *'sorcerer'*
Elymas, nicknamed Bar-Jesus, was a Jewish sorcerer and false prophet who opposed Paul and Barnabas at Paphos, and attempted to turn the proconsul, Sergius Paulus, away from the Christian faith. Because of his deceit and trickery, Paul struck him temporarily with blindness.
Acts 13:4-12

Epaphras *'charming'*
Epaphras was a leader, and possibly the founder, of the church at Colossae. Epaphras visited Paul while he was a prisoner in Rome, and was for some time imprisoned with him. Paul wrote his letter to the Colossians in response to what Epaphras told him about the church. Paul held Epaphras in high esteem, calling him a 'dear fellow-servant' and 'a faithful minister of Christ'.
Colossians 1:7; 4:12;
Philemon 23

Onesimus *'profitable'*
Onesimus was a runaway slave who, through meeting Paul in prison in Rome, became a Christian. Paul sent Onesimus back to his master, Philemon, with a letter asking for Onesimus to be accepted back as a Christian brother.
Philemon

Philemon *'friendship'*
The letter to Philemon is the only surviving personal letter of Paul's. Paul entreats Philemon to

Aquila and Priscilla earned their living making tents.

Onesimus with his master, Philemon.

The Forum, Rome.

Claudius.

Nero.

receive back his runaway slave, Onesimus, as a fellow Christian, reminding Philemon that he himself owed his conversion to Paul.
Philemon

Epaphroditus *'handsome'*
Epaphroditus, a member of the Philippian church, was sent by his church to take a gift from them to Paul who was imprisoned in Rome. He worked so strenuously that he became ill and almost died. Paul wrote that he 'put his life in danger so that he could help me'.
Philippians 2:19-30; 4:18

Eutychus *'fortunate'*
During Paul's last day at Troas, the young man Eutychus fell asleep as Paul carried on speaking to the people until midnight. Eutychus fell to his death from a third-floor window. Paul immediately went down to him, put his arms round him and miraculously brought him back to life.
Acts 20:7-12

Claudius *'lame'*
Claudius, Roman Caesar A.D. 41–54, expelled the Jews from Rome for rioting.
Acts 11:28; 18:2

Nero
Although Nero is never mentioned by name in the Bible, he was the cruel Roman Caesar, successor to Claudius, who was responsible for the most horrific persecutions of Christians in Rome. Tradition has it that both Peter and Paul suffered martyrdom at the hands of Nero.

Felix *'happy'*
Felix was the Roman governor of Judea who tried Paul, keeping him in prison for

two years, hoping to receive a bribe from him.
Acts 23:23–24:27

Festus *'swine-like'*
Festus succeeded Felix as Roman governor of Judea, and continued Paul's trial.
Acts 25–26

Agrippa *'causing pain at birth'*
King Herod Agrippa II, as ruler of Galilee, had Paul brought before him by Festus, the Roman governor, and listened sympathetically to Paul's defence. Agrippa said Paul could have been released, if he had not appealed to Rome.
Acts 25

Jason *'healing'*
Jason looked after Paul and Silas during their stay in Thessalonica. Some zealous Jews went to Jason's house looking for Paul and Silas, but, not finding them, dragged Jason and some other believers before city officials and accused them of breaking Roman law. They forced Jason to pay before freeing them.
Acts 17:1-9

Lydia *'native of Lydia'*
Lydia, a business woman from Thyatira who traded in purple cloth, believed in the Lord through Paul's preaching and invited Paul and Silas to stay at her home.
Acts 16:11-15

Some Bible Facts and Figures

What's in the Bible?

A summary of the books of the Bible

OLD TESTAMENT

GENESIS
The beginnings, describing the creation, the rebellion and sin of man, and the early history of God's people, through whom he introduces his plan of redemption.

EXODUS
The history of Israel's departure from Egypt and the leadership of Moses; God's covenant with Israel and the giving of the Law; the construction of the Tabernacle.

LEVITICUS
The laws by which God's people can approach and maintain fellowship with their holy God.

NUMBERS
The census of the people, and their wanderings in the wilderness, during which God prepares them for the Promised Land.

DEUTERONOMY
Moses emphasises the covenant and the Law to the people before his death.

JOSHUA
The story of Israel's conquest of Canaan and the division of the land among the tribes.

JUDGES
The continuing history of the Israelites as they learn that their turnings from God lead to oppression by enemies, which leads to repentance and deliverance through a judge.

RUTH
The story of tragedy and love in the lives of ordinary people who become ancestors of David and of Jesus.

1 SAMUEL
The history of Israel from the rule of Samuel, the last judge, to the reign of Saul.

2 SAMUEL
The record of David's reign.

1 & 2 KINGS
The last days of David's reign, to Solomon's reign and the division of the kingdom, after which the kings of both kingdoms are presented in historical order up to the release of Jehoiachin from prison in Babylonia, about 561 B.C.

1 & 2 CHRONICLES
The official histories of the kingdoms of Judah and Israel, including the genealogies and history from the reigns of David and Solomon to the captivity.

EZRA
The story of the return of the Jews from the Babylonian captivity, and the rebuilding of the Temple.

NEHEMIAH
A further account of the return from Exile; the rebuilding of the walls of Jerusalem, and the renewing of the covenant.

ESTHER
The story of a Jewess who becomes Queen of Persia and saves the Jewish people from destruction.

JOB
The story of the sufferings and faith of a man who learns to accept the sometimes baffling will of God.

PSALMS
Poems, prayers and praises written by David and others, expressing to God the emotion of personal experience.

PROVERBS
The wise and practical sayings of Solomon and other wise men.

ECCLESIASTES
A book revealing how the search for happiness and satisfaction in earthly things apart from God always ends in vanity.

SONG OF SOLOMON
A love song presenting the courtship and marriage of man and woman, and illustrating the relationship between God and his people, and Christ and his Church.

ISAIAH
Prophecies concerning Judah and Jerusalem, vivid messages of redemption for God's people, and the hope for a Messiah.

JEREMIAH
Prophecies predicting the fall of Judah, the people's sufferings, and the final overthrow of their enemies.

LAMENTATIONS
A lament expressing grief over the fall of Jerusalem and the destruction of the Temple.

EZEKIEL
Pronouncements of God's judgement on the Jews, and messages of comfort in their captivity.

DANIEL
A story of some of the events of the captivity, and prophecies of Christ and the endtimes.

HOSEA
Hosea's personal grief over his unfaithful wife illustrates God's relationship with Israel.

JOEL
Prophecies of God's judgement of Judah, and the blessings that will follow repentance.

AMOS
Predictions of judgement against Israel because of idolatry and oppressing the poor, and against surrounding nations, and glimpses of the Messiah's kingdom.

OBADIAH
Prophecies of the destruction of Edom and the deliverance which will be found in Zion.

JONAH
The story of the prophet Jonah and of God's concern and mercy towards nations who are willing to repent.

MICAH
The pronouncement of judgement on Israel and Judah; the prediction of restoration and the Messiah's reign.

NAHUM
Prediction of the downfall of Assyria.

HABAKKUK
A prediction of the Babylonian invasion, the destruction of the Babylonians, and the restoration of God's people.

ZEPHANIAH
A prediction of the overthrow of Judah because of idolatry, pride and materialism; and a foreshadowing of the ultimate deliverance and restoration of God's people.

HAGGAI
Prophecies and exhortations concerning the rebuilding of the Temple.

ZECHARIAH
Prophecies relating to the rebuilding of the Temple and the coming of the Messiah and triumph of the kingdom of God.

MALACHI
Pronouncements of judgement for Israel's sins and predictions of blessings for the repentant, and of the coming of Christ.

NEW TESTAMENT

MATTHEW
A history of the life of Christ, emphasising Jesus as the fulfilment of God's covenant with Israel and the importance of Jesus' teachings.

MARK
A history of the life of Christ, with special emphasis on the last week in Jerusalem, the crucifixion and resurrection.

LUKE
The history of the life of Christ, emphasising the person of Jesus and the people whose lives he touched.

JOHN
The life of Christ, written to reveal that Jesus is the Christ, the Son of God.

ACTS
The giving of the Holy Spirit, and the development and spread of Christianity in the Spirit's power told in terms of people and places.

ROMANS
Paul's explanation of the doctrine of justification through faith in Christ.

1 CORINTHIANS
Paul's letter to the church at Corinth, correcting their errors, rebuking their sins and exhorting them to practise Christ's love.

2 CORINTHIANS
Paul's letter revealing his concern for the Corinthians and guiding them into lives of love and unity.

GALATIANS
Paul's proclamation of Christian liberty, firmly maintaining that man's justification by God's grace is through faith alone, not through works of the Law.

EPHESIANS
Paul's treatise on the person of Christ and the Church, God's household, through which God's wisdom and grace are revealed.

PHILIPPIANS
Paul's love-letter, revealing the joy and beauty of the Christian life.

COLOSSIANS
Paul combats errors and heresy by proclaiming the uniqueness and sufficiency of Jesus Christ as the only Saviour of all.

1 THESSALONIANS
Paul's concern for the people and an exhortation to faith, purity and holiness, waiting in hope for the Lord's return.

2 THESSALONIANS
Paul's letter concerning the second coming of Christ.

1 & 2 TIMOTHY
Letters from Paul concerning the Church, and the qualifications and duties of church officers.

TITUS
Paul's letter to Titus, emphasising church order and sound doctrine.

PHILEMON
Paul's most personal letter, asking his friend to receive a runaway slave as a brother in Christ.

HEBREWS
A defence of the Christian faith, emphasising the sufficiency and finality of Christ, and the superiority of the Christian faith over Judaism.

JAMES
A letter concerning the practical aspects of the Christian faith, and emphasising that faith is shown to be alive and active by the work it produces.

1 PETER
A letter exhorting the people to a life of purity and spirituality, as God's chosen, a royal priesthood.

2 PETER
A reminder of the truth of Christ against heresies, and warnings to remain in this truth, looking towards the second coming of Christ.

1 JOHN
The fundamentals of the Christian faith revealed in Jesus Christ.

2 JOHN
The primary importance of love in Christian fellowship, and warnings against false teachers.

3 JOHN
A letter concerning hospitality towards travelling Christian teachers.

JUDE
Strong condemnation of false teachers, and admonitions to remain in the true faith of Christ.

REVELATION
A revelation stressing the lordship of Christ, the overruling sovereignty of God, and his final victory over all sin and evil.

Some ways into your Bible

Some fascinating Bible statistics

	Old Testament	New Testament
Number of books	39	27
Number of chapters	929	260
Number of verses	23,214	7,959
Number of words	592,493	181,253
Longest book	Psalms	Luke
Shortest book	Obadiah	3 John
Longest chapter	Psalm 119	Matthew 26
Shortest chapter	Psalm 117	Revelation 15
Longest verse	Esther 8:9	Revelation 20:4
Shortest verse	1 Chronicles	John 11:35 ('Jesus wept.')
Middle book	Proverbs	2 Thessalonians
Middle chapter	Job 29	Romans 13–14
Middle verse	2 Chronicles 20:13	Acts 7:7

Total number of verses in both Testaments: 31,173.

Middle chapter of the Bible: Psalm 117

Middle verse: Psalm 118:5

Most mentioned character: David (1,118 times)

Longest word: Mahershalalhashbaz (*Isaiah 8:1*)

NB *These figures are based on English Bibles and may vary according to the translation.*

Bible translation facts
• More than 6,500 languages are spoken in the world.
• Of these, 2,167 languages have some or all of the Bible (355 complete Bibles, 850 New Testaments).
• About 4,333 languages are still without any part of the Bible.

The smallest Bible ever published was the Mite Bible published by Oxford University Press in 1896. Its pages were 28 x 41mm (1.62 x 1.12"), it was 900 pages long and 13mm (0.5") thick.

A Bible reading plan

If you would like to read the Bible systematically and carefully, the following reading order will be helpful. Although this plan does not include every book of the Bible, it will give you a good overview of Scripture if followed regularly.

New Testament
1. Mark
2. John
3. Luke–Acts
4. 1 Thessalonians
5. 1 Corinthians
6. Romans
7. Philemon
8. Philippians
9. Ephesians
10. 2 Timothy
11. 1 Peter
12. 1 John
13. Revelation (1–5 and 19:6–22:21)

Old Testament
14. Genesis
15. Exodus (1–24)
16. Numbers (10:11–21:35)
17. Deuteronomy (1–11)
18. Joshua (1–12 and 22–24)
19. Judges (sample)
20. 1–2 Samuel (sample)
21. 1–2 Kings (sample)
22. Nehemiah
23. Amos
24. Isaiah (1–12)
25. Jeremiah (1–25, 30–33)
26. Isaiah (40–55)
27. Ruth
28. Jonah
29. Psalms (some examples of the major types)
30. Job (perhaps 1–14 and 38–42)
31. Proverbs (1–9)
32. Daniel (1-6; sample chapters 7–12)

Noah's boat

The boat God told Noah to build (133 metres x 22.2 metres x 13.4 metres) was big enough to hold 432 double-decker buses.
There was plenty of room for the 35,000 or so animals that were saved from the flood with Noah and his family.

BIBLE VERSES FOR SPECIAL OCCASIONS

Birthdays
Joshua 1:1-9; Psalms 1; 23; 25; 37:3-7; 39:1-7; 90; 91; 139; Proverbs 3:5-8; 26:3-4; 41:10; 43:1-3; 46:4; Lamentations 3:22-26; Luke 1:46-55; John 6:35; 8:12; 10:1-30; Romans 8:28-39; 11:33-36; Ephesians 1:3-14; Philippians 4:4-7; Hebrews 10:23; 1 John 1:7-9

Baptism, dedication of children and confirmation
Joshua 1:5-9; 1 Samuel 1:27-28; Psalms 1; 23; 111; 121; Ecclesiastes 12:1; Matthew 3:11-17; 10:32-33; 28:18-20; Mark 10:13-16; John 3:1-21; 15:1-17; Acts 8:36-40; 16:30-33; 22:16; Romans 6:1-14; 1 Corinthians 12:12-13; Galatians 3:26-28; Ephesians 3:14-21; 4:1-6; Philippians 1:1-11; Colossians 2:6-14; 1 Timothy 6:11-16; Titus 3:4-7; 1 Peter 3:18-22; Jude 24

Thanksgiving
Deuteronomy 6:10-19; 8; Psalms 33; 65; 95; 100; 103; 104; 107; 111; 116; 126; 136; 145; 147; Isaiah 12; Luke 12:13-34; Acts 14:17; 1 Corinthians 3:5-9; Colossians 2:16-17; Hebrews 13:15-16; Revelation 5

Wedding day
Genesis 2:18-25; Ruth 1:16-17; Psalms 67; 84; 100; 118:24-29; 121; 127; 128; 139; Matthew 19:4-6; John 2:1-11; 1 Corinthians 7; 13; Ephesians 5:22-33; Colossians 3:12-21; 1 Peter 3:1-7

Retirement
Deuteronomy 33:27; Joshua 1:7-9; 1 Samuel 7:12; Psalms 23; 71:14-24; 93:12-15; Isaiah 26:3-4; 43:18-21; 46:4; John 14:27; 1 Corinthians 1:8; Philippians 3:7-16

CHRISTMAS AND NEW YEAR READING PLAN

December 20: *Luke 1:26-38*
Jesus' birth foretold

December 21: *Luke 1:39-56*
Mary and Elizabeth

December 22: *Luke 1:67-80*
Zechariah's song

December 23: *Colossians 1:15-20*
Who Jesus is

December 24: *John 1:1-18*
The Word became flesh

Christmas Day: *Luke 2:1-7*
The Saviour is born

December 26: *Luke 2:8-20*
The shepherds and the angels

December 27: *Matthew 2:1-12*
The Magi worship Jesus

December 28: *Luke 2:21-32*
Jesus is presented in the Temple

December 29: *Luke 2:36-38*
The redemption of Jerusalem

December 30: *Matthew 2:13-18*
Jesus is kept safe

December 31: *Psalm 90*
Teach us to number our days

New Year's Day: *Exodus 33:7-23*
Show me your glory

January 2: *Philippians 3:7-14*
Pressing on to the goal

January 3: *Joshua 1:1-9*
Be strong and courageous

January 4: *Matthew 6:25-34*
Do not worry

January 5: *Romans 8:28-39*
More than conquerors

January 6: *Philippians 4:4-9*
Rejoice in the Lord

EASTER READING PLAN

Palm Sunday: *Luke 19:28-44*
The approach to Jerusalem

Monday: *Luke 19:45-48*
Jesus at the Temple

Tuesday: *Philippians 2:5-11*
Obedient to death

Wednesday: *1 Peter 2:21-25*
Christ suffered for you

Maundy Thursday: *Luke 22:7-71; John 17*
The Last Supper; Jesus' arrest

Good Friday: *Luke 23; Isaiah 53*
The crucifixion

Saturday: *Matthew 27:62-66*
The guard at the tomb

Easter Day: *Matthew 28:1-15*
The resurrection

Easter Monday: *John 20:24-31*
My Lord and my God!

Tuesday: *1 Corinthians 15:12-58*
Victory over death

Wednesday: *Acts 2:22-41*
Why Jesus died

Thursday: *Romans 1:1-7*
Jesus Christ our Lord

Friday: *Romans 6:5-14*
United with him

Saturday: *Colossians 3:1-4*
Raised with Christ

Sunday: *Revelation 1:4-18*
Alive for ever and ever

Ascension Day
Luke 24:50-53; Acts 1:1-11

Pentecost (Whitsun) *Acts 1:8; 2:1-2; 19:1-7; Ephesians 4:30*

If you want to have an idea of what's in the Apocrypha, here is a suggested reading plan.

Apocrypha
1. Tobit
2. Ecclesiasticus (sample chapters 1–23)
3. 1 Maccabees (1:1–9:22) or 2 Maccabees
4. Judith
5. The Wisdom of Solomon (1–9)
6. 2 Esdras (3–14)

When you are in need . . .

Bible verses to look at when you need help

The Bible includes many promises that can help and encourage us in times of sadness, difficulty or stress. Here are some verses that show us God's help. Read and meditate over them:

• When you feel afraid
'I sought the LORD, and he answered me; he delivered me from all my fears' *Psalm 34:4.*
See also Psalms 27; 46; 56; 91; Matthew 8:23-27.

• When you feel alone
'So do not fear, for I am with you; do not be dismayed for I am your God' *Isaiah 41:10.*
See also Psalms 23; 73:23-24; Isaiah 49:14-16; John 14:15-21.

• When you are anxious or worried
'Cast all your anxiety on him, because he cares for you' *1 Peter 5:7.*
See also Isaiah 43:1-13; Matthew 6:25-34; 11:28; Philippians 4:4-7.

• When you have been bereaved
'Blessed are those who mourn; for they will be comforted' *Matthew 5:4.*
See also Psalm 23; John 11:21-27; 1 Corinthians 15:51-57; 1 Thessalonians 4:13-18; Revelation 21:1-5.

• When you feel discouraged
'Why are you downcast, O my soul? Why so disturbed within me? Put your hope in God' *Psalm 42:5.*
See also Psalms 34:18; 40:1-3; Lamentations 3:20-23; Romans 8:28-39; 2 Corinthians 4:7-18.

• When you have doubts
'I do believe; help me overcome my unbelief!' *Mark 9:24.*
See also Isaiah 40:27-31; Matthew 11:1-6; John 20:19-29; Acts 17:22-28.

• When you feel you have done wrong
'But God demonstrates his own love for us in this: While we were still sinners, Christ died for us' *Romans 5:8.*
See also Psalm 51; Luke 15:11-24.

• When you feel distant from God
'Come near to God and he will come near to you' *James 4:8.*
See also Psalm 139:1-18; John 10:29; Acts 17:24-31.

• When you are ill or in pain
'My grace is sufficient for you, for my power is made perfect in weakness' *2 Corinthians 12:9.*
See also Psalm 103:1-4; Romans 8:18-25; 2 Corinthians 4:16-18.

• When you need peace
'You will keep in perfect peace him whose mind is steadfast, because he trusts in you' *Isaiah 26:3.*
See also John 14:27; Romans 5:1-5; Philippians 4:4-7.

• When you are tempted
'We have one [a High Priest] who has been tempted in every way, just as we are – yet was without sin' *Hebrews 4:15.*
See also Luke 4:1-13; Ephesians 6:10-20; James 1:2-6, 12-18; 4:7-8; 1 Peter 5:8-9.

• When you are tired or weak
'Come to me, all you who are weary and burdened, and I will give you rest. Take my yoke upon you and learn from me, for I am gentle and humble in heart, and you will find rest for your souls' *Matthew 11:28-29.*
See also Joshua 1:5-9; Isaiah 40:28-31; 2 Corinthians 4:16-18; 12:9-10; Philippians 4:12-13.

• When you need guidance
'In all your ways acknowledge him, and he will make your paths straight' *Proverbs 3:6.*
See also Psalm 48:14; John 14:16; 16:13.

Model prayers of the Bible

Complaint	*Numbers 14:13-19*
Confession	*Psalm 32; Psalm 51; Ezra 9:5-15*
Dedication	*2 Chronicles 6:14-42*
Dependence	*2 Chronicles 20:6-12*
Despair	*Psalm 73*
For believers	*Ephesians 1:16-23; Ephesians 3:15-21*
For blessing	*Psalm 90*
For deliverance	*Isaiah 37:14-20*
For healing	*Isaiah 38:3, 9-20*
For restoration	*Daniel 9:4-19*
For unity	*John 17*
In national crisis	*2 Kings 19:14-19*
Intercession	*Genesis 18:16-33; Exodus 32:11-13*
Petition	*Acts 4:24-30*
Praise	*Luke 1:46-55*
Recommitment	*John 2:2-9*
Thanksgiving	*1 Samuel 2:1-10; Psalms 16; 65*
The Lord's Prayer	*Matthew 6:9-13; Luke 11:2-4*
Trust	*Psalm 23*

Some key Bible passages

The creation story	*Genesis 1:1–2:7*
The fall	*Genesis 3:1-24*
The flood	*Genesis 6:1–9:17*
The call of Abraham	*Genesis 12:1-9*
The Ten Commandments	*Exodus 20:1-17*
The shepherd's psalm	*Psalm 23*
The birth of Jesus	*Matthew 1:18–2:23; Luke 1:26–2:40*
The golden rule	*Luke 6:31*
The Sermon on the Mount	*Matthew 5–7*
The Beatitudes	*Matthew 5:3-11*
The Lord's Prayer	*Luke 11:2-4*
The prodigal son	*Luke 15:11-32*
The good Samaritan	*Luke 10:29-37*
The Last Supper	*Matthew 26:17-30; Mark 14:12-26*
The death of Christ	*Luke 23:26-56; John 19:16-42*
The resurrection of Christ	*Matthew 28; Luke 24; John 20*
The ascension of Christ	*Acts 1:1-12*
The coming of the Holy Spirit	*Acts 2:1-21*
The conversion of Paul	*Acts 9:1-31*
The love chapter	*1 Corinthians 13*
The faith chapter	*Hebrews 11*

Where to find help in the book of Psalms

Psalms to read when you're feeling:

Afraid *3, 13, 27, 46, 56, 59, 64, 91, 118, 121*
Alone *9, 12, 13, 27, 40, 43*
Angry *17, 28, 36, 37, 109*
Burned out *6, 63*
Cheated *41*
Confused *10, 12, 73*
Depressed *27, 34, 42, 43, 88, 143*
Disappointed *16, 92, 102, 130*
Distressed *13, 25, 31, 40, 107*
Guilty *19, 32, 38, 51*
Impatient *4, 13, 27, 37, 40, 89, 123*
Insecure *3, 5, 12, 91*
Insignificant *8, 23, 86, 90, 139*
Insulted *41, 70*
Jealous *37, 73*
Joyful *96, 149*
Like giving up *29, 43, 145*
Lost *23, 139*
Overwhelmed *25, 69, 142*
Proud *14, 30, 49*
Purposeless *25, 39, 90*
Self-confident *24*
Sorry/repentant *51, 66*
Stressed *12, 31, 34, 43, 56, 62, 84*
Thankful *30, 33, 66, 96, 103, 104, 113, 118, 136, 138*
Threatened *143, 144*
Trapped *7, 17, 42, 88, 142*
Vengeful *3, 109*
Weak *13, 18, 23, 28, 29, 62, 70, 86, 102*
Worried *37*
Worshipful *19, 29, 148, 150*

Psalms to read when you're facing:

Competition *113*
Criticism *35, 56, 120*
Danger *11*
Death *23*
Decisions *1, 25, 62, 119*
Discouragement *12, 42, 55, 86, 107, 142*
Discrimination *94*
Doubts *34, 37*
Enemies *3, 25, 35, 41, 56, 59*
Evil people *10, 36, 49, 52, 109*
Hypocrisy *26, 50*
Injustice *7, 9, 10, 17, 56, 94*
Insults *35, 43*
Lies *5, 12, 120*
Old age *71, 92*
Persecution *1, 3, 7*
Poverty *12, 34, 146*
Punishment *6, 38, 39*
Sickness *6, 22, 23, 41, 116, 139*
Slaughter *46, 83*
Sorrow/grief *6, 23, 31, 71, 77, 94, 123*
Success *18, 112, 126, 128*
Temptation *38, 141*
Troubles *34, 55, 86, 102, 142, 145*
Verbal cruelty *35, 120*

Psalms to read when you want:

Acceptance *139*
Answers *4, 17, 119*
Confidence *46, 71*
Courage *11, 27*
Fellowship with God *5, 16, 25, 37*
Forgiveness *32, 38, 40, 51, 86, 103*
Friendship *16*
Godliness *15, 25*
Guidance/direction *1, 19, 32, 37, 89, 146*

Healing *6, 41, 103*
Hope *16, 17, 18, 23, 27*
Humility *19, 131, 147*
Illumination *19*
Integrity *24, 25*
Joy *9, 16, 33, 47, 84, 96, 97, 98, 100*
Justice *2, 7, 14, 26, 37, 82*
Knowledge of God *18, 19, 29, 65, 89, 97, 103, 145, 147*
Leadership *72*
Miracles *60, 111*
Money *15, 16, 49*
Peace *3, 4, 85*
Perspective *2, 11, 73*
Prayer *5, 17, 27, 61*
Protection *7, 16, 18, 23, 27, 31, 91, 125*
Provision *34, 81*
Reassurance *15, 23, 26, 112, 121*
Rest *23, 27*
Salvation *103, 146*
Security *34, 84, 91*
Vindication *9, 35, 109*
Wisdom *1, 16, 19, 64, 111*

Animal, vegetable, and mineral . . .

Why are some mountains of the Bible important?

Mount	Height (in feet above sea level)	Bible reference	Biblical significance
Ararat	16,946	*Genesis 8:4*	Noah's ark came to rest
Sinai (also called Horeb)	7,500	*Exodus 3,19* *1 Kings 19*	God revealed his name and his Law to Moses Elijah fled there from Jezebel
Ebal Gerizim	3,100 2,900	*Deuteronomy 11:29*	Moses reminded Israel of the Law's blessings and curses
Nebo	2,700	*Deuteronomy 32:49*	Moses died here
Halak	1,640	*Joshua 11:17*	Southern boundary of Joshua's conquest
Hermon	9,100	*Joshua 11:17* *Matthew 17:1*	Northern boundary of Joshua's conquest ?Jesus transfigured here
Tabor	1,900	*Judges 4:6* *Matthew 17:1*	Deborah's forces fought Sisera ?Jesus transfigured here
Gilboa	1,700	*1 Samuel 31:1*	Saul killed in battle
Carmel	1,750	*1 Kings 18:20*	Elijah defeated prophets of Baal
Moriah		*2 Chronicles 3:1*	Early name for Mount Zion
Zion		*Psalm 48:1-2*	Site of the Temple
Beatitudes (location uncertain)		*Matthew 5–7*	Jesus' Sermon on the Mount
Olives	2,600	*Zechariah 14:4* *Matthew 26:30*	Site of Bethany, Gethsemane, Jesus' ascension and his predicted return

The foothills of Mount Hermon, northern Palestine

Some animals in the Bible

Antelope *Deuteronomy 14:5*
Ape *2 Chronicles 9:21*
Baboon *2 Chronicles 9:21*
Bat *Leviticus 11:19*
Bear *1 Samuel 17:34-36*
Boar *Psalm 80:13*
Camel *Job 1:3*
Cattle *Genesis 12:16*
Coney, or **rock badger** *Deuteronomy 14:7*
Deer *Deuteronomy 12:15*
Dog *1 Samuel 17:43*
Donkey *Genesis 12:16*
Fox *Song of Solomon 2:15*
Gazelle *Deuteronomy 12:15*
Goat *Genesis 27:9*
Horse *Genesis 47:17*
Hyena *Isaiah 34:14*
Ibex *Deuteronomy 14:5*
Jackal *Isaiah 34:13*
Leopard *Jeremiah 13:23*
Lion *Judges 14:5-6*
Mule *1 Kings 1:33*
Ox *Deuteronomy 14:4*
Pig *Leviticus 11:7*
Rabbit *Leviticus 11:6*
Rat *Leviticus 11:29*
Roe deer *Deuteronomy 14:5*
Sheep *1 Samuel 16:11*
Weasel *Leviticus 11 :29*
Wild goat *Deuteronomy 14:5*
Wolf *Matthew 7:15*

Camels from an Assyrian relief.

Musical instruments of the Bible

Instrument	Hebrew	Bible references
Wind		
Ram's horn	*shophar, yobel*	*Exodus 19:13; Psalm 81:3; Joshua 6:4*
Trumpet	*hasoserah*	*Numbers 10:2-10; Psalm 150:3*
Flute	*'ugab*	*Job 21:12; 30:31; Luke 7:32*
Double pipe	*halil*	*1 Kings 1:40; Isaiah 5:12*
String		
Lyre	*nebel*	*2 Samuel 6:5; Psalm 33:2*
Harp	*kinnor*	*Genesis 31:27; Psalm 43:4*
Percussion		
Tambourine	*toph*	*Exodus 15:20; 1 Samuel 18:6; Psalm 149:3*
Cymbals	*selselim, mesiltayim*	*1 Chronicles 13:8; Psalm 150:5; Nehemiah 12:27*

Some birds in the Bible

Black kite *Leviticus 11:14*
Cormorant *Leviticus 11:17*
Desert owl *Leviticus 11:18*
Dove *Genesis 8:8*
Eagle *Leviticus 11:13*
Falcon *Deuteronomy 14:13*
Great owl *Leviticus 11:17*
Gull *Leviticus 11:16*
Hawk *Leviticus 11:16*
Hen *Matthew 23:37*
Heron *Leviticus 11:19*
Horned owl *Leviticus 11:16*
Osprey *Leviticus 11:18*
Owl *Leviticus 11:17*
Partridge *Jeremiah 17:11*
Pigeon *Luke 2:24*
Quail *Exodus 16:13*
Raven *Genesis 8:7*
Red kite *Leviticus 11:14*
Rooster *Matthew 26:34*
Screech owl *Isaiah 34:11*
Sparrow *Psalm 84:3*
Stork *Leviticus 11:19*
Swallow *Psalm 84:3*
Swift *Isaiah 38:14*
Thrush *Isaiah 38:14*
Vulture *Leviticus 11:13*
White owl *Leviticus 11:18*

Even the sparrow finds a home
and the swallow a nest for
herself. . .
Psalm 84:3

Who are the heavenly beings?

What are the titles of Jesus in the Bible?

The beginning and the end (Greek *Alpha* and *Omega*) *Revelation 1:8*

Anointed One *Psalm 2:2*

Author of life *Acts 3:15*

Branch *Zechariah 6:12*

Bread of life *John 6:35*

Bright Morning Star *Revelation 22:16*

Christ (Greek 'Anointed One', or Messiah) *Matthew 16:16*

Daystar *2 Peter 1:19*

Everlasting Father *Isaiah 9:6*

Gate *John 10:7*

Good shepherd *John 10:11*

Holy and Righteous One *Acts 3:14*

Holy One of God *Mark 1:24*

I am *John 8:58*

Immanuel *Isaiah 7:14*

Jesus (Hebrew, 'Yahweh saves') *Matthew 1:21*

King of kings *Revelation 17:14*

Lamb *Revelation 5:6-14*

Lamb of God *John 1:29*

Last Adam *1 Corinthians 15:45*

Light of the world *John 8:12*

Lion of Judah *Revelation 5:5*

Lord (Greek *Kyrios*) *Philippians 2:9-11*

Lord of lords *Revelation 17:14*

Man of sorrows *Isaiah 53:3*

Master *Luke 5:5*

Messiah (Hebrew for the 'Anointed One') *John 1:41*

Mighty God *Isaiah 9:6*

Nazarene *Matthew 2:23*

Prophet *Acts 3:22*

Prince of Peace *Isaiah 9:6*

Rabbi *John 1:38*

Resurrection and life *John 11:25*

Root of David *Revelation 5:5*

Root of Jesse *Isaiah 11:10*

Saviour *Luke 2:11*

Son of David *Matthew 1:1*

Son of God *Mark 1:1*

Son of Man *Matthew 8:20*

True vine *John 15:1*

Way, truth and life *John 14:6*

Wonderful Counsellor *Isaiah 9:6*

Word (Greek *Logos*) *John 1:1*

Word of God *Revelation 19:13*

What are some of the names for the Holy Spirit in the Bible?

Counsellor *John 14:16*

Eternal Spirit *Hebrews 9:14*

Holy Spirit *Luke 11:13*

Power of the Most High *Luke 1:35*

Spirit *Romans 8:26-27*

Spirit of Christ *Romans 8:9*

Spirit of his [God's] Son *Galatians 4:6*

Spirit of holiness *Romans 1:4*

Spirit of the Lord *Judges 3:10*

Spirit of sonship *Romans 8:15*

Spirit of truth *John 14:17*

How is the Church described in the Bible?

Believers *Acts 2:44*

Body of Christ *1 Corinthians 12:27*

Bride *Revelation 21:2*

Called *Romans 8:30; 1 Corinthians 1:2*

Children of light *Ephesians 5:8*

Chosen people *1 Peter 2:9*

Christians *Acts 11:26*

Church *Matthew 16:18; 18:17; 1 Corinthians 1:2*

Citizens of heaven *Philippians 3:20*

Disciples *Acts 6:1; 11:26*

God's building; God's field *1 Corinthians 3:9*

God's children *John 1:12; Romans 8:14-23*

God's elect *1 Peter 1:1*

God's fellow-workers *1 Corinthians 3:9*

God's household *Ephesians 2:19*

God's temple *1 Corinthians 3:16*

Heirs of God *Romans 8:17*

Holy City *Revelation 21:10-27*

Holy nation *1 Peter 2:9*

Israel of God *Galatians 6:16*

Light of the world *Matthew 5:14*

Living stones *1 Peter 2:5*

People belonging to God *1 Peter 2:9*

Pillar and foundation of the truth *1 Timothy 3:15*

Royal priesthood *1 Peter 2:9*

Sanctified *1 Corinthians 1:2*

Saints *Ephesians 1:1, 15, 18; 3:18*

Salt of the earth *Matthew 5:13*

Sheep *John 10:3*

Soldiers of Christ *2 Timothy 2:3-4*

Strangers in the world *1 Peter 1:1*

Which Bible people saw God?

- Jacob dreamt of 'a stairway resting on the earth, with its top reaching to heaven, and the angels of God . . . ascending and descending'. *Genesis 28:12-13*

- 'Moses and Aaron, Nadab and Abihu, and the seventy elders of Israel went up and saw the God of Israel.' *Exodus 24:9-10*

- Moses saw the back of God. *Exodus 33:23*

- Micaiah saw 'the LORD sitting on his throne with all the host of heaven standing on his right and on his left'. *2 Chronicles 18:18*

- Isaiah saw 'the Lord seated on a throne, high and exalted'. *Isaiah 6:1*

- Ezekiel saw 'what looked like a throne of sapphire, and high above on the throne . . . a figure like that of a man'. *Ezekiel 1:26*

- Daniel saw thrones 'set in place, and the Ancient of Days took his seat. His clothing was as white as snow; the hair of his head was white like wool. His throne was flaming with fire.' *Daniel 7:9*

- Stephen looked up to heaven 'and saw the glory of God, and Jesus standing at the right hand of God'. *Acts 7:55*

- Paul wrote, 'And last of all he [the risen Christ] appeared to me also.' *1 Corinthians 15:8*

- John wrote, 'I was in the Spirit, and there before me was a throne in heaven with someone sitting on it.' *Revelation 4:2*

Angels

The word 'angel' literally means 'messenger.' As used in the Bible, it applies mostly to supernatural beings of the unseen world, used as messengers in the service of God or Satan.

Angels played an important role in the life of Jesus:
- An angel announced the birth of John *Luke 1:11-17*.
- An angel named him *Luke 1:13*.
- An angel foretold to Mary the birth of Jesus *Luke 1:26-37*.
- An angel foretold to Joseph the birth of Jesus *Matthew 1:20-21*.
- An angel named him *Matthew 1:21*.
- Angels announced to shepherds the birth of Jesus *Luke 2:8-15*.
- They sang hallelujahs *Luke 2:13-14*.
- An angel directed the child's flight to Egypt *Matthew 2:13, 20*.
- Angels ministered to Jesus at his temptation *Matthew 4:11*.
- An angel came to Jesus in Gethsemane *Luke 22:43*.
- An angel rolled away the stone at his tomb *Matthew 28:2*.
- An angel announced to the women his resurrection *Matthew 28:5-7*.
- Two angels presented him to Mary Magdalene *John 20:11-14*.

Jesus talked about angels:
- Nathanael would see angels ascending and descending upon him *John 1:51*.
- He could have 12 legions of angels to deliver him *Matthew 26:53*.
- Angels will come with him *Matthew 25:31; 16:27; Mark 8:38; Luke 9:26*.
- Angels will be the reapers *Matthew 13:39*.
- Angels will gather the elect *Matthew 24:31*.
- Angels will separate the wicked from the righteous *Matthew 13:41, 49*.
- Angels carried the beggar to Abraham's side *Luke 16:22*.
- Angels rejoice over the repentance of sinners *Luke 15:10*.
- Little children have guardian angels *Matthew 18:10*.
- Jesus will confess his people before the angels *Luke 12:8*.
- Angels have no gender and cannot die *Luke 20:35-36; Matthew 22:3*.
- The devil has evil angels *Matthew 25:41*.

Artist's impression of Jacob's dream.

Some Bible names and their meanings

Aaron *enlightened*
Abel *shepherd, a meadow*
Abigail *source of joy, father's joy*
Abraham *father of a multitude*
Absalom *father of friendship, or of peace*
Adam *man*
Agrippa *causing pain at birth*
Ahaz *possessor*
Amos *burden, one with a burden*
Andrew *a man, manly*
Anna *grace, gracious*
Apollos *destroyer*
Aquila *an eagle*

Balaam *foreigner, Lord of the people*
Barnabas *son of consolation*
Bartholomew *son of Talmai*
Bathsheba *daughter of an oath, or of seven*
Benjamin *son of the right hand*
Bernice *bringer of victory*
Boaz *fleetness, strength*

Cain *acquisition, possession*
Caleb *a barker, dog*
Cephas *stone, rock*
Cornelius *of a horn*
Cyrus *sun, splendour*

Dan *judge*
Daniel *God is my judge*
David *dear, beloved*
Deborah *bee*
Delilah *dainty*

Ehud *the only*
Eleazar *God my helper*
Eli *God is exalted*
Elijah *Yahweh my God*
Elizabeth *oath of God*
Elisha *God as a Saviour*
Enoch *teacher*
Esau *hairy*
Esther *myrtle*
Eve *life, living*
Ezekiel *God will strengthen*
Ezra *help*

Felix *happy*
Festus *joyful*
Gabriel *man of God*
Gad *good fortune, fortunate*
Gaius *lord*

Gideon *a hewer, tree-feller, great warrior*
Goliath *expulsion, expeller*

Habakkuk *God is strength*
Haggai *festive*
Ham *hot, black*
Hannah *grace, prayer*
Herod *heroic*
Hezekiah *might of Yahweh*
Hosea *deliverance, salvation*

Immanuel *God with us*
Isaac *laughter*
Isaiah *salvation of Yahweh*
Ishmael *whom God hears*
Israel *soldier of God*

Jacob *supplanter*
James *supplanter*
Jason *healer*
Jehoiakim *set up by Yahweh*
Jehoshaphat *Yahweh judges*
Jehu *Yahweh is he*
Jeremiah *exalted by God*
Jesse *God exists*
Jesus *the Lord saves*
Jethro *pre-eminent*
Jezebel *chaste*
Joab *Yahweh is father*
Job *afflicted, persecuted*
Joel *whose God is Yahweh*

Judas betrayed Jesus for 40 pieces of silver.

John *God's gift, grace*
Jonah *dove*
Jonathan *God is given*
Joseph *he shall add*
Joshua *Yahweh is salvation*
Josiah *God supports*
Jotham *Yahweh is upright*
Judah *praise*
Judas *praised*
Jude *praised*
Judith *Jewess*

Laban *white, beautiful*
Lazarus *God my helper*
Leah *weary*
Levi *joined*
Lot *covering, veil*
Lucifer *light-bringer*
Luke *light-giver*
Lydia *contention*

Malachi *my messenger*
Manasseh *forgetting*
Mark *polite*
Martha *lady*
Mary *loved by God*
Matthew *gift of Yahweh*
Melchizedek *king of righteousness*
Micah *who is like God?*
Miriam *loved by God*
Moab *the desirable land*
Mordecai *consecrated to Merodach*
Moses *drawn out of the water*

Nahum *consolation, comforter*
Naomi *gracious, pleasant*
Nathan *gift (of God)*
Nathanael *gift of God*
Nebuchadnezzar *may the God Nebo defend the boundary*
Nehemiah *consolation from God*
Nicodemus *conqueror of the people*
Noah *rest*

Obadiah *servant of Yahweh*

Paul *little*
Peter *rock, stone*
Philemon *affectionate*
Philip *lover of horses*
Priscilla *ancient*

Rachel *ewe*
Rahab *gracious*
Rebekah *flattering*
Reuben *see, a son*
Ruth *friend*

Samson *distinguished*
Samuel *name of God, placed by God, heard of God*
Sarah *princess*
Saul *asked for*
Seth *sprout*

Ruth would not desert her widowed mother-in-law.

Simeon *one heard*
Simon *one heard*
Solomon *peaceful*
Stephen *crown*

Thaddaeus *man of heart*
Thomas *twin*
Timothy *honoured by God*
Titus *honourable*

Uriah *light of Yahweh, Yahweh is my light*
Uzziah *power of Yahweh, strength of Yahweh*

Zechariah *remembered by Yahweh*
Zedekiah *justice of Yahweh*
Zephaniah *treasure of Yahweh*

Mary Magdalene, the first to see Jesus alive again.

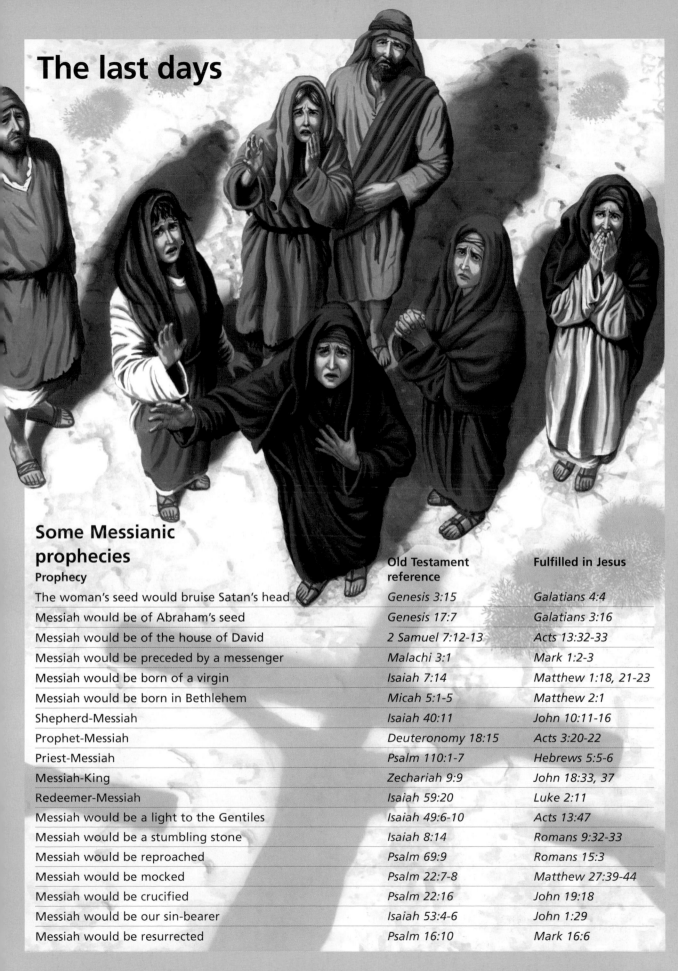

The last days

Some Messianic prophecies

Prophecy	Old Testament reference	Fulfilled in Jesus
The woman's seed would bruise Satan's head	Genesis 3:15	Galatians 4:4
Messiah would be of Abraham's seed	Genesis 17:7	Galatians 3:16
Messiah would be of the house of David	2 Samuel 7:12-13	Acts 13:32-33
Messiah would be preceded by a messenger	Malachi 3:1	Mark 1:2-3
Messiah would be born of a virgin	Isaiah 7:14	Matthew 1:18, 21-23
Messiah would be born in Bethlehem	Micah 5:1-5	Matthew 2:1
Shepherd-Messiah	Isaiah 40:11	John 10:11-16
Prophet-Messiah	Deuteronomy 18:15	Acts 3:20-22
Priest-Messiah	Psalm 110:1-7	Hebrews 5:5-6
Messiah-King	Zechariah 9:9	John 18:33, 37
Redeemer-Messiah	Isaiah 59:20	Luke 2:11
Messiah would be a light to the Gentiles	Isaiah 49:6-10	Acts 13:47
Messiah would be a stumbling stone	Isaiah 8:14	Romans 9:32-33
Messiah would be reproached	Psalm 69:9	Romans 15:3
Messiah would be mocked	Psalm 22:7-8	Matthew 27:39-44
Messiah would be crucified	Psalm 22:16	John 19:18
Messiah would be our sin-bearer	Isaiah 53:4-6	John 1:29
Messiah would be resurrected	Psalm 16:10	Mark 16:6

What were Jesus' seven last sayings on the cross?

1. **'Father, forgive them, for they do not know what they are doing.'** *Luke 23:34*

2. (To Mary) **'Dear woman, here is your son.'** (To John) **'Here is your mother.'** *John 19:26-27*

3. (To the criminal on the cross) **'I tell you the truth, today you will be with me in paradise.'** *Luke 23:43*

4. **'I am thirsty.'** *John 19:28*

5. **'My God, my God, why have you forsaken me?'** *Matthew 27:46; see Psalm 22:1*

6. **'It is finished.'** *John 19:30*

7. **'Father, into your hands I commit my spirit.'** *Luke 23:46*

The I Ams of John's Gospel

I am the bread of life *6:35-48*

I am the living bread *6:51*

I am the light of the world *8:12*

I am from above; I am not of this world *8:23*

I am the gate for the sheep *10:7*

I am the good shepherd *10:11*

I am the resurrection and the life *11:25*

I am the way, and the truth and the life *14:6*

I am the true vine *15:1*

The number of the beast?

In Revelation 13:18, 666 is given as the number of the beast. What does this mean? Any number of villains in history have been identified with the 'beast': the infamous Roman emperor Nero, the wicked emperor Caligula, the persecuting Diocletian – or even the Roman emperors as a whole. Other candidates have included the Roman Empire itself, Muhammad, Martin Luther, Napoleon and several popes!

The number 666 has also been used as the basis for calculating the year when the beast might appear.

However, it is possible that the number does not stand for any particular person or institution, but simply for 'the beast'.

In the Bible seven is the number of perfection, completion and fulfilment (Genesis 2:2; Exodus 20:10; Leviticus 16:29-30; Revelation 1:12). However, six never reaches seven; it fails to attain perfection, and forever misses the mark. Hence, the number of the beast – 666 – is failure after failure after failure. The mark of humanity.

What events will occur before Jesus' second coming?

- **Apostasy** *Matthew 24:10*
- **The rise of Antichrist** *Matthew 24:5, 23, 26*
- **Betrayal** *Mark 13:12; Luke 21:16*
- **Earthquakes** *Matthew 24:7; Mark 13:8*
- **False Christs** *Matthew 24:24; Mark 13:6, 21-23*
- **False prophets** *Matthew 24:11, 24; Mark 13:21-23*
- **False signs and miracles** *Matthew 24:24; Mark 13:22*
- **Famines** *Matthew 24:7*
- **Increase of evil** *Matthew 24:12*
- **International strife** *Matthew 24:7*
- **Persecution of believers** *Matthew 24:9; Mark 13:9-13*
- **Pestilence** *Luke 21:11*
- **Unparalleled distress** *Mark 13:17-19*
- **Wars and rumours of wars** *Matthew 24:6; Mark 13:7*
- **World-wide proclamation of the gospel** *Matthew 24:14; Mark 13:10*

The most popular English translations of the Bible

Amplified Bible, The The unique feature of this translation is the addition of thousands of alternate (amplified) readings in brackets to help the reader understand the text. It was first published in 1964.

Authorised Version (AV) *See* King James Version.

Douay-Rheims Bible A Roman Catholic translation produced in the early seventeenth century about the same time as the King James Version. For the most part it was translated from the Latin Vulgate. Until the 1970s, when the New American Bible was completed, the Douay-Rheims Bible was the standard English translation of the Bible for the Roman Catholic Church.

Good News Bible (GNB) *See* Today's English Version.

Jerusalem Bible (JB) Roman Catholic translation first published in 1966.

King James Version (KJV) Until recently, the King James Version was the most widely used English translation of the Bible. It was first published in 1611, authorised by King James I of England; in Britain it is called the Authorised Version (AV). Its stately language has had a great influence on spoken English and on English literature over four centuries. Most popularly known biblical phrases and quotations are from the King James Version. In recent years, modern translations have replaced the King James Version in many churches.

Living Bible, The (TLB) A thought-for-thought translation of the Bible, widely used since its initial publication in 1971. In the 1970s, it was the best-selling book in the United States.

New American Bible (NAB) A translation sponsored by the Roman Catholic Church. Sometimes called the Confraternity Bible, it was first published in 1970 and is the translation now mostly used by Catholics.

New American Standard Bible (NASB) A translation first published in 1971, it gained popularity among evangelicals as an accurate word-for-word translation.

New English Bible (NEB) A thought-for-thought translation published in 1970. The New English Bible was more popular in Britain than in the United States.

New International Version (NIV) A popular translation that has been accepted by evangelicals since its publication in 1978. It has recently surpassed the King James Version as the most widely-used English translation of the Bible.

New Jerusalem Bible. (NJB) Revision of the Jerusalem Bible first published in 1985.

New King James Version (NKJV) A popular revision of the King James Version, it was first published in 1982. Many difficult and archaic words have been updated, and the words 'thee' and 'thou' have been replaced with the contemporary 'you'.

New Living Translation (NLT). A complete revision of the Living Bible, first published in 1996.

New Revised Standard Version (NRSV) See Revised Standard Version.

Revised English Bible (REB) A revision of the New English Bible first published in 1989.

Revised Standard Version (RSV) The standard Bible used by most mainstream denominations. The translation was sponsored by the National Council of the Churches of Christ in the USA and was first published in 1952. In 1990 a revised edition called the New Revised Standard Version (NRSV) was published to replace the former edition.

Today's English Version (TEV) This modern translation, published by the American Bible Society, has been popular since its publication in 1976. It uses simple English and tends to be a thought-for-thought style of translation. It is also called the Good News Bible.

Index